FANFROLICO AND AFTER

FANFROLICO
AND AFTER)

JACK LINDSAY

THE BODLEY HEAD
LONDON

© Jack Lindsay 1962
Printed and bound in Great Britain for
The Bodley Head Ltd
10 Earlham Street, London WC2
by C. Tinling & Company Ltd, Liverpool
Set in Monotype Plantin
First published 1962

To N.L.

Alone in the Blue Mountains

Though you in your hermitage
of cold and scornful stone,
of tranquil and ruthless light,
refuse to accept these pages,
what other name can I write
over the arch of the ruin
made my sole monument?
Your rejecting word I ignore
and call up your name once more,
though you will pay no heed,
though you will never read
these words in your mountain-lair.

So long for you alone
I wrote, all my thoughts I bent
on you as friend and foe
so long, no name I know
but yours for this empty space
now Ray and Phil are both gone
and the spiralling fury of Time
bores remorselessly on.

As a bitter tribute then take
these pages that strip me bare
in death's thin bleakening ray.
Turn for a moment I say
turn from your obdurate place
in that clarity of stone,
that terrible folly of light,
turn for a moment this way
your abstracted face.

                              J.L.

CONTENTS

ILLUSTRATIONS

PLATES

LINE DRAWINGS

FOREWORD

THIS is my third volume of autobiography. It brings to a head the extended conflicts which I have tried to describe in *Life Rarely Tells* and *The Roaring Twenties*. In the first book I dealt with my childhood and youth, spent mainly in Brisbane; in the second, with my efforts to develop as a poet after having dedicated myself to the aesthetic ideas of my father Norman Lindsay. The setting there was Sydney and I attempted to show the relation of our ideas to the stage reached by Australian culture.

In the present book I cover my arrival in London, the foundation of the Fanfrolico Press in which we set out our views on life and art, and the various struggles that culminated in the year 1936—though a final chapter rapidly carries things forward to 1941 when I was called up into the Army. There is no need for me to give any preluding summary of our ideas; what they were, will come out fully enough in the account of the Press. The book can thus be read as complete in itself, a record of an odd Australian invasion of British culture, which had drastic effects on the invaders if not on the invaded.

As this is in large part a biography of ideas, I have had to deal with the aims and methods of my work; it is of course for the reader, not me, to decide how well or ill they were carried out in the works in question. I cannot but think however that the exposition of my change from an extreme Existentialism to Marxism has a certain interest in relation to contemporary problems of thought.

Acknowledgements are due for several of the illustrations: to Michael Ayrton for his portrait of Constant Lambert; to J. Symonds and his *The Great Beast* (Rider) for the photo of Crowley; Messrs J. Cape for that of Heseltine; Betty May and her *Tiger Woman* (Duckworth); P. R. Stephensen for his own photo and that of Winifred Stephensen; Mrs Owens for that of Philip Owens; H. Chaplin for that of B. Penton. No photo of Elsa could be included as she always refused to be photographed.

J.L.

A*

FAN-
FROLICO

1. ACROSS THE WORLD

STANDING in the ship's stern, I watched the wake of foam wallowing and twisting behind us, with a few melancholy seagulls swerving above. Western Australia was rapidly fading out into the dazzled east, sinking flatly into the unimpressed waters. I felt a cord of some sort snap and twang, recoiling smartly between my eyes that watered in the stiff breeze. Now at last I realized I was crossing the world in search of a strange place labelled Britain, perfidious land of shopkeepers and breeding-ground of the greatest line of poets known to men. The rope of the knot-registering contraption spun and dragged tensely, as if I trailed one furious strand of resistance into the sundering waters; and I turned with an effort to join John Kirtley in the interminable deck-circuit on which we were to prowl for a month and more, passengers caged in a narrow bucketing space of caulked planks and shivering rattling metal. My thrill of fear was dissipated in boredom and I hoped for an albatross-poem to roost in the shrouds of my mind; but nothing broke the deadly routine. We walked as if we had to cover the thousands of miles by foot as well as by steam-power.

The tedium of crossing the Indian Ocean at the most sweltering time of the year took its toll of us. After Freemantle all hope of anyone interesting or even personable appearing in the second class was abandoned. There were no girls at all between the ages of five and forty. Never can a P. & O. liner have contained less charm inside its second-class barriers. Not even one ugly young woman. With the handsome girls of the superior end of the ship I now and then exchanged a glance, as on my endless prowl I neared the barrier FIRST CLASS ONLY: a glance haughtily class-conscious on my part and unseeing on theirs.

After a while, however, we found there was a bulky sculptress who blocked our way by modelling someone's head on a stand, making a thumb-slash and then standing back with fine and crushing abandon on any onlooker's feet. I gave her clay only hasty side-looks, but noted to my surprise that her technique was adequate if unexciting. Our only acquaintance, a tough amused farmer, who drank beer with us, warned

13

against catching the lady's eye, as she was on the look-out for commissions. 'She's got a grip of iron,' he said, and pretended that he'd almost succumbed to her sales-campaign; but the salesman who could have put anything over on Mr E. was not yet born. We liked him for his instant and absolute distrust of all the things that the world tried to sell us—wives, curios, God, deckgames, or newspaper-print. He was clearly more than rich enough to travel first. 'It's better this end. People aren't skiting all the time.'

The ship slid on through the vastness, smoothly or in long pitching movements. In the bar you felt the furious turning of the screw, clutched your glass and listened to your teeth chattering; in the cabin the bunks shook with an incessant screech and grinding, and sweat poured down the lines either side of your nose. The great glaucous gliding water-masses gave way to dull and dingy waves heaving vaguely after the ship. Heat-mists hovered in the sky moted with a heavy mealy light. Then shoals of fly-fishes skimmed the wave-ridges or a porpoise gracefully cavorted.

I read nothing, wrote nothing, did not think. I sweated and watched the hypnotic waters. Some days there was a canvas tank rigged up in which we could plunge and swim a few strokes. The deckgames I evaded, though Kirtley, a good cricketer, succumbed to the bat and drove balls into the rope-nets hanging all round the pitch. One afternoon the first-class area amidships and forwards was opened to the second-raters, and I alone refused to pass the barrier into the more commodious, better-furnished, and less screw-racketed quarters. However, I paused long enough by the bulky sculptress to be engaged in conversation; and thereafter had the job of dodging her to make the deck-prowls more varied. Apart from anything else, I couldn't afford to buy her gins.

Then at last our oceanic days were over and we arrived at Colombo, where we stayed three days, waiting for some overdue mail-steamer. With the sardonic Mr E. we wandered along the swarming streets, drove out to the beaches to sip beer or coffee on spacious terraces and watch the coconut-palms against the sky, dark with blue brilliance, while the foam hissed and crisped along the sands. We watched the nimble fingers of girls moving pins about as they made lace, and strayed into a ramshackle Buddhist temple garishly painted with damnation-scenes, where an old priest told us either to get out or to pay up. Mr E. chuckled at the similarity of all religions, as he chuckled at the other passengers buying ebony elephants made in Birmingham as mementoes of Ceylon.

He enjoyed himself stimulating the shopkeepers to ever-greater exertions of salesmanship and then buying nothing; we enjoyed watching him. We didn't want to use up our money by going by train to Kandy and the uplands.

On to Aden, where we stayed a day and night: a place of shattering sunlight caught between mountains of cinder-and-ash and a sea of molten silver. A triangle of grass, with Queen Victoria at its centre dumpily defying the heat, was kept almost green by the water-sprinkler going round and round without pause. Except for the post office round a corner on the right, all the buildings were pubs, with equally long and stifling rooms. We dodged across the slabs of heat, from gin to gin, and paid to see the Authentic Mermaid, who turned out a stinking stuffed seacow. Waiting for the boat back to the ship, we threw coins for the arrowy-diving boys in the water.

Now at last the ship shook herself and set off at full speed, rushing up the Red Sea and leaving red-sailed fishing-craft quickly behind, till we reached the Canal and went leisurely along. We arrived at Port Said by dark, with only a few hours for a trip ashore; Mr E. went off, but we stayed on board, watching the skurry of lights and shadows on the landing-stage, with the sense of a vast starry gateway to Europe opening ahead of us, till Mr E. returned, to chuckle over the way he had diddled the vendors of dirty postcards and tickets for the marriage-of-lady-and-donkey.

We came out into a Mediterranean turbid with recent storms and believed that the world was round. For after climbing up a long slope, now we felt that we slanted downhill and smelt a new air. Nearing Crete, we saw a filagree of lofty snow before we saw the earth, a long delicate fretwork of silver breathed rigidly on the sky. Gradually the fine pattern hardened and the lower sky took on the dark blue of a sprawling island. What vision could have better expressed the conviction of a descent into Europe from an eyrie of poetry? I was entering Europe via the sky-gates of Mount Ida, with the metallic pulse of the boat turned into the clashing of the shields of the Kouretes as they danced around the divine babe.

By the time we were close to the western end of the island I was talking to the girl who had come aboard at Port Said, red-haired and pleasantly ugly, who had been visiting China and who assured me that chopped-off heads, hung on a wall there, had turned into stone over the centuries. Everything she had seen was as fabulous as that. And that night, caught by the tubular sculptress, I lay with her on a rug in one of the scanty recesses of our second-class decks and even kissed her rough dry lips smelling of tobacco.

The great rugged hills of Calabria were the first clear forms of Europe, and then the Straits of Messina brought the towns of men

Drawing by Norman Lindsay from the title-page of *Lysistrata*

unimportantly into the picture, huddled and flattened in the scene of vast sky and water. That night Stromboli was outlined in dull fire, a hulking pyramid against the flattened sky; and later we passed between Corsica and Sardinia, with glimpses of red-burnt barren earth, ancient as a dream-symbol. We landed in Marseilles and wandered with Mr E. along the sea-front, drinking *vin rouge* and watching the tarts with blood-red lips and tigerish eyes. Europe at last; somehow looking disordered, corrupt, shabby, and rotten-rich with its unrealized inheritance, beside the rowdy and yet well-run Australian scene still rawly fresh in our minds. Kirtley bought some snails cooked and restored to their shells with congealed fat, which we took back to the boat and finally threw out of the port-hole.

The suit Norman had bought me was still fairly presentable, and I had my silver-headed Malacca cane. But my shapeless hat and my shoes worn away on one side of each heel betrayed me; and I can still recall the shame I felt when we exchanged some comments with a steward on the boat. I was leaning flushed and negligent on my elegant cane; and the steward, sharp with all the snobbery of the flunkey, made some sarcastic balloon-pricking remark. I smiled on, but from that moment to this have never attempted to be correctly-dressed or to delude myself about any possibilities of even a third-rate elegance.

The furious dock-life brought me back to a sense of realities. I watched for hours a gang who had loaded a barge with huge cases before they noticed that they had driven down another barge under one of its ends. They then had to unload again before they could free the second barge, swearing magnificently all the infuriated while. We sailed out on a silvery afternoon, with the harbour and islands burning in soft tufted lights, a magical scene. Then, along the Spanish coast, I saw for the first time the yellow-greens of Europe, a new dimension of colour after the hard blue-greens of Australia. The broad velvety fields gave a soft feeling of abundance, of earthly promise, which I could not fit into my aesthetic where the luxurious image-of-beauty was bred from the rough-tough bitter soil, a compensating antithesis. We punctually passed Gibraltar, which for me was the Pillar of Herakles, and rounded the easternmost point of Portugal, into the grey and heaving waste of the stormy Bay of Biscay. I enjoyed the floundering decks, the wild waters, the screaming woodwork of the cabin; the change from the steam-heat of the equatorial line to the icy and ghostly tumult which hedged Britain, that ancient Land of the Dead.

I began to feel dimly alive. I still had read nothing, written nothing, thought nothing. Kirtley and I did not even discuss our plans; for I had none and he did not want to talk of his, probably they were confusedly dependent on what he found in London. Only the apotheosis of Crete had struck through my bemused torpor. The last days aboard were variegated however by conversations with the idiot girl from Lancashire, who carried a large stone from the Hill of Olives in her handbag—'for luck'—and by evasions of the sculptress. We hid from her any of our London trails and were distressed to find that Mr E. hid his from us; he didn't believe in carrying on shipboard-friendships. No doubt he scented that we would soon be on the rocks and might want to borrow money. The ship's world of six weeks was breaking up.

2. LONDON AND PARIS

EVERYTHING grew smaller as we neared our destination, which turned out to be the Regent Palace Hotel. Kirtley had picked up that name from someone on the ship, and I was ready to go anywhere, the Ritz or a Limehouse joint. The weather was dingy, the docks lacked the spaciously enchanting hurlyburly of Marseilles, the train from Tilbury swung us through ever-worse slum-backyards. Liverpool Street was a cavern cobwebbed with smoke and foul with the smell of decaying fish. Everything grew smaller and dirtier. We had never imagined that men could live in such a dwarfed and sootied world. A taxi drew us out of the station catacombs along narrow bedraggled streets. London.

We stared out at Fleet Street and the Strand, confirmed in our impression of a grey diminutive world, wholly lacking in dignity or charm, parochial and constricted. The impact of London so depressed us that we did not dare to speak of it for days; above all we felt fooled and humiliated. To have come so far for this. However, at least we weren't refused admittance to the hotel. Kirtley booked two small bedrooms and a porter dumped our things in them. I wrote down Kirtley's number on a piece of paper, which I then lost, and had the feeling that we were parted for ever. The fact that I could find out his room from the enquiry desk below did not dawn on me. In any event I still had an extreme repugnance from even such a mild instance of authority as an enquiry-clerk in a large hotel where I felt an interloper, liable at any moment to be excluded by a disgusted management. A poet, with a deboshed felt-hat—out with him!

But Kirtley came along to my room, which I had attempted to humanize by putting copies of *Zarathustra* and Blake on the spindly bedside table. We slunk downstairs to a meal, and then went out to look at London.

Our aimless walk increased the feeling of desolation and smallness. The cold wind poured along the Strand with its two-decker open-topped buses and its cruising taxis; the agitated lights merged to build a narrow frail world, lowering the skies and stinging our eyes. In doorways or along the kerbs were puffy-faced tarts with coats pulled tight round their fat legs; their predatory eyes picked us out at once as bronzed colonials and we ran a gauntlet of hoarsely alluring whispers. I felt the power of rhymes stirring afresh in me after the oceanic sleep and demanding a defiance of the impinging world in what was for me a new way. Australian society I had repudiated on the general grounds that, while nothing human was alien to me, the element in people which accepted the State and the cash nexus was inhuman and therefore alien; but here I felt a more immediate shock of rejection. The intrusion of State and cash nexus was pervasive. I felt the persons of the many beggars as the visible sign of an inhumanity that hit me harder than I knew.

> *Chimney-pots like decaying teeth in rows*
> *stick broken into a mumbling sky.*
> *Street after street, where cleanness never blows,*
> *goes shabbily by.*
> *The frowsy beggar at the pubcorner stands*
> *with bunch-of-carrot hands.*
>
> *We have known mangy faces and rubble-shacks,*
> *but not this dingy graveyard where*
> *the miminy mourners move with mortgaged backs*
> *and snoffling care.*
> *Share with the wind a house of stringy-bark slats,*
> *but not with mingy rats.*

I had never felt moved to write that kind of verse in Australia; now for a while I didn't want to write anything else.

We strolled in misty Hyde Park and on principle visited a few pubs. But neither of us was given to drink for its own sake, and anyhow the beer was dull and heavy after the lagerish Australian brands. We were condemned to the grey wintry streets. Even Sydney, rising on the sheep-tracks of convict-days, seemed a well-devised city next to London, where, after the fire of 1666 wiped out the medieval bases, only a commercial greed, I felt, had determined the medley of mediocre buildings. The residential squares of the 18th and early 19th centuries, or the Victorian terraces, could not affect the overall impression; they were unavailing refugees from the prevailing lack of style and civic purpose, or pompous reflections of the deadening cash nexus in the family sphere. Trafalgar Square as the imperial centre was an excellent admission of the lack of human dignity: the Hero hoisted aloft so that all personal features might be lost in the inane, while Landseer's blandly hypocritical lions digested their prey below with an air of poodle virtue. I liked only the statue of Charles I and occasional dusk-moments on the Embankment. However I ventured into the National Gallery and was warmed by the Titians and Rubenses, the first originals of those artists I had seen; at last I felt the handshake of friends.

Kirtley arranged to call on W.P., editor of a print-collectors' quarterly, with whom he had corresponded. I went with him to the suburban villa, but took no part in discussions. Looking drowsily at artbooks, I gathered that on the strength of our admired *Lysistrata* Kirtley hoped to work up some financial backing; but after protracted negotiations nothing happened. I had dropped a line to Walter de la Mare, who at once asked me to Taplow. I spent a pleasant day of late-winter frost there, during which he drove with me to Burnham Beeches. I recall only one comment of his: 'I don't know much about flowers, but my favourite reading is seed-catalogues, they're so full of lovely and intriguing names.' At tea one of his sons remarked, with an obvious intention of belittling Norman's work, that Beardsley had had an overwhelming effect on modern black-and-white artists; and as I didn't consider Norman at all influenced by Beardsley, I amiably agreed. However, though I had enjoyed the day, I made no effort to follow it up and never saw de la Mare again; I felt our worlds did not really meet and I was an impostor in his presence.

I felt the same with Ralph Strauss and Holbrook Jackson, to whom Norman had given me letters of introduction. I had a genial dinner with Strauss at his flat, where he insisted on giving me a letter to J. C. Squire. My contact with Jackson consisted of a chat about typography at his office. He sat with scholarly stoop, bored into me with his lively dark eyes, leaned back and chatted with the wary fluency of someone who had editorially met too many young writers. After some hesitation, I sent Strauss' letter to Squire and was asked to call at the offices of the highly-influential *London Mercury* in one of London's very few old buildings, near Temple Gate. Squire received me affably; but in the course of his advice to a young colonial aspiring to the London literary scene, he dropped a plain hint that he'd read an article of mine on Abercrombie's *Phoenix* in the Sydney *Bulletin*. (I had praised the play and jeered at Squire for abusing it as disgusting, as an 'abominable and

unconvincing farce'.) Nothing could have been more adroit or in-
offensive than the hint and the following inference that rash raw colonials
would be forgiven if they now showed the right sort of respect and tried
to tread in the footsteps of their betters. Perhaps Squire read my
stupefaction as remorse; he ended his long and sensible discourse by
taking me down for a couple of beers at the pub nearby. His encouraging
handshake however was not a token of entry into the hearty world of
week-end poets, but my definite farewell to all malingering on the edge
of that world. I was annoyed at myself for getting into a false position,
for being polite to the man who had attacked the Phoenix Society for
their 'bad taste and brazen effrontery' in staging Wycherley, I forswore
all letters of useful introduction and decided to abandon myself to my
destiny—do nothing, write poetry when moved, and co-operate with
Kirtley if asked.

About this time I dropped into the Café Royal, which was in the
throes of genteel transformation, discarding its sawdust floor, marble-
topped tables, gaudy gilt decorations, and red plush seats. I had a drink
in the corner that wasn't being rehabilitated, and heard a young fellow
at the next table talking about Australian poetry and insisting that the
coming man was Jack Lindsay. This remarkable speech stunned me, so
that I didn't introduce myself; but I took it as an omen that I was
right in avoiding the respectable literary world.

Meanwhile Kirtley, who paid all basic expenses, decided the Regent
Palace bed-and-breakfast was too costly. Though flats and apartments
were not then so plentiful, we could have easily found something cheap
and suitable if we had had the least idea how to set about it. What we
did do was to take a bus in Regent Street which had St John's Wood on
the front. Kirtley hoped it would take us to Lord's: which it did. We
found a house-agent close to the churchyard with Joanna Southcott's
remains and he gave us a list of furnished houses. We took the first we
looked at, in Blenheim Street, a small prim detached three-storeyed
brick-house, with basement leading out into a neat backgarden. It
belonged to Lady Somebody, who wanted to go to the South of France,
and was full of muslin curtains, gesticulating bronzes by inferior Italian
artists (two of them lifesize), and tiny bric-à-brac. Kirtley's references
satisfied the agent and we moved promptly in, spending our whole first
day in stowing the myriad bits of movable junk into the cupboards. We
left out only large and apparently unbreakable objects like the prancing
Bacchante, with windblown frills covering all the more interesting parts

of her anatomy, who stood before the front window on the groundfloor, shaking a thyrsus tipped with a frosted electric lightglobe. She came in anyway as a convenient hat-and-coat rack. From Priory Street we laid in a stock of tinned food, eggs, bacon, bread. Our meals tended to consist of the same items in a different order, but were eaten in a charming room that looked out into the tender intricate lights of the garden with its acacia trees, its lilac and laburnum, where I tried to keep the grass down with a pair of Lady Somebody's scissors. I took the attic room for myself, to be as high as possible above the sourfaced neighbours who peered curiously in at our front window—though we tried to baffle

Drawing by Norman Lindsay from *Lysistrata*

them by draping the muslin curtains round the thyrsus and thus dislodged ancient dust by tugging in vain at the cords of the velvet side hangings of rusty red.

I paused, scribbling angry doggerel, to recall P. R. Stephensen, whom I had known at Queensland University and who had looked in on me at Sydney on his way to Oxford as a Rhodes scholar. I wrote to him at Queen's, and several days later got a reply from Paris; I had forgotten about vacations. He exclaimed gleefully at our arrival and invited me to come straightaway over to Paris. I went, with Kirtley's gruff encouragement.

P.R.S. met me at the Gare du Nord, running along the platform with his usual zest, chattering in argot to grumpy porters and carrying me off under his arm to the nearest café for *vin rouge*. Norsely fair, clearly handsome, athletic and bristling with a compact energy, he was able to stamp any moment with a casual effect of historic importance. I already

liked Paris; but after ten minutes in his company it was ten times more
lively and charming, the French girls ten times more attractive, chic,
amorously-bottomed, and French. The wine glowed with red earth-
fires and for the first occasion since we left Sydney I knew that I had
done absolutely the right thing in coming to Europe. The taxi we took
darted madly through the traffic with a high-pitched squeak of warning,
P.R.S. and the driver excitedly discussing the cost of living and narrowly
missing the demented policemen. Paris lay all around me, with avenues
revolving and flashing away, people actually enjoying life under the
leisurely café-awnings, girls who were girls whether seen from the left,
right, front or back, from below or above, the Seine broadly emerging
through leaves and bookstalls, and myself deposited at the Hotel de
l'Univers, near the Panthéon.

In a few moments P.R.S. (never called Percy or Reginald, always
P.R.S. or Inky) was hauling me out with brisk hilarious gestures and
introducing me to the street-scene with impresario generosity as if he
himself had invented it all only the day before for my special benefit
and was gratified that the world was behaving so well. His keen brisk
enjoyment irradiated the persons and things all around, merging with
the spring sunlight to stress the peculiar momentary individuality of
each movement, each pattern of light and shadow, each gesture. One
realized that aeons had gone to bring about this magnificent unrepeat-
able performance, and felt infinitely grateful for the wayward chance and
the infinite pains that had come together to produce the transitory vista
which seemed struck in eternal bronze. What setting could suit his
spell-binding better than Paris, a carefully-staged show with all the
Renoir colours and the Dégas tones of spontaneity? He was part-French
as well as part-Scandinavian; in Brisbane I had met his fine-mannered
old grandfather, as French as a gavotte by Rameau. Paris effervescently
stimulated the vivacity that companioned his air of trim purposiveness.

During my stay he introduced me to a friend of his, Winifred, with
whom he was already in love and whom he was to marry. She was a
classical ballet-dancer with soft small big-eyed face, incredibly finely-
bodied and gracefully slight. I never saw her dance on the stage, but
can imagine her as the merest piece of thistledown blown charmingly
about by the wind of the music, an ondine floating as weightless as the
reflection of lilies on the shimmering surface of the tremolo of the violins.
In character she was gentle as her flower-face suggested—something
not always true of blossom-girls; and as strong and steady as her dance-

image was light and swan-gliding. Also there was J. D. Hall, whom I had known as a fellow-undergraduate at Brisbane; he had turned to Economics and was already, I think, a Fellow of Trinity at Oxford. For ten days we had a consistently happy time, talking and wandering round, mainly in the Latin Quarter. Heaping up the saucers on the terrasse of the Dôme and sneering at the bourgeois Rotonde on the opposite corner of the Carrefour Vavin with its grill-room and dance-orchestra, which was cashing in on the legends of Modigliani's boozing in the days when it was a humble zinc. Having an apéritif with Baudelaire's ghost at the Closerie des Lilas and then saluting P.R.S.'s swashbuckling predecessor, Maréchal Ney, in his statue outside. Watching the traffic of the Avénue de l'Opéra from the Régence where Napoleon had played dominoes, with the finely-proportioned Comédie-façade to remind us of the elegant pretences against which the swooning Romantic (de Musset) fell into the arms of his Muse. Or night-roaming among the mollshop-cafés near the Markets and the Boulevard de Sévastopol.

Once when Hall was discoursing on the economic world-situation, at the Dôme, I put in some caustic comments about Malayan tin, which I had heard Mr E. make on the boat; and P.R.S. patted me on the back. 'You see the poet isn't such a fool. What a pity Michelle is away in the country. She would have been just the person for him.' I wasn't sure in what way Michelle would have suited me, but regretted her absence. Walking in the Bois de Boulogne, I was overwhelmed again by the radiant yellow-greens, the veil on veil of filtered light. 'I can understand Turner at last. The greys of dampness in the English landscape. The delicate gauzes of light, as here, drift on drift, vane on turning smoky vane, golden flat on flat as in a stage-set but fumed in flower-crucibles. A strange new world. Have you noticed how low the night-skies are after Australia, sagging with their stars, as if slung only a little above the housetops. Australian light is a single infinity, depth beyond depth, and yet only one depth.'

P.R.S. took me and two young Russians from the Embassy on an underworld-exploration. We visited bars and cellars thick with smoke where throaty singers bawled witty songs of which I couldn't follow a word, and then took a look at cheap dimly-lit brothels where stolid workers sipped bocks at splintery tables from the corners of which a huge swarthy tart picked up coins with an unlikely part of her anatomy, a coin-swallowing contortionist, while other tarts, mostly slummocky, lounged about in bits of underwear or less. I spoke to one girl, slenderly muscular, with a faint dark down on her legs and upperlip, and found her of Italian origin, recently come up from the Savoy.

Somewhat dazed by the spectacle of torpid vice at its plodding routine, we came up for night-air and found another taxi, making for a more normally-somnolent café—for the hour was late. The Russians noticed that the driver spoke with a compatriot accent, and suddenly one of them recognised him as the colonel of the regiment in which he had served during the 1914 war. When the car stopped, the three Russians rapturously embraced, and the ex-colonel was asked to join us in a coffee. A rapid exchange of reminiscences went on; but as my Russian was worse than my French (P.R.S. knew the language not at all badly), I could not make out what was said. However, our Russians did not tell the White that they were Soviet diplomats—though one of them grew too talkative. The other whispered some code-word that I was to repeat to the blabber, who sat on my other side; but in my confused state I translated what I took to be the code-word's sense saying, '*Taisez-vous !*' to the dismay of the young Russians and the ex-colonel's bewilderment.

The last episode of the night I remember was an encounter with two bicycled gendarmes who came upon us as we were all urinating against a notice *Défense d'Afficher*. They dismounted and remonstrated, but in a few moments P.R.S. was slapping them on the back and giving them a speech on the superior humanity and lack of prudery in the French nation. They shook hands all round and rode on again. We sang the Marseillaise.

Winifred had asked me to call on her in London. I called and became friendly. She lived in a rambling one-floored weather-board house (with the doors all at different levels) near the 'World's End', Chelsea, in a lane that was half slummy, half rustic, a remnant of a London now quite vanished. A handsome confident girl lived with her, whom I didn't much like, though I once took her a large bunch of flowers—the only time I think I have presented a bouquet to a girl. Probably Winifred, a kindly, tactful and understanding soul, egged me on into doing it. Anyhow, having blushingly given the flowers, I felt such a fool I avoided the girl thereafter.[1]

---

[1] Winifred Edwards had been a member of various classical ballets in America led by such important dancers as Giuseppe Bonfiglio, Sergei Pernikoff, and Ivan Bankoff. In 1924 she retired from the theatre while her young son (by her

Through Winifred however I met a group of people who were to play a crucial part in my life. This group centred on Young, an Australian musician, who was a pioneer in evoking community-songs at football-matches and the like, and his ex-wife Edith. The marriage had broken up, and Young was living with a strange and lovely girl Elza, while Edith had turned to a young artist Roe. Among their friends were the painter Ronald Dunlop and Philip Henderson, then trying to write poetry. Edith and Roe had just taken over the house in Ebury Street, Chelsea, where Peter Warlock the musician had been living. Shortly before his removal he had acquired the habit of stripping all his clothes at a certain stage of drink and running about in the street. The Ebury ladies still peeped through their midnight curtains in the hope-fear of seeing his white form speed along the pavement, chanting snatches of some relevant hymn or ballad-refrain. There were also tales of his having become so obstreperous on one occasion that he was locked in the lavatory for a considerable length of time; he emerged from his dungeon sobered and disconsolate, declaring that he was henceforth dishonoured.

Edith had a slow wondering way of speaking, while she fastened her large, grave and kindling eyes on you, bearing you down with the full weight of her mental processes: as if only that moment she had thought out what she was saying, and understood what she thought—so that you were inescapably involved with it all, half-responsible for the momentous discovery she was making, with all its exciting and illuminating implications. You felt flattered, even if in fact she were only asking by what bus you had come. Everything, the bus number or the interpretation you made of Blake's Prophetic Books, was equally remarkable and full of clues to the ultimate mystery. Not that the mannerism was superficial; it held a genuine childlike element, an unslackening sense of strangeness in the revolving world. I found it pleasant to talk over cups of coffee with her and Roe into the early morning, and then to sleep on the couch, with Roe rushing to his office of commercial art and Edith wondering at the strangeness of an early morning, the eerie quality of the light, the peculiar way water boiled, and the secret messages in a newspaper.

first marriage) was at school in England. She had a small private income from Australia, and was working hard at private lessons in both stage and ballroom dancing, in the large studio room which her flat in Kensington contained, and was also teaching in a school. (She stayed only briefly at the World's End house.) She even tried to teach me to dance; but her failure in this impossible task was no slur on her expertise.

Young, prognathous, keen and earnest, introduced me to his colleague
John Goss. I listened to them both joyously singing chanties. A
forceful woman-singer, met at Curwen's musical publishing house, gave
me a long lecture on the sort of songs I was to write for her, and
presented me with some of Graves' poems set to music as exemplars.
What I did write, however, were unsingable curses on the English
scene—and an essay *Travel Narrows the Mind*, about the girl on the
liner with her tales of decapitated heads weathering into stone sculptures.
This I sent to the *Manchester Guardian*, which, to my surprise, accepted
it. A fluke that gave me incorrect ideas about the ease with which I
could make something out of freelance journalism.

Ronald was a Quaker, slow in his way of speaking, but not out of
Edith's sense of wonderment; rather he was deliberately rebuking the
world and its devils. His irritated wife retorted by throwing things
which he returned with dumb courtesy. A portrait he had painted, the
whole head a sodden red-purple, uncomfortably impressed me. What I
saw was his own pale face of renunciation, large and heavy, flat as a
sheep's, hanging against the red lump, the battered face of denied life.
I wrote a furious poem of White and Red in conflict, abstraction and
dead-matter, the driven sheep and the battered corpse uniting in the
Lamb of God and defeated by the red cock of resurrection. What I was
expressing was my own divided self as I stood in the bought-and-sold
streets of London.

However, it was Elza who most interested me, though for the moment
I kept warily out of her way and she said next to nothing as she sat in
her lonely beauty, lithe and pale, among the chattering others. Dressed
always in long pre-Raphaelite drape-clothes of rich and simple colour.
For the moment I shall cite only a few words from the novel *Lisa* that
Edith wrote later about Elza and myself. (Lisa Morrison is Elza.)

There was Mrs Morrison with her head thrown back a little wearily,
resting against the wall, seeming cast there, I thought, like a shadow. . . .
In her black frock, fitting almost affectionately to her slim body, she looked
curiously unreal, yet more real in her quivering evanescent beauty than
any of the others gathered round Mrs Dalrymple on the hearth rug—more
real in her way than anybody I had ever known. . . .
Lisa gathered up her body, as it were, and sat lightly on a stool, resting
her head on her hand, looking at the ground as though lost in contempla-
tion, alone in her thought-world.
I found myself picturing her with me by the sea. The white waves

would be choppy, blown by a following wind landwards, and a gull would wheel in sight suddenly, like a rare thought, to surprise the laziness of our minds as we lay amongst the thyme-strewn grass. The wind would bring colour to her pale cheeks, and those lips, I thought, would not droop so much, might smile, as I made a cushion for her head.

Edith is there trying to depict Elza through the eyes of one who was to be her fated lover—through my eyes; and she does it subtly and truly. All her wondering excitement at the strangeness of things had become concentrated on Elza, who had followed her in her husband's affections. But her intentness was in no way a mere effort to understand what Young was feeling; it was a pure effort of wonderment, without a speck of jealousy or envy.

There was indeed already something of a cult of Elza in the group, and that was one of the reasons I felt wary. They all spoke to me about her with something of bated breath, and she herself said nothing, seemed hardly to notice me at all. I wondered if they were creating a myth in order to give words to a serene and stricken silence as many worlds away as a statue. And then, watching her, I felt that all their comments were a hopeless effort to catch the strange and proud spirit certainly laired in her long supple body, which, when it moved, moved with the sudden and yet effortless gliding of water.

The General Strike loomed up. I still did not read newspapers, but could hardly escape hearing of this event. Mrs Kirtley had turned up with her ironic smile, taken one look at our house, and gone off with her son to Germany; so I was left alone in charge, living on eggs and sausages. The night before the Strike I drifted about Fleet Street, drinking in the pubs and trying to hear what people said. I ended among a group of printers and began haranguing them on the need to fight to a finish, to fight for a complete overthrow of the system. They listened with an air of amused toleration till one of the older men said, 'Weren't we told to look out for provocators?' At the note of hostility I drank up and retreated: which was taken as a confession of my guilt by some of the younger chaps. They started hustling me, keen for a chance to knock me down. So I ran for a bus going Strandwards and caught it, pursued by one of the more obdurate lads. Thus ended my first effort to fraternize with the English proletariat.

My mood of revolutionary hope, which ran counter to all the positions I had accepted under Norman's influence, was the first strong revival of the political enthusiasms of my undergraduate days; it revealed the powerful effect of the English social scene upon me. The new leaven was going to take a long time to work out, but it was already present. I continued to fume with a sense of excluded importance as the Strike continued. I would have liked to help, but had no idea how to set about it, unaware that P.R.S. in Oxford was one of the few students there working hard under the Coles to help the strikers. I strode about London, now mostly a city of the dead, with a savage satisfaction. Several times I walked across to Chelsea and chatted with Winifred; and I wrote an article, discussing Wellsian Utopias and arguing that the Strike involved human factors which made really fundamental change possible. In many ways an innocent article, but expressing a naïvely deepgoing response to the situation. I tried it on the *Guardian* and on the *Statesman*, and had it promptly rejected; I realized that after all I didn't fit into any journalistic niche in the English scene.

3. NINA HAMNETT

SUDDENLY the Strike was over. I didn't understand how and why, but felt let-down; the possibilities of humanizing the deadly world seemed nonsense. I had tried to say in my article that the serious artist could not be moved by reformist tactics, but that every impulse from below to break through the existent vicious-circle must at once engage his total sympathies. With the collapse of the Strike I simply forgot this idea. Soon after I visited P.R.S. in Oxford, dined at Queen's, was suitably impressed by the college-beer, and met S., who had been a student under Lascelles Abercrombie at Leeds. S. had a cool hard insolence of daring; and the three of us drank in small dank river-pubs or swaggered into any premises forbidden by the proctors—easy enough for me, but involving some hair-breadth escapes for the other two. One afternoon, at an outlying pub, I felt my anarchist compulsion come on me and exhorted some yokels to pull down the pillars of a worthless world, keeping respect only for art and intellect. I recall the fascinated bewilderment of one lad who continued the discussion in the Gents.

P.R.S. took me barging with Ramsay Macdonald's daughter; and one afternoon, watching cricket, we met a close relation of Sir John Simon, who gave us the inner-story of the Strike's breakdown. A story that meant nothing to me, but I understood P.R.S.'s denunciation of the right-wing T.U. leadership.

On the last night I returned to my lodgings at a late hour, groped my way into the dark room, undressed, and climbed into a bed already tenanted by an Indian, whose inconsequent explanations I couldn't follow. The landlady arrived in curlpapers and insufficient wrap, asserting that I'd only taken the room till the previous noon. There was nothing for it but to seize my case and wander out into a moonlit Oxford at about 2 o'clock a.m.; but luckily I met a policeman who gave me an address, where I knocked up an uncomplaining landlady and fell into bed.

Back in London, I carried on alone in Lady Somebody's house, which was steadily becoming more dusty. One day Jack MacLaren, a friend of

Woodcut by Lionel Ellis from *Theocritos*

Winifred's, who had been a beachcomber in the South Seas and still carried a whiff of that spacious oceanic existence, turned up with Thomas Burke, then famed for his Limehouse stories. We went for a drink in a near pub, a pleasant miniature place, a toy-pub blown out of an illustration to *Pickwick Papers*. Burke, a smallish screwed-up man, talked in a literary way, admired by the simple Jack. When I said I disliked London and wanted to get out somewhere on my own, he replied, 'No, I cannot live away from people. Unless I am in the thick of them, I feel that I'll go mad. In any solitude the enemy of souls comes too close. I cannot withstand him.' Jack looked respectful, but I said there was no need to be afraid of the enemy of souls; the problem was to use his temptations against him.

We went on into town and ate in Charlotte Street, then tried the Fitzroy Tavern. An automatic piano was clattering. A woman came up and asked me if I were some Danish sculptor who I think was holding an exhibition. She was Nina Hamnett. Not long over from Paris, she had just had a show at the Claridge Galleries and hadn't done badly. She looked rather like the Colonel's Daughter at first glance, perhaps a bit seedily down on her luck, but able to retreat when necessary to a Cheltenham croquet-garden, and her voice was as distinct and colourless.[1] But in fact, together with a fair talent as a draughtsman, she had an insatiable hunger for life—though her mediocre mind prevented her from bringing the talent and the hunger together in her art. I have met few people who had less interest in ideas except perhaps as a tag on which to hang personalities. In the process even personalities were reduced to the most banal level of anecdotage. She was an odd indomitable character: a bohemian snob who collected names. Not that it mattered to her whether the significance of your name lay in a title, a boxing championship, a criminal record or skill in training fleas, an abnormal beer-capacity or high achievement in art. Her aquiline blunt-tipped nose, her brow sloping a little back and her chin slightly retreating, suggested accurately enough her eager appetite for persons and places,

---

[1] In registering this image I was unaware that she was actually the daughter of an army officer and grand-daughter on the maternal side of Capt. Archdeacon, the surveyor of West Australia; educated at the Royal School, Bath, for the daughters of officers, before she went to the London School of Art. Her youthful body is immortalized in Gaudier-Brzeska's torso carved on a piece of marble stolen from a Putney stonemason's yard. (I have just noticed that in *Is she a Lady?* she mentions hearing her voice on a recorded broadcast and it 'sounded just like Itma's drunken Colonel!')

B

as if her childhood had been spent with that prominent nose pressed against windowpanes which she now had no compunction about smashing in all directions, without loss of her ladylike accent. Her rather large baggy ears increased the effect of an omnivorous thrust forwards through all winds, windows, and other obstacles.

We had several drinks together and Nina was delighted to add the author of *Limehouse Nights* to her list of acquaintances. Then we moved to another pub, nearer Tottenham Court Road, where were D. B. Wyndham Lewis and others. I sat back, enjoying the scene from a remote distance, over a bellyful of beer. 'At last I have found my proper Hell,' I told myself. 'Now I am at home.'

I had arranged to meet Nina next day. I took along some copies of *The Passionate Neatherd*—unbound sheets—which were the only specimens of our printing to hand. She had with her a young American from Paris, Robert McAlmon, who ran his own press and was a pal of Joyce: peevishly handsome, with depressed lines on his longish face. However, I liked his sudden rude remarks about England. I recall saying, 'In Oxford they think it frightfully advanced to put up a Corot reproduction,' but have no idea where I had picked up the information. McAlmon looked even more bored, his fine features pinching into gloomy silence, when I produced the sheets. I knew now they'd fall flat, but couldn't get out of showing them. Nina read out a few lyrics and charitably laughed. Over our beers I tried to convince McAlmon that I had a long poem *Between Two Kisses*, which was a sort of surrealist experiment; but he knew that no experiment of mine could interest him and merely grew gloomier.

Nina however wasn't put off. I became very friendly with her and we went about a lot. Passing down Howland Street, she pointed out the house where Rimbaud and Verlaine had stayed and said that she had lost her maidenhead in the same rooms; and she told the anecdote which she was proud of: 'I asked Sickert if the L.C.C. would put up one of their blue plaques, and he said: They'll put up one for you at the front and another for them at the back.' She took me to a party at Augustus John's studio where I met Tommy Earp, who, I found to my surprise, knew Australian poetry well: the work of Brennan, McCrae, Dowd and others. 'If we print McCrae here,' I said, 'you must write the preface.' And Tommy, with his red beaming face, his cropped hair, and his quavering drawl like a point scribbling on a slate, replied that there was nothing he'd like better. I met also Tallulah Bankhead, then at her height as a gallery-girl crush, with her violet-blue eyes and her hot-honey-and-milk voice, with her ash-gold hair under one of the horrible toques of the time; for some reason she took much interest in our proposed press and offered to introduce me to various N.Y. personages. who could help; but I didn't call on her as she suggested. I had a complete scepticism always as to success gained through the right contacts; and perhaps also I remembered McAlmon's boredom. More important was my first meeting, on this occasion, with Peter Warlock, if meeting it can be called. For he had already passed-out when we arrived, and was moaning feebly with closed eyes in the bathroom, where various drunks were trying to revive him with doses of brandy or douches of cold water. I regarded his tipsily-pasty face, which I revered as belonging to the original of Coleman in Huxley's *Antic Hay*, and took my turn at water-sprinkling. 'He was talking of God and then 'collapsed,' said Eugene Goosens. I replied, 'It serves him right for such ungentlemanly behaviour.' I remember that not-very-bright remark because it was the only quip of mine at this period which received uproarious response. Which only shows how drunk everyone was.

Finally I found that Nina and myself were the last revellers left in the studio with Augustus. As Nina was still looking for bottles with something left in them, I tried to tell him how affected I had been in Brisbane by a book of his Welsh landscapes and pictures of his wife. One painting, which showed the brightly-clad woman in a splendid cabbage-garden, recurred to my mind with luminous clarity, and I tried to describe it. 'The rich blue greens . . . neglected beauty . . . I can only recall one poem, attributed to Ausonius, *On Budding Roses: Vidi concretas per gramina flexa pruinas.* . . . The clotted hoarfrost on the bent grass, rounded drops rolling together on the cabbage-leaves. . . . Break-up of the classical generalizations, the poet really looking at nature. Somehow you know, looking at those Welsh cabbages, I mean your colours, in sweltering Brisbane. Quite lost. And now I'm here.' I went on a long time like that, and Augustus said absolutely nothing. Only now it occurs to me that he was owl-drunk.

I also went with Nina to a performance of *Façade* and heard Edith Sitwell performing through a large painted face. I had mentioned to Nina that about the only book I could read on the liner had been Sacheverell's *Hundred and One Harlequins*, with its rhythms that suited the continuous ever-changing sea; and she introduced me to him. My expressions of gratitude seemed to make him yet more depressed, but

THE GOING TO BED

IOHN: I feele my selfe a litle ill after supper. My stomacke greeueth me. Mine Oast I will go to rest. I haue great desire to sleepe. The sleepe is alreadie fallen into mine eyes. Let some bodie shew me my chamber.

HOST: When you will my daughter shall shew you the way.

IOHN: God night mine Ost. Godnight, God-night hostesse. God giue you good night and good rest euerie bodie.

GAUDINETTA: You must mount this way sir. See your chamber. See your bed. There are the priuies, and here is your chamber pot.

IOHN: Draw these curtines. Lend me a kercheffe or a coiffe: I haue a night cap in my bosome.

GAUDINETTA: Your sheetes are cleane.

IOHN: Looke that they be verie drie I pray you.

GAUDINETTA: I haue ayred them at the fire.

IOHN: Pull of my hosen. Couer me with my gowne. I haue too litle couering. Giue me another pillow, I cannot lye so low.

GAUDINETTA: Are you well now? will you haue yet more heling? would you nothing else?

91

A page from The Parlement of Pratlers

no doubt he was merely shy. Afterwards we went to a nightclub not far from the Fitzroy. As I took out a banknote I realized that I would have to pull myself up. Nina wasn't in the least mercenary. Having decided that I was Somebody, she wouldn't have bothered if I had announced empty pockets and proceeded to borrow from her; but I had irrupted in the guise of a well-off Australian and had been too weak-willed to change my labels. At the moment I was sitting with a superbly beautiful girl who said almost nothing and encouraged me to talk with her serenely imperial smile. After a while Nina came back and made some praising comment on another woman. The superb one paused, held her long cigarette-holder away, and slowly turned her head. 'Yes, a handsome lump of meat,' she said in a voice of lucid insolence, but without any stress or even interest.

I admired her inordinately, rose and said good night.

I dropped clean out of Nina's world thenceforth. I had come to know Tommy fairly well and had eaten at his flat. (The legend went that he had inherited a large part of a foundry; and that he had sold hearth after hearth to finance a cheerful if not riotous flow of good liquor at the Ritz. He had been president of the Union at Oxford and at one time meditated standing for Parliament as a Liberal.) I had even found some pleasure in McAlmon's morose company as long as we kept to the shortcomings of the English.[1] But now I decided that I must pull out, save my cash, and wait for some deeper impulse to show itself in me, something which convinced me of its connection with my poetry.

I had been seeing little of Winifred and her group; but now they asked me to a dance, which was to raise funds for some art purpose. I went, and under the stimulus of whisky I actually danced. Again the illusion that I was a rich young Australian came out in some half comment, and for once I didn't object. There was a lot of whisky flowing. Elza was there; and my confused attraction and revulsion gave way to a simple high-spirited wish to draw her out of her mystical reverie. As usual she was dressed in a long clinging dress of rough texture; this time the hue was dark. And her hair was plainly done, smoothed down over her ears and knotted at the back. Her eyes were still uninvolved in the scene, but her lips were slightly parted with a breath of excitement.

I felt masterful for once. I kissed somebody else, perhaps just to make sure that I could act as recklessly as I felt. And somebody else. And then

---

[1] I had somehow become acquainted with A. J. Symonds, who was much interested in fine printing. During a dinner at his flat overlooking Baker Street, Marrot (of the bookshop and publishers) made an attack on modern verse and for some reason picked on uses of the word 'bland'. I cited from *Helen*, without mentioning my authorship, 'Or the bland fillets of the wind'. He guessed the lines were mine and was scathing.

I kissed Elza. I was dancing with her and had guided our steps into a side corridor, away from the large hall. She did not return my kiss, but she made no resistance, and afterwards her bright eyes looked directly in on the dancers, on me. And her lips were a little more opened. Her slender body felt strong, pliant, but still locked as it lapsed in my arms. Young, I saw, was watching us with a stare that made his heavy jaw yet heavier; but I didn't care. We went on dancing.

Two days later I called on her as arranged; for then Young was away on one of the tours arranged, I think, by the *Daily Express*. She was alone in her room. Let me again cite *Lisa*. Whether the details are exact, I cannot recall; but the atmosphere is exactly evoked. (*Lisa* was published in 1930; and Edith sent me a copy. But though I was then in throes of trying to understand Elza, I did not read the book beyond the first page—as if there was a taboo on it and I must penetrate Elza's world by my own efforts alone. I read the book in the British Museum Reading Room for the first time this year, 1961, and was astonished at its insights, though inevitably there was much that Edith did not see, deceived despite her sharp scrutiny by Elza's own account of herself at that time.)

My first impression was of strangeness, of being in a sort of bizarre tent. A divan in a corner covered with some sort of scarlet cloth, a chest of drawers, tall and narrow, painted black, and the white walls, white ceiling arching into a concave peak and then sloping down to an alcove over the window, from the window a diffused, rather pale light throwing one side of Lisa's face into shadow—all these impressions, although they came in succession, seemed to come in one glance, as I stepped rather diffidently over the threshold. It is as I imagined, I said to myself, she creates about herself an atmosphere of legend.

As I came close up to her I saw that she was wearing a dark dress fitting close to her body in her usual style, and a heavy silver necklet—of old coins, they seemed to be—as ornament. Her hands moved nervously. She did not look up.

She made tea and answered quietly to my fervent account of what I hoped to do in England. There was never at any time the faintest suggestion of coquetry in her manner; I cannot remember her ever laughing, though she had a gentle and subtly-lingering smile. Although I had kissed her at the dance, I felt no self-assurance; there seemed no link between the gravely-aloof dispenser of tea and the girl who had sunk with entire passivity into my arms. I talked on to cover my uncertainty and at last stood up to go. I reached the door, still talking, and turned to say goodbye. She had come up close, but without the least flicker of emotion on her pale tranquil face with its fine modelling, its Florentine clarity of outline. I took her in my arms and she stayed there. I kissed her and she gave a faint sigh, closing her eyes.

Afterwards, we went out and ate in a small café nearby, then returned to her room. When I left about eleven o'clock, I felt that I had possessed her wholly and that she was now an integral part of me, and at the same time that she was more a stranger than ever, someone whom I least

Drawing by Norman Lindsay from *Lysistrata*

understood of all the persons in the world. A minglement of rapture and fear. As if at last I had entered the unknown dimension of England, the alien thing which I had been decrying because I did not comprehend its meaning, its reason for existence. Something parasitic and yet beautifully gathering all the pang of lost things, the broken hopes and yearnings of the many centuries. Already I had a fair idea that she was ignorant, lacking any sense of history, perhaps hardly educated at all; and I guessed that her silences were in part protective. Yet I felt in her the unspoiled essence of all art, all poetry, strangely naïve and spontaneous, and also compressing an immemorial wisdom and lore. Whereas the sophisticated wenches in Nina's world had left me at root repelled, since I felt in them only a delectable well-polished surface with nothing individually significant on the other side, in Elza I felt that the surface was unimportant. Her beauty was wholly a projection of a strange inner life for which she had no words, though she found a certain release in the accessories with which she surrounded herself as emblems of her difference, her sojourn in a dim sea-cavern of oracular repose. The only analogy I could find was in the paintings of Giorgione, where each woman, where indeed all nature, is listening—listening to an unheard music. She was a prisoner of her senses, which were tuned to a system of harmonies denied by the world. Helpless and asking me to rescue her— from what? I too was helpless, deliberately rejecting any of the normal defences against a derisive world, an inquisition in which the threat of starvation was the primary and unceasing weapon used to bring about conformity, the acceptance of the mechanism of the cash nexus.

This close similarity which I felt between Elza and myself was one of the elements of my fear. How could I protect her when I could not protect myself, had no wish to? And yet I knew I could not evade the fascination of her enigma; I could know myself only in knowing her.

These ecstatic fears and foreboding filled me in a confused way, and drove me out of the bus, so that I walked some miles home. But they reached my mind only in fits and starts, in fragments of consciousness; if I had known what they really implied, I should have fled from London.

4. ELZA

I DID not go to her room again, but she came almost every day to St John's Wood. She offered herself simply, without words, with an emotion that could be either complete trust or reckless despair. I tried to sound Winifred and Edith about her. I had no idea if she had drawn Young away from Edith or had been taken by him after his marriage had broken down. I didn't like to ask Edith questions directly, and she always expressed the greatest liking and respect for Elza. I felt however that Winifred didn't quite accept the legend; I let her know how things had gone and got the impression that P.R.S., learning of our relations, wasn't altogether pleased. Also, the MacLarens, I thought, did not like her. I got hints that she was not the immaculate dreamer she seemed. M., a stalwart whom I had known at the Queensland University, and who had been surveying in the Sudan, was now in London and was haunting her place, I found.

Meanwhile in Lady Somebody's house we had our hasty meals and lay in the attic, or had a bath together and wandered naked round the house. She had a gay tenderness, a childlike readiness to lark. What with my careless and anxious way of living, eating little and erratically, I had a recrudescence of adolescent skin-trouble and was afraid to strip. But when she saw the carbuncles on my back, she kissed them and said, 'Poor dear.' I felt as if she were a medieval Saint who embraced lepers, and at the same time a Thais of the ancient world. But that seemed a *fin-de-siècle* fancy; and despite her Byrne-Jones aspect, she was at these moments radiantly a creature born from the waters of poetic immediacy, without any ancestry, and yet incarnating a dream of aeons, a thing of beauty with humanity perfected. Perhaps it was now that I was finally lost.

Suddenly S. descended on me from Oxford, with his hard wit, his challenging hand-clasp, his cold air of ruthless daring. He gave the effect of having tried everything once already, and of now dangerously seeking the sin-against-the-holy-ghost, passionate and bored. We made the round of local pubs and found Kilburn, where he was more at home, restoring confidence to the most draggled of aged tarts by his ubiquitous glance of brazen desire, P.R.S. also turned up, and Elza promised to cook a duck for us. Young was home, but she managed to dash across, produce the dinner, and dash off again. That night we had the conviction of having cracked the rafters of the heavens, and I danced a mime of the Crucified Faun to *L'Après-midi* on a gramophone. S. tried to dance with the prancing Bacchante.

Then things were quiet again. Kirtley came back from Germany and announced that he would have to give up the house at the end of the six-months' lease. Elza went on visiting me, with his caustic tolerance. She and I never discussed the future. She, who used no make-up, gave herself with a calm and eager submissiveness, with open eyes in which there was a questioning look. As though she understood neither herself nor me, and was looking on from afar.

I knew that things were now strained between her and Young, but she told me nothing and I did not ask. Nor did I mention M. to her. I had met him once when I was in Chelsea on a visit that I could not get out of without seeming to evade Young and the others. I disliked his large confident presence, his husky seducer's voice, the way he watched Elza; and remembered acutely how in our Brisbane days he had had Rosaline at his beck and call, a lithe loose wild-eyed girl with long slim hands, to which I had written sonnets in the Elizabethan manner and which, limply, she had let me kiss, keeping the rest of her tenuous self for M.'s complacent devouring. He had come to London, he said, after a touch of the sun, and he seemed a bit queer, huskily lowering his voice and talking suddenly of Sudanese things we couldn't follow.

Young was doubtless worried about M. and myself; but I think that the more he had come up against the power of dead resistance in Elza, and the more he tried to hold her, to impress himself upon her, the more she coldly withdrew. There is a passage in *Lisa* where Munt (Young) states his attitude to Lisa, a matter on which Edith must have been well informed. I cite it for this reason and because it shows him torn by the same divided emotion that I was to feel: the wish to make Elza stand on her own feet, and the fear of using any of the available ways of doing so:

'You needn't waste pity on her. She's the lucky one.'
'Why? What do you mean?'
'She's the only one of us all who lives apart in her own inner world, and doesn't feel. She is cold, I tell you. Damnably cold. I don't believe she

has ever felt a real emotion for anyone in her life. You can see how apart from everyone she is, by her eyes. Her eyes never grow warm—or seldom,' he added quickly, smiling as he spoke, as though he had suddenly remembered a pleasing reflection.

'Why are you attached to her, then?' I asked, interrupting his reverie.

'God knows! Perhaps because of her very coldness. I never know what she is thinking. She doesn't talk very much, but all the time you can feel her making her observations—acute ones. It is disconcerting. She is clever, too. No, perhaps not exactly clever. . . . Most women you understand almost at once—what they will say—what they will do under certain circumstances. You know what it will be like kissing them, you can feel their flesh under your hands—and know it is flesh—and while you pet them you know how they will respond—and it is all so stale.' He sighed wearily.

Turning on me, he said: 'With Lisa you never know, not from one hour to the next; I often imagine when I come home she will have vanished.'

'Like fire and air,' I murmured, forgetting him.

'You can never get at her—so you are always left searching. To Armstrong she is the legendary woman, he says, but he is so full of literary ideas, I don't take much notice of him.'

'Can she not earn her living at anything? That would solve one of her difficulties, surely.'

'What at? But I see—you would urge her to be independent—it would make your problem easier. The heroic girl struggling away at uncongenial work! You would not advocate her being an artist's model, I suppose? That would expose her to temptations. Oh yes! Sully the white bird. It would please you, no doubt, to see her struggling with a tray of greasy plates in a restaurant—perspiring—with the young men looking at her calves. . . . Do you know I wish I had never seen her. . . . Ever since I first saw her at Leo's,' he said, 'I have never had an hour's freedom—not an hour without strain. Sometimes it is almost unbearable.'

To Young, the leader of community-song, who had something coarse as well as genial about him, Elza had been turning her cold impenetrable side: the side which seemed to me her lonely pride. And suddenly she told me that she had left him. Told me without the least emphasis or show of emotion: as if she had merely spoken of going to Harrod's to shop. I asked no questions but I noticed that she had a bandaged wrist. From my other sources of information I learned that she had tried to commit suicide by severing a vein. The effect of this story on me was considerable. My fear of her was deepened, and I felt a sharp repulsion.

Suicide, like murder, was to me an act possible only for creatures of a low quality of life. But the shock also drew me towards her, driving away all my suspicions that she was a well-disguised tart whom anyone could have; the deed stamped her with an undeniable

MY FRIEND

Her heavy hair drips with gold
From the sweat of the gods she bathes in.
The fires in her eyes are sparks from the steel
Of the giants and the gods of the air clashing
    swords.

On a web of air we walk by day
And bask in caves of flesh by night.
Milk from my breasts she feeds upon—
Men look at her, and not at me.

She pities me, this child of love,
Sold me her lover for a kiss,
And now the gold drips from my hair . . .
Was ever love so great as this?

39

A page from *I See the Earth*, with a
drawing by Jack Lindsay

sincerity and showed her position with Young as one of long-suffering martyrdom.

She told me that she was moving into a basement in Eaton Square. First however the place had to be decorated. I offered to help her. There was a large front room with a kitchen behind. We set to work

distempering the walls a faint under-sea green. I concentrated on the
ceilings; and distemper ran down my arms, into my eyes and hair, as I
tried to produce the maze of wavy lines she wanted. Young had sent
over a few pieces of furniture and she had picked up some second-hand
things. Nothing definite was said about Young, yet somehow she made
me feel that he had been incredibly cruel to her: not by any physical
ill-treatment, but by a tyrannical inability to understand her, to cease
from trampling on all the fine things of her spirit. She infused me with
an emotion of passionate resentment against him, a fathomless contempt, which had the effect of binding me all the closer to her—
increasing my conviction that I alone of all men could appreciate
her, could come in time to find and unlock the buried fountains of her
spirit.

The second night I did not go back to St John's Wood. She did not
ask me to stay and I said nothing about any plans. I stayed and we slept
on the divan which Young had sent over. It was her own property, she
said. The next day we went on with the distempering and with the
clearance of lumber from the kitchen, then we drank beer at the Antelope
—something unusual for Elza, who seldom drank anything but a little
wine—and again I stayed. At the end of a week I was still there. In a
strange spell of happiness we carried on with the redecoration and
wandered up and down King's Road hand in hand, buying vegetables
or spaghetti and looking in the shop windows at our incomparable
reflections. I carried back to Eaton Square on a wheelbarrow an old
chest of drawers that she bought and meant to paint.

One evening Edith called in and smiled on our ménage. She read a
poem I had written on the wall:

> *Pull down the blind and bring*
> *this twilight of kisses. Pull*
> *love down over the mind*
> *and shut out people passing.*
> *Pull down the blind.*

> *O that this kiss might be*
> *a silence enduring and strong*
> *to shut out for ever*
> *men the faceless noises*
> *endlessly passing along.*

Give me your mouth and draw
love down over the mind.
Let the world suddenly die—
pull down the blind.

'How brave you are,' she said to Elza, who smiled her most mysterious smile and said nothing.

At long last I felt an urgent need to write. I began a verse-play with a Norse setting, *Ragnhild*, which was to be a counterpart and contrast to *Helen Comes of Age*. Ragnhild, a wild dreamy Irishwoman, has been captured by Frithiof. She does her best to set his brother Asmund against him, and draws on a bard, Viglund, to fall in love with her. At the end, meaning to stab herself, she stabs Frithiof in the eye. She persuades Asmund to accuse Viglund of the murder, and the bard is killed. The whole point of the play lay in the enigmatic and contradictory character of Ragnhild, in whom I wanted to express all my love and fear of Elza: the element in her that seemed to me strangely pure, gentle, dedicated, and uncompromising, the element that was bewildered with anguish and capable, I thought, of compulsive violences. Frithiof was given something of what I felt to be Young's hostile half-insights:

Frithiof: *Standing there as if you have been discovered*
in some great act of guilt that you yet were proud of,
as you are always standing
when I come into a room that you've been filling
with an ooze of sullen and thick silence.
What is it you always do when you're alone
that gives you such a sly anger of surprise?
Ragnhild: *I am not alone. And I have been talking.*
And I am not angry yet,
Frith: *Go, Ingebiorg.* (She goes.)
Now we're alone. You always seem alone,
and silent too. Even when you've just spoken,
your words remembered in the echo of thought
seem bellnotes that tinkle harshly from your mind
across the dulcet hush of the air
into my mind.
Not noises uttered at me between your teeth;
and when I speak I scrape that harsh silence.

Ragn: *I shall go also.*
Frith: *Don't go. What have I done?*
I haven't seen you now for three days.
Where have you been hiding yourself away?
telling your sulks to birds looking sideways at you?
dancing to wild cattle in a glade
in hopes to lure the bull-king from his cow?
going for walks at midnight?

Those lines, which start off a long altercation between Ragnhild and Frithiof, I wrote at Eaton Square. But we weren't there for long. The woman letting the basement saw that I was with Elza, and said the terms of occupation had been broken. So we moved to a room further down King's Road, losing all our hard work of decoration. What we wanted to keep of the furniture, I took off in various wheelbarrow-trips. Elza had no money. Young had been going to make her a small allowance, visiting her in her basement; but naturally when he heard I was with her, he dropped this arrangement. Apart from the few pounds earned from the *Guardian*, I had had all this while only the £40 odd with which I had landed; and now there was very little left. I had lost any belief that Kirtley would manage to float the Fanfrolico Press. What with his going-off to Germany and my preoccupation with Elza, a rift had come between us. He was having trouble with Lady Somebody or her agents, who asserted that we had broken large quantities of her valuables. Except for a few pieces of cheap crockery and perhaps a dent or two in the Bacchante I denied the damage; but though Kirtley said little in his testy way, I felt that I was blamed.

We moved from our nondescript room to a basement near Baron's Court. I was learning some facts about Elza. She was married to Robert Craig, a son of Gordon Craig, and had a child Robinetta, aged about six. Robert and the child were living in Paris, where he was acting as a guide for tourists. She always spoke fondly of Robert and I failed to get any clear idea as to why she had left him. This definite background of hers relieved my mind a lot; also the existence of Robert made her dependence on me seem less absolute. About her earlier years she was vague. She gave an incoherent impression of having lived in Paris, born in a family closely related to the poet Hérédia; yet she knew French very imperfectly—a smattering she had picked up when living in Paris with Robert for a year or two before her return in 1925. Her mother, I gathered, had been mad to some degree; and as the subject affected her painfully, I made no effort to press it. At least the Craigs were undeniably real.

She was in touch with Mrs Craig (who had long been parted from Gordon). Mrs Craig called unexpectedly one day on the basement and I was shut in the kitchen. I heard her excessively upperclass dulcetly-false voice and caught a glimpse of her as she departed in the taxi that had been waiting. Elza was excited by the visit. She had an ambivalent attitude to her mother-in-law, which she had obviously taken over from Robert. Mrs Craig, according to this version, was an extremely charming, well-bred woman, with fine taste in clothes and furniture (she used her knowledge of antiques to add to her income); but she was completely superficial, conventional, and self-centred. She used her charm unscrupulously to dominate her sons and was armoured in every way against the attack of reality, assured of her good intentions whatever she did. There were three sons: Robert, who was intelligent but restless, unable to settle down to any of the jobs that Mrs Craig used her social position to gain for him, secretaryships and the like; one who, badly upset by his war experiences, had been drowned a few years back; a third who suffered from various nervous disabilities but seemed to have found his place in a City job. Elza blamed Mrs Craig for the drowning of the second son, who had swum out in desperation until he sank, though Mrs Craig resolutely treated the episode as an accident. Robert, it was clear, had been very attached to the dead brother, who seemed highly talented; and I felt that the latter's death had much to do with his own inability to accept a role in his mother's world. Mrs Craig, according to Elza, even used her physical charm to keep her sons tied to her suspender-belt, coquettishly allowing them into her toilet with entire 'innocence'.

I felt much sympathy for Robert, who had severed his class-connection with a certain flamboyant and insulting verve. I gathered that he had picked Elza up not long after the war and fallen in love with her. Against his mother's bitter resistance he married her and she bore Robinetta. His mother then accepted the position and did her best to groom Elza and fit the couple into her world. Elza was grateful to Mrs Craig for much that she had learned from her, yet had abetted Robert in all his resistances; it was his refusal to take the conventional profitable line, without being able to find an alternative, which seemed to me to have bound her to him. She had made a few attempts since her marriage

Drawing by Nina Hamnett of Betty May in the Fitzroy Tavern

to earn something, as a fashion-model and as an actress, briefly taking
the main role of Lawrence Houseman's *Prunella*; somebody had also
wanted her as Joan of Arc in a film, which had come to nothing. Once
again I could not make out why her efforts had flagged away. One of her
best friends had been the painter Nicholson, for whom she had often
sat. (I had an impression that the Craig boys had been embittered at
public school by the fact that their father was an illegitimate son of Ellen

Terry; they had been made to feel something of a pariah position.)

Mrs Craig's visit proved that the family did not look on the marriage with Robert as broken, and I tried to sound Elza on this point. Something unpleasant had happened in Paris, but whether or not she blamed Robert I did not know; she had rushed away, leaving him and the child. Had she any intention of rejoining Robert if he came to London? what about the child? how had she kept herself before living with Young? To these matters and others of the same sort I could get no clear answer. Not that I pestered her with questions; but at moments she seemed impelled to talk about herself, and I tried to put together the scattered ends, generally in vain.

She had a cult of Epstein's *Rima* and took me to see the monument in Hyde Park; it was clearly important to her to find if I liked it. I liked it. She took me out into Epping Forest via Waltham Abbey, and she stripped in a small copse where, lying quietly, we caught a glimpse of shy deer. She had a passionate feeling for birds and all wild creatures. I tried to put this side of her into *Ragnhild*, using tales she told of herself—how, for instance, she used to search the harvest-fields for nests and fledglings, which she carried tenderly to the hedges. Such country memories rang more true than her vague accounts of childhood in some mouldering park on the outskirts of Paris.

However, on the whole I had come to accept her account of herself. For instance, one evening we were in Piccadilly Circus and she saw Marie Tempest billed in a play; she sent a note in and a pair of tickets promptly appeared; after the play we had a chat with Marie. Then came a blow. I learn from her dislikers that she had certainly been having an affair with M. about the time she first gave herself to me, and for a while afterwards, and, worse, that M. had been invalided back to London through catching syphilis in the Sudan. For some days I was filled with a cold revulsion, though I said nothing. Then the pathos of Elza's charm overcame me again and I gradually forgot.

London was now a different place, irradiated by our secret delights and revealing furtive moments of a strange poetry. Elza talked of Regent Street and its vistas before the big shopkeepers got together to kill it. With her I rediscovered the parks and older squares, and strolled through the evening of Chelsea embankment. Along the river, here or near the Tower, I could gratefully recall that London was Turner's city and had in many ways made him, at least its docks and watersides, its Covent Garden of spilt plenty. In the full moonlight the blackened buildings

with their rain-streaked whites became the flats of a faery-play, and we
hunched our shoulders under the cloaks of an enormous secrecy. The
traffic-lights spun in mad patterns of pursuit and flight, and the puddles
were scummed with hell-flares. We rode in the front seats of the open
tops of buses in the rain, drawing the tarpaulins over our knees, visiting
fantastic arenas of hoarse activity, Clapham Junction and the Elephant
and Castle, under the wet glittering darkness drawn close down like a
circus tent. One afternoon we came out of Hyde Park with twined
fingers and no weight at all in our bodies, and I felt someone's glance
upon us, turned and saw Lord Balfour watching us with eyes of over-
brimming benevolence. Only a moment, but the memory remained
clear, an old man serenely blessing life.

A working arrangement had been reached with Kirtley. I was to
carry on somehow on my own till the year-end, making a new version
of the *Satiricon*. Meanwhile he'd go ahead organizing the Press. The
first book would be a replica of our Australian *Lysistrata*; the second,
the Petronius, re-using the illustrations Norman had made for the
pre-war edition printed by Strauss.

At Elza's insistence I was growing a beard. Visiting my bank in
Broad Street to draw almost all that remained of my meagre account, I
saw the clerk stare with horrified compassion, but did not tell him my
unshaven state was deliberate. Then P.R.S. turned up at our basement,
full of adventurous spirits and soaking me in renewed hope. All sorts of
ways of making money were instantly possible; the only real question
was how to enjoy ourselves. Away from London, the treadmill round,
the pleasure-lash whistling over the backs of the tormented city-throng.
Why not Brittany? We got out a map of France. I closed my eyes and
jabbed a pin down. 'It's landed right in mid-sea,' I said. 'We drown.'

'Nonsense,' he replied. 'It's on an island.' He snatched the map.
'Ile de Bréhat. Off Paimpol. Icelandic Fisheries. Splendid choice.
Let's go there.'

'To Debussy's sunken cathedral if you like.'

Having acquired a beard, I needed a new photo in my passport; but
as I knew no clergymen, etc., I went to Australia House to ask someone
to vouch for me. The official I saw was sympathetic, though concerned
to find out why I had grown such a luxuriant beard. He chatted on, and
happened to bring up the fact that the Australians were playing cricket
at Lord's. My blank ignorance of this world-shattering event must have
made him doubtful of my Australianism; however he signed my photo.

Now came the crucial matter. I used my last shillings to cable Norman with a request for £50. This was the only time I ever asked him for money; and he sent the sum by return cable. In the next few years we took his pen-and-inks, old ones or new ones specially drawn for us, without making him any return in cash. But as the Press was established on the basis of propagandizing his ideas, we felt no compunction. Money, however, was a different thing, and I had qualms about the request. I quieted my conscience that otherwise I did not see how I could be sure of finding time for Petronius, which was essential for the launching of the Press.

5. ILE DE BRÉHAT

WINIFRED had decided to join us in our Breton holidaying, and we set off late in August, sailing from Southampton to St Malo. P.R.S. impressed the *douanes* with his versatile French and we found cheap rooms near the Quai. I don't know what went wrong with our train-calculations, but we spent the next night stranded in mid-Brittany at St Brieuc. We arrived so late, with no connection, that we decided not to tramp through the slumbering township on the quest for rooms. We settled down on the railway station, using what rugs and coats we could muster to keep out the early-morning cold, and woke cramped and sore-boned. A train turned up before we could find any café, and we made for it, warned by a porter, '*Vous serez écrasé!*' At last we arrived at Paimpol, to drink warm coffee and *cidre bouché*, and to roam about the port with its ancient lugger and its old men dreaming on lumps of granite. There was no launch to the Isle till the next day, so we walked along the coast, and then found a cheap hotel.

That night I felt abysmally lost and scared for the first time since I had left Australia. But with P.R.S.'s cheerful face over morning coffee and with the pleasant chugging across the blue waters to the island, I grew assured. The port was small, but had houses hung at different levels and angles; and the island itself was a perfect miniature, a clump of warm rocks and pine trees dropped with fine precision of tone upon the wavering waters, against a scudding sky. Actually there was much more of it than appeared at first glance. We drank to our arrival at the first café, with nets drying on the wall; and then reconnoitred inland. We decided to put up, not at the port, but at an hotel a couple of miles in, by a small village. It was cheaper: also there were dining-tables in the open under pergolas of vines.

Here we all stayed two or three weeks. I played chess with P.R.S. at the café down the road and drank *cidre*; and I finished putting together *Dung of Pegasus*, an autobiographical fantasia, which was later published serially as by Peter Meadows in *The London Aphrodite*. P.R.S. in his large way notified the proprietor that a great work had been completed under his roof; and the man begged to be allowed to present us with a bottle of champagne for the honour of having his hotel mentioned as the address at the end of the book. The champagne was bad, but its delivery was a solemn ceremony, with speeches and handshakes, and we drank it seriously under the shadow of the broad vine-leaves.

We found a small cottage in the open ground facing the hotel, which was called Prairie de l'Allégoat. The landlady, Veuve Lambolet, lived thriftily in a lean-to at the back, with a goat tied to a post. The cottage had one room below, one above, with a later room tacked on at one side at the front.

The tide was out as the others went to catch the launch, which had to be approached by a winding track of stones slippery with seaweed. Winifred had bought pottery at Paimpol and packed it carefully in a large crate. The fisherman nonchalantly carrying this crate on his shoulders slid on a slimy stone and brought the pots down with a crash. As everyone crowded into the launch, P.R.S. took me aside with an unusual air of seriousness and asked if I had definitely broken with Janet. Caught by surprise, I could only answer, 'No, of course not.' What then about Elza ? 'I don't know, we've never discussed it, I suppose things will work out, she's married too.' The questions distracted and disturbed me, and in my confusion I mentioned that Norman had once called Rose and Janet the only two intelligent women he knew. P.R.S. rightly made a sarcastic comment, but looked relieved. My perturbation however went on and lay heavily on me after we had waved our friends out of sight and were climbing back to the Prairie from which no sea was visible. I found it hard to speak, until the dusk smudged out the world with swabs of blue, and I could look Elza in the eyes again, because there was only we two left alive in a softly-breathing world.

We spent about three months in the Veuve's cottage and came to know the island and its people well. We watched the men make apple-pulp in the rough stone presses, and drank their cider. Watched them working barefoot in the seaweed spread for manure and going home with a song, tramping or riding in the island's one sturdy cart. Watched an old woman minding a cow with a length of rope round its neck, herself dressed in black with a big poke-bonnet tied under her chin and her face as cracked as a ball of crumpled paper. We wandered over the island, which was really two islands joined by a narrow strip, and bathed among the rocks, thinking at every swirl of shadow that we had stirred up the octopods which figure ferociously in Hugo's novel about the

Mary Butts, by Jean Cocteau

Channel Islands. We climbed to the tiny Noah's-ark of a church perched on a hilltop and inevitably dedicated to St Michael; and there we found a rock-hollow where we might lie out of the winds, read poems, and strip in the sun, unseen by anyone but a floating bird or St Michael on one of his fiery clouds. We strolled among pine trees where lay the mossy ruins of old fortifications, on afternoons with the broadsheets of light poured on the reddened trunks, or at dusk, sometimes blundering into huge spiderwebs spun stoutly from tree to tree. We came out on the shore with its clusters of golden seaweed at ebbtide, the seamews wheeling in the amber-tinted air or a soft radiance suffused like gold-dust in the distance, a smack's wake glimmering purple on the smooth sea. Bats flickered in the dimness like our own uncertain thoughts momently troubling us.

There was dancing in the cobbled square before the battered thatched Mairie and the small dark stuffy church. I liked sitting on the terrasse with a cider and watching the heavy bodies lightly revolving, the strong shoulders and torsos of the girls with their veiled eyes. An accordion and a fiddle or two provided the music; and as twilight came on there would be moments of brief indecorum in the shadows, a scuffling and a burst of laughter from the lads, a clucking of black-shrouded women, and a rapid thinning of the last lingerers. The warmth of cider in my bones and the blessed mutter of the vanishing world and Elza enigmatically but consolingly silent at my side.

In the café I played chess with a grey-bearded landscape-painter who was slightly lame. There was also a villainous-eyed marquis from Guincamp with a fat mistress sewn into a shiny black dress, the seams of which she was always on the edge of bursting wide open with a cloud of stale scent and a dead white flash of expanding globular breasts and buttocks. Her voracious mouth twisted and swelled as she chewed shellfish and other pulpy live things of the sea. Once, when she and the distrait marquis insisted on seeing us home on a dark night, I remarked, as we neared the Veuve's kitchen-garden, *'Prenez garde: la forêt des choux.'* She gave her belly-gurgle of a laugh and with her pudgy fingers pressed my hand somewhere deep into her cleft person—the only time she seemed to notice my existence. Another acquaintance was M. Negroponte, technically British (having been born in Egypt) with a son who had served in an English regiment in the war. He wore a peaked cap, a check coat, and a twinkling air as if he were always about to produce a shattering witticism; he treated Elza gallantly, as if she were so fragile that she must be helped over every rut in the road (which was nothing but ruts) and every crack in the café floor. The one local intellectual, the grey-eyed chemist, a Voltairean, who had once been to sea and spoke English, discussed Breton superstitions and expressed a great desire to read Conrad. Vibert, an artist who lived in a vast place with an uncomfortable studio like a church, had taken over the café to have something to do. We spent some dull afternoons in his studio, looking at his excellent collection of pictures. Clearly the artists and the others were ready to put up with my bad French for the privilege of looking at Elza. I translated my pinewood poems into French and typed them out. The lame artist read them with an encouraging nod and turned his gaze back to Elza; but the fact that I was translating Petronius gave me a certain standing. The marquis woke up, pressed my hand, and asked us to dinner at the hotel, with drinks afterwards at his villa.

Gradually, even with our bad French, we absorbed the island's scandals. The marquis took drugs; his mistress, after administering cocaine, cuckolded him in all her seams with a young fisherman. The woman with big eyes in violet cavities and a pasty-face was a Lesbian. Vibert looked so disconsolate because he was waiting for his wife to return. Much younger than he, she regularly selected a lover from the summer visitors and went off with him; but she always came back for the winter. Sure enough, she did turn up, a short high-breasted woman with a hard handsome face, thick eyebrows and down-curving lips. The islanders hated her and would have beaten her up if they had had a chance, but she always went round with a leashed Alsatian. She did not frequent the café or the chilly studio-nave, so our acquaintance was limited to acknowledging her curt nod as she strode defiantly by, with a cigarette in her hand and the dog tugging at its strap. Vibert had grown much happier; he beamed on us and praised *l'amour*.

A Canadian girl with red chapped face, earnest and stupid, turned up at the hotel and hung round us as fellow-souls. She was hoping to develop the art of cutting silhouettes and made many efforts at Elza's profile. Once she burst in at a moment when we should have made sure the door was locked, and hastily retreated. A few hours later she returned, keeping up a feeble pretence of calling on us for the first time that day. She too had blundered on some of the scandals. 'I really do think you are the only properly married couple on the island,' she said with pious vehemence. We both laughed loudly, and the poor girl blushed and stammered her way out. But before long she was back to ask us what she ought to do if Mme Vibert spoke to her.

One day we were urgently asked to visit some people whom we didn't know at the other end of the island. We went, were given a pleasant meal and much wine, and at last were shown the surprise for which we had been invited. A wireless set, probably the only one on the island, was brought out and tuned in after long delays, volubly-discussed breakdowns, and peculiar noises. Everyone looked at us expectantly and I felt that we were letting them down. Finally I realized that we were listening to someone speaking English with an Australian accent; but who he was, what he was saying, and where he spoke from, I never found out. However I was now able to make ecstatic gestures of recognition and pleasure, and our hosts were satisfied.

One of the fishermen was being married and he asked us to the wedding reception in the village hall. Wine was lavishly poured and I even managed to dance with the bride, a broad handsome girl; but stolid as she was, she was obviously glad when I stopped treading on her toes and delivered her over to her man. She excited much comment among the women of the village through having something pink in her costume; and several of them said that everyone knew she was a cracked vessel but she needn't announce it to the world. A week or so later I saw the couple returning from their honeymoon on the mainland. The large comely fisherlad was striding ahead and greeting everyone, while the girl struggled along behind, with a huge portmanteau on her back bowing her down.

Now and then we went across to Paimpol, to cash a pound or two at the bank, an ancient mouldering place that smelt of Balzac. There was a counter with bars in front of it, and notices on curling paper in faded violet ink. After much banging, a decayed clerk with long frayed moustache emerged from some lair, dusty and snuffy, and tried for a long time to find some excuse for refusing to do business. My only defence was to ignore his objections and keep on presenting the notes, with a demand for francs. He at length withdrew to make his calculations, returned resentfully wheezing, and slowly counted out the money, taking back some small sum at the last moment as he thought up an extra charge.

We liked the port and the old lanes in which sabots clinked, the old woman standing patiently in a doorway made of three great slabs of granite, with a dour room glimpsed through the window, a blurred photo-enlargement ringed with the mourning wreath of glittering white and black shells or beads, whitewashed timber-joists and wallpaper showing the rough granite surfaces beneath, a pewter candlestick, a fragment of worm-eaten carved timber, men in blue jerseys and patched trousers stained with tar and perhaps even wine-red stockings. The stalwart woman serving us coffee in the port café was hostile till I mentioned that I was Australian, not English. Pausing in her sewing, she called in her small wiry husband to meet me. Come from so far away to see France? I ceased to be a foreigner battening on the exchange and was treated as a friend, under the stained photos of ships and engravings of shipwrecks.

I picked up a torn copy of Loti's *Pêcheurs d'Islande* with plentiful small woodcuts more interestingly full of local colour than the novel. To return to the island we usually went by autobus via Ploubazlanec to Arcouest, passing baroquely-muscled Christs at crossroads and finding time for a drink in the sailors' bar of the hotel overlooking the sea. The patron liked to tell the tale of his prize-setter having been out-scented by the fat white dog of his wife, and the setter knew he was being

AFTER SCENE XVII

A page from *Hereward*

ridiculed, apologetically snorted, and put his head between his paws. There was a marvellous moment as the bus came up to the point above the promontory where we suddenly saw the Channel spread in an

intolerable lustre and sown with burning yellow-gold rocks. From here
the passage to the island was short.

I was working steadily at the *Satiricon* and revising *Ragnhild*. Perhaps
the struggle to define Ragnhild forced me to think about Elza instead of
evading the ambiguous aspects of her story, as I would have liked to do. I
remembered M. and the sly hints made by the others. I tried to find out
why she had left Paris. She had moments of black despair when she
retreated inside herself and crouched or lay on the floor, unable to move
or speak. How can I help you if I don't know the truth? Tell me, what
is it? what crushes you down? She told me a broken tale of Robert
falling badly ill and their friends in England ignoring appeals for aid:
doubtless they were all owed money. She had to do something. What
could she do? For the sake of the child and Robert, who knew nothing
of it all, she sold herself. There had been no other way.

Mingled with these admissions were obscure and fragmentary
remarks about an unhappy childhood, a beautiful distracted mother, a
noble garden grown wild, frogs croaking where the lilies were lost in
the matted reeds and ivy strangling the mutilated Venus. Somehow she
had been cheated of her birthright and all her life she had been striving
to find the cheat out, to regain what she had lost. Before meeting Robert
she had drifted from job to job, serving in cafés, in a tobacconist's, a
draper's, even kicking her incompetent legs up in a third-rate chorus-
row. Always victimized, seduced, driven out, making another hopeless
start, dreaming of her lost birthright.

I believed her tales, yet felt that she omitted some essential fact
making sense of the scattered details. My heart was wrung with pity and
I was afraid, chilled and repelled. I hated this entry into the pitiful
secrets of another soul, another body; and yet, if we were to go on
together, I must have some coherent image of her, something I could
trust. Suddenly, from a remark she made about an operation, I chal-
lenged her: 'So you had gonorrhoea?' She paled and nodded. 'Do you
want to go back to Robert?' She made no definite answer. It seemed
that she did not hold him responsible for any of her troubles. True, his
rebellion against his mother's world had made it impossible for him to
find an easy job, but it was the incapable rebellion which in fact en-
deared him to her. Though I did not press the point, I felt sure from
her random remarks that on her return to London, before taking up
with Young, she had lived by selling herself.

I ran out of the house and wandered along the shore by the pines.

But I couldn't think. I felt only a horror. It was not so much that I made a moral judgment of Elza's past; for her personally I felt only an aching impotent pity. What I couldn't decide was her nature, her character; and unless I decided that, I could not understand in the least what was my own relation to her. The horror I felt was a horror of the void, of the dark void I touched in her. A void in which all personality broke down and was lost in a faceless anguish. She seemed to have no distinctive character at all: to be an image of pure beauty and the wound of ancient wrong. To save her was to find out how to give her a personality in place of a strange elemental confusion of terrors and aspirations, which lacked any centre.

I longed for the harsh clarity of Australian light. In Elza I felt the chiaroscuro of a rich culture which had broken down under its own weight and which now existed in a dark cavernous penumbra, lighted by unknown crannies and cracks, with no way out into the unequivocal day.

But from another angle she was a child, a poor lost child, who could not tell me the truth about herself because she did not know what it was, did not possess the words to define the complex outrage inflicted upon her, could not find the simple line of growth that would have carried her out of the knots and cankers tethering her to an unrealized past.

> *When I pierce your secrecy, Time shudders and dies*
> *and your abandoned mouth, curled from the teeth, replies*
> *but Childhood wonders and broods from your distant eyes*
>
> *Some implacable terror your passion condones*
> *from the other side of language come your small moans*
> *I see you a faint red flame kindled in a nest of bones*
>
> *And I possess in one moment as I press on*
> *through closing cones of warmth Time-to-be and Time-gone*
> *the ravished Child and the dancing Skeleton.*

I came home to find her crouched where I had left her hours before. Nothing roused her, neither caresses nor exhortations, complaints nor tears. Only at last she revived in an embrace, coming up entire from the depths without a word or a sign to express her change from a deathly

numbness to a serene liveliness of all the five senses. I was left torn by a
conviction of her duality. She had some absolute integrity and pathos,
an immediacy of communion with nature and with all things living
(except men in their social existence); I watched her eyes as she watched
birds. And yet she had something absolutely broken, a submissive fear

THE
SEVENTH
MIME:
THE
COBBLER

METRO:
Cerdon, I've brought these ladies to your shop,
I want you to display your special wares,
those that have real craft put into them.
CERDON:
I'd a right instinct, Metro, when I took
a liking for you... Bring in the big bench,
here, for the ladies. Drimylos, wake up.
It's you I'm calling. What, a-snooze again!
O Pistos, smack him nicely on the nose
until he yawns this sleepiness away.
No, take that spine and stick it underneath
his nodding chin, to tickle him awake.

A page from *Herondas*

that attracted outrage and made her the casual prey of any passer-by.
Possessed by corruption, she was uncorrupt.

I lay in our engulfing wooden bed, the roof only a few inches from
my face, the wind whistling and blurting through the paper where the
wood had cracked apart. I appreciated the *houhou! houhou!* of Loti's
wind, ranging from a cavernous noise of tremulous rage to the little

flutings of an owl; his lovers lying awake and thinking of the dark sea that would one day flow over them. I thought of the dark sea and longed to put out my hand, saying the one unknown word that would make us recognize one another.

For one thing, I could not think of Elza and Janet at the same time; my will was cut clean in half. And this inner uncertainty of mine, about which I was unable to think, could not but react on Elza, increasing her helplessness. To evade my problem, I told myself that Elza belonged both to me and to Robert; she too was a divided being. If only I could have said to her, 'I love you and I shall never return to Janet, my wife in Australia, we are one from henceforth,' things might have turned out differently. But I couldn't say that for many reasons, one of which was that I had no firm image of Elza, only a series of Ragnhild-contradictions. Thus the division inside her in turn intensified my own inner divisions and confusions.

Chequered by the abrupt moments of impasse, which ended because we dared not sustain them beyond a point, our days of roaming and versifying went on. I borrowed a wheelbarrow from the Veuve and collected the *boulets* of compressed coal-dust which were the only fuel on the isle, and burned them in the tiled stove, on which we heated small salted fish. Once as I was carefully chopping some kindling on the tiled floor, the Veuve, who could interpret every sound that went on in her one asset, the cottage, burst in to remonstrate, plead, weep. If I cracked one of her tiles, she would be a lost woman. I was therefore all the more worried when a few days later I spilt a bottle of ink abed, on her beautiful linen. (I can't recall why I was trying to write in such an uncomfortable position.) At all costs I had to conceal the linen, for cash had now run short and I couldn't possibly pay her for the damage and also get back to England. As she did all the washing, the concealment was difficult but I managed it.

Suddenly the time was come to return. We departed in a last flurry of the Veuve's reminiscences and found a large number of people come to see us off, ranging from the lame artist and Vibert to the chemist and the carpenter. The fisherman who carried our luggage refused a tip. (Perhaps it was our thrifty way of living that had made the Bretons like us.) We said *Kenavo*: Till we meet again.

6. WAITING

WE had to spend the night at Paimpol. At the hotel was another marquis, this time an anglophile sportsman from Dinant. We breakfasted with him and his daughter, a puppy-fat girl who sulked on being told not to eat so much butter. Attracted by Elza, he pressed us to stay at Dinant a few days: at which his daughter flounced out of the room, glaring back at us from the doorway. I was tempted, but our finances were too low. We caught the night-boat at St Malo. The weather was rough and Elza lay down, but I felt exultant and stayed up all night, walking the decks and watching the wild waters or drinking whisky with a young engineer, who expounded a *mystique* of machines. We argued and then went out again into the wind.

I dozed through the train-journey. The sun rose like a poached egg of bleary gold amid spectral trees, in a yellowish mist. Indeterminate England again, full of strange possibilities. We went to a flat that Kirtley had taken, in some suburban area: where, I have forgotten. We were unhappy there. Kirtley and Elza disliked one another. While she didn't mind cooking her simple dishes of rice or spaghetti and vegetables for me, she couldn't fit in with house-running on a conventional scale. Within a few days there was discord and she was refusing to cook. Kirtley, who had lived a life of irritable bachelorhood, tended by his mother with her quizzical humour, considered her a pretentious nuisance; and I was miserable as a feeble go-between, trying to keep the peace by placating both parties. Finally Elza drove me to assert myself and to ask for a definite statement of what was happening, what was my role in the Press. Nothing was more painful for me than that sort of thing. I have never had any personal sense of rights and dues, and I had a more-than-Australian objection to woman's (irrational) protests intruding in the masculine world of careless comradeship. But she insisted and at last I gave in.

Kirtley had arranged to take over a room on the second floor at the corner of Bloomsbury Square. Thus the Press had the excellent address of Five Bloomsbury Square, though our semi-circular window looked

Jack Lindsay
Painting by Lionel Ellis, 1928

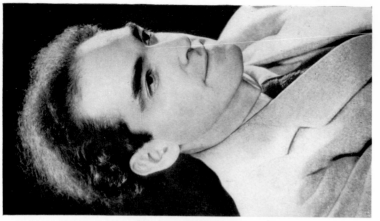

Brian Penton

Winifred Stephensen, 1929

P. R. Stephensen *c.* 1934

out into Bloomsbury Way. The Chiswick Press had been persuaded
to print an edition of the *Lysistrata* which followed in all respects our
hand-printed version. I felt that it was unfair to saddle Kirtley with my
problems at this difficult moment; but when I did tackle him with some
apologetic comments about the strain of the existing arrangement, he
made things easy for me by agreeing at once, suggesting that we had
better part, and offering me £5 a week in advance of royalties on
Aristophanes and Petronius. I gratefully offered to help in the office.

I sent the Veuve Lambolet a money-order for her linen, and received
a letter of amazed thanks; and I sent the chemist some books by Conrad.
We moved to a small flat in a converted house near Earls Court, mainly
composed of what had once been a corridor; and I promptly fell ill
with influenza, with a mild touch of something like brain fever, a
feeling of maggoty pressures in a body of heaving heat. Doubtless
the effect of standing-up for myself. I then started going fairly regularly
into the office to do editorial work and the like. Noticing a reference to
Blake's coming death-centenary, I felt the impulse to write something
about him.

I wrote *William Blake, Creative Will and the Poetic Image* at high
speed. The first chapter was a long commentary on the epistle to Butts
in which Blake says that his outward eye sees a Thistle, which his
inward eye turns into an Old Man grey. I used this to expound my
notion of the transformative force of the poetic image and to develop
the thesis of the creative act as a negation alike of the processes of
abstraction or of naturalistic and expressionist submergences in the
material of life. (In the latter category I should have placed both
surrealist automatism or D. H. Lawrence's primitivism.) Here is the
conclusion of chapter I, in which I attempted to say that 'the recoil of
the senses' and the fertilization of 'an eternally active mind' were alike
necessary:

There is no harm in seeking to express the essential dualism inside all
unity by some such set of symbols as long as we remember that, like all
antinomies, they must be mingled to produce actuality.

Indeed, the only way to penetrate deeper into unity is to clarify and
tighten our conception of the married opposites that are its actualization:
Being and Becoming, Life and Death, Force and Inertia, Joy and Torment,
Individuality and God, Spirit and Matter—there are scores of headings
under which we can define various facets of the dynamic synthesis of
unity. We shall find when we return to life that instead of being obliterated

C

by the harsh simplicities of the idea, the nuances of thought and emotion which are begotten by the idea meshed in nerves and blood are multiplied mysteriously. Moreover, Blake of all people insisted on a mystical sharpness of thought, and to approach him with anything less than an effort to achieve his own savage and sensitive precision of ultimate values is an insult.

How then is the tree to become part of myself? Only by growing up on the other side of my eyes, still the tree that is there to be photographed, still carrying the peculiar complex of form and colour which makes it different from any other tree on earth, yet subtly smudged by the lights of my imagination and re-etched by the circling forms of my identity so that it sits somewhere into the ever widening, ever contracting, mosaicked unity of mind. Until this is done, it is an undigested unit in my mind, not a dynamic factor in its unity.

This is the only means by which my spiritual content can be increased. And it is a process which, the more it is put into action, the wider and richer grow its implications and potentialities. Just as the trees in nature, though infinite, if tamely photographed in my head, produce no spiritual action and fade into less than the wraith of a geometrical problem, so the tree-in-my-head, the universal idea of a tree, is also but a wraith if it is left to itself, a bloodless corpse hung on the gibbet of God. But once the tree-in-my-head begins its sport of chafing and knocking with its spiralling energies upon the trees of earth, an infinite series of aesthetic combinations is begun, an eternal game of hide-and-seek with Venus.

Infinity ceases to be a mathematical or philosophic counter. It becomes a symbol of aesthetic emotion, that point where the disdainful tree-in-the-head, having done its best like a shaping wind with the tree let in by the eyes, fades, and the wind fades off the leaves. The constructive imagination swoops on the material, sinks through it, sifts it, impregnates every element it desires with something of its fire, blasts the rest out, and then curves back to the closing heavens.

It finds a thistle and it leaves an old man.

I cite that passage as a sample of the positions we were to set out at length in the Press—and also to bring out the fact that my method, however erratic and idealist, was always dialectical and concerned with the unity of opposites. (The term *God* was never used for any form of unity; it expressed nirvana, void, the abstraction from the *pleroma* of reality.) The book went on to discuss the crisis in culture represented by Blake, whom I saw as the first poet consistently taking the creative consciousness itself as his material. But my existential dogmas, my lack of any concrete understanding of history, prevented my analysis from leading anywhere. I tried to distinguish Form-image from Colour-image: the latter expressing the attempt at a new qualitative synthesis following the crisis brought to a head by Blake.

I sent the MS to Benn. It came back with a polite letter from Victor Gollancz, who had not yet achieved his own firm. Having thus proved to my own satisfaction that nobody wanted the work, I put it aside.

Elza now said that Robert was on a visit to London and she wanted to see him. On what terms they were to meet, she gave no hint, and I did not ask. But I suggested that he should come to our flat. He came and I found him much what I expected: a good-looking well-built product of the public school, with a charm of manner in which were merged both his mother's fine taste and the broadened humanity brought about by his revolt against that mother. Except to tell Elza that their child was well in Paris, he seemed to have no special reason for seeing her. He had indeed more to say to me; for he had roughed out an account of his own life, which had grown into an attempt to criticize his father Gordon Craig for not having fought hard enough for his ideas in the stage-world. Though the correlation was only sketchily made, Robert had some idea of linking what he felt his father's inadequacies as a family-man with the dilettante element in his work; and I felt there was a good thesis in the project, but one needing more knowledge of the European Theatre than either Robert or I had. However, I read and criticized the MS in some detail. Robert seemed thankful, but nothing came of the work. As it stood, it was too slight.

We had several meetings, with the MS our main theme of discussion. I liked him and was jealous of Elza meeting him alone, but didn't like to say so. He appeared to accept without question her living with me. The three of us never in any way raised the problem of our relationship or of Elza's future. After a while Robert returned to Paris.

Kirtley meanwhile was building up the Press, though his comments on the English people and climate grew daily more sarcastic. Once he startled me by saying that though there was every sign of a satisfactory response from the book trade he felt inclined to chuck the whole thing. My heart sank. I foresaw an ignominious return to Sydney on more money borrowed from Norman. And what was going to happen to Elza? While I still theoretically considered myself bound-for-life to Janet, I couldn't imagine myself ever losing Elza. A part of me hoped that she'd find some way of living which would remove her from emotional and financial dependence on me (on anyone); and yet I had resisted any return to Robert, the only visible alternative to her remaining with me. In fact I couldn't now imagine life without her and was involved in a set of contradictory needs and hopes. Whether she really wanted to stay with me and was prevented from going to Robert solely by economic problems, I had no idea.

But soon afterwards Kirtley suggested I should take over the Press on his departure, clearing him from all claims on my part or on Norman's for work done. Neither Norman nor I had in effect any claim on him; there had been no contracts or even verbal allocations of profit and loss. As he was shouldering the whole risk, I had felt that the final word in any monetary consideration should be his. Now I at once snatched at his offer, though he warned me that I should have no capital, only such goodwill as the first two books had built up. The proposition was too much like something brought about by the fate of my poetry to be refused; I had no business experience whatever, but that seemed irrelevant.

In any event I soon had a strong ally. P.R.S. had called on us with his usual irrepressible energy; but over a pint it turned out that he was at a loose end. A Rhodes Scholar who had been a Communist at Oxford, he wasn't cut out for an academic career; nor was he the kind of person who could tamely step into some job in business or the civil service. He wanted a position permitting him to display his panache in a stormy wind; and in our discussion about the possibilities of the Press it became clear that as a champion of Fanfrolico he would find just the outlet he wanted. I was overjoyed. Here seemed to me the fated fellow-fighter to match the fated battle-chance. P.R.S. did not accept the Apollinian Universe of N.L. as I did, but he shared enough of our Fanfroliconian attitudes to take his place in the ranks with unreserved loyalty.

Winifred was now in her large flat, where she let P.R.S. or his Oxford friends use some of the spare rooms. Among the friends was Tom Driberg, who stayed there awhile in a hard-up period. He had broken from his family, quarrelled with his mother, if I remember correctly, and for a while was working as a dishwasher in Soho. He had come down from Oxford, the tale went, after giving a dadaist concert with all sorts of peculiar instruments, such as typewriters. The star-piece came at the end. There was the sound of a chain being pulled offstage, then of a water-cascade, and someone entered with a notice: Gentlemen will adjust their clothing before leaving the premises. 'There's only one hall in England that can perform the symphony, as it alone has a water-closet almost on the stage.' T.D. was hoping to start a magazine and I wrote him a brief piece on Beethoven. He was a gentle-mannered quiet person, who not long after rose to fame as William Hickey of the *Express*, starting off the modern type of newspaper column in England. I recall a long conversation with him on a bus, in which I tried to justify my writing verse-dramas of the most unfashionable kind. He agreed to each point with such amiable readiness that I felt driven to find fresh and more vehement reasons at each acquiescent nod.

I recall also having a bath in that flat and towelling myself so vigorously that I knocked over a whole glass shelf and its contents. I was so annoyed at my clumsiness that I didn't even apologize except in a vague mumble; and when Winifred divagated into a panegyric on T.D.'s good manners, I could say even less.

7. FIRST FANFROLICO DAYS

ELZA, who was always good at finding places to live in, secured the top floor and roof of 30 Museum Street for 30/- a week, and we moved there. The place was very handy both for the office and for the British Museum Reading Room. There were two fair-sized rooms and an asphalted roof thick with smuts and grit. I still had something of my Australian habit of never locking doors, but was cured of it by having most of my (sparse) clothes stolen in the first week.

Though I had been in close touch with the office during Kirtley's last days there, I went along with much trepidation on the first occasion of my own control. Nothing was changed, and yet everything was changed. P.R.S. was there, happily brisk, turning over the ledgers, devising all sorts of systems and oblique attacks on the book-trade; and I felt sure that together we should be inspired to do the books which would both sell and express our point of view. I threw myself whole-heartedly into the work. Now, while the Press lasted, I did all the typographical designing: often a laborious job—for instance I drew out every single page of McCrae's large *Satyrs and Sunlight*. I also corrected proofs, did most of the editorial work, and translated or wrote a number of the books; our line of country necessitated further a lot of research in the B.M., which I carried out. And though P.R.S. bore the weight of the selling and advertising side, I had to make the final decisions as to our financial strategy, which all the while was highly complicated. Though we took over a running concern, we had no capital, as Kirtley had warned; and if the Chiswick and Curwen Presses had not been ready to give us credit (largely against their better commercial judgment), we could not have carried on a week. Only by the most careful juggling with cash and credit, and by getting each book out exactly on time, did we survive. The slightest margin of error or accident—a book delayed a few days at the printers, or the bookbinders (the worst snag) holding us up a few days longer than we had calculated, and our system was liable to crash. Also, needless to say, we could not afford any failures. Every book had at least to pay its costs by sales at publication; and the main ones had to make a considerable profit.

Kirtley, before deciding to go, had arranged to publish at 15 guineas a selection of translations which I had done under the title *Propertius in Love* and for which we had a number of drawings by N.L. Enough orders had already come in to ensure the book's success; but I considered the price too high. All we could do was to make the binding costly and so on. However, though I kept on feeling a bad conscience about the book, it sold out and the money was a help to get us started.

The original intention had been to follow up the translations with my verse-play *Marino Faliero* and Kenneth Slessor's poems, *Earth Visitors*. We carried on with this plan. Oliver Simon at the Curwen Press was very helpful; now as always he was ready with advice and took special care with any of our work under his hands. The *Satiricon* had been the first book printed in the newly-cut Poliphilus type; for *Marino* Simon got the Walbaum type and had the book handset. *Lysistrata* had been praised by reviewers, but *Marino* was ignored or treated as pseudo-Elizabethan. I encountered John Rodker on the day that the *T.L.S.* found the play wanting in every respect, and he remarked that the passages cited by the reviewer disproved his point. I gave him a copy of the book and we remained mildly friendly. An anxious, intelligent man, he lived near the other end of Great Russell Street and was publishing his own limited editions of works like *The Arabian Nights* in lively versions by Powys Mathers.

Soon after we had moved to Museum Street, I looked in at the Plough, which was only a few doors away. Whom did I encounter at first glance but Nina Hamnett again? I said I'd been on Bréhat, thinking the island something out-of-this-world; and found that she had stayed there a while before us. She put me in my place by asking if I'd ever seen any salamanders, as she had, by lantern-light. Without knowing it, I had come to live close to the other main Bloomsbury pub of the intellectuals. Elza did not drink beer and disliked pubs and every form of rowdy or disorderly living in which her peculiar aura of silence could not function. I myself had no interest in drinking for its own sake; but I felt the pull of the group-excitement, the chatter, the meeting with new characters who had something to say about art and life. Not that I often spent an evening at the Plough. But there were after-office chats with P.R.S. over a pint, which now and then led to more than a pint or two. Elza never asked me not to drink, never reproached me, but she made me feel that she suffered. If I drank more than a half-pint, I couldn't help thinking of her; and though I was near enough to be able always to tell her where I was, I had a feeling of truancy, which I resented. I still held fast to my Australian ethic of the sexes. Beer was a male prerogative; men drank in a bar and wives stayed at home. Besides, if she felt lonely, she had only to walk a few yards and join me.

I was still sending a few brief letters to Janet in Sydney. In them I gave some scraps of news and stressed the indeterminacy of my position. Later I learned from Elza that Janet, doubtless intuiting that something was wrong, had written suggesting that she could come across, taking a job as stewardess if the money couldn't be raised. (I feel sure however that her father would quickly enough have given her the money if she had announced her decision.) Elza intercepted the letter and tore it up; and she herself wrote an anonymous letter in which she informed Janet that I was in love with a very beautiful woman.

I find it hard to imagine what I should have done if I had received Janet's letter. I still considered her my wife, tethered to my rational side and representing the Australia to which I assumed I would return as soon as the commission of the Press, dropped in my hands by Apollo's well-disguised emissary, Kirtley, had worked out in definite failure or success. Yet at the same time Elza was more and more pervading my life. I cherished a half-feeling that she didn't need me, and yet did everything to make her do so. I wanted her to stand on her own feet, and yet encouraged only that side of her which kept her dependent. For one thing, because of my uncertainty about her, I didn't want her out in the world, mixing with other men; it suited me for her to grow emotionally attached, cut off from other sources of strength or satisfaction, and thus unable to seek any of the ways-out from our dilemma, which I fondly pretended to myself were always open to her. I was deeply aware of the broken element in her, which called out my tenderness and my pity as nothing else in life ever had; and yet I refused to believe that this was the essential thing in her make-up. For if it was, I could never be so callous as to break our union and complete her brokenness. I clung to our romantic concepts. The poet followed the signs of his fated career through delight and anguish to some battle-moment of significant death; the woman, his image of desire, also sought the fate which was the structure of her character, discovering herself in her lovers. What mattered for both was the poetry, the image, the tension most powerfully precipitating the drama in which they recognized their deepest desire and fear; the dualism inherent in experience ensured that the tension operated most effectively at the tragic level, where fulfilment was realized only in the moment of most intense loss, life only in death. I tried therefore to convince myself that, at the deepest level, Elza was using me for her own development and self-realization, as I was using her—though in very truth I wasn't using her at all; I was desperately bound to her by my fears and hopes, my unknown needs. Daily more hopelessly bound and refusing to admit it.

Someone sent in a hand-written copy of Sir John Harrington's *Matamorphosis of Ajax*. I wrote to Jellinek, whose name was on the MS; and he called in a large, genial person connected with the law, who said that the idea was really Philip Heseltine's. I wrote to Heseltine and he in turn called in. We at once got on well together and I decided to do the book, in which Elizabeth I's godson propounded the virtues of the water-closet, defending his invention with multifarious texts and appeals to authority, which were both a serious effort to overcome opposition and a Rabelaisian parody of scholastic method.

Soon after we settled in Museum Street, Elza took me down to Chelsea to meet a friend of hers, Jeanne, the model of Lionel Ellis, a young painter from Plymouth. There was a flush of suppressed excitement about her, a most unusual thing, as she told me of her friend and waited for the bus to deliver us up at the studio's doors in King's Road. Jeanne turned out to be a well-built young woman, with a mop of untidy hair, who dressed in something of a more careless version of Elza's own clothing. She had a small voice, muffled or sweetly piping, part of the effect she gave of a little girl dressed up in mama's clothes without being quite sure which things went with which. I got on well at once with Ellis. He had a slight beard and one eyelid hung over its eye: which, he said, helped his painting vision. A gentle and withdrawn character, he did not lack tenacity, but was oddly dependent on Jeanne for his plastic inspiration. Though taken up for a while once with drawing the buttocks of large horses, he showed generally no interest in any other theme than her body; at the moment, as a source of income, he was working on the murals at St Stephens. I admired his big nude and his studies of Jeanne. He had a keen sense of humour and enjoyed life quietly from his corner, though I thought he was too averse from struggle and rated his own dignity too high. He remarked that it was oppressive to see a beautiful girl, so he studied her carefully till he found a flaw somewhere in her looks, her limbs, her walking or her talking; then he felt free from her. A delightful companion, he developed light veins of fantasy with his intimates. Thus, tickled by a phrase in

C*

Dung of Pegasus about childhood-games in an old store-room, 'ridiculous crockery of giants', he kept working out all sorts of variants: the one I best remember consisted of references to the snow we had on our heads as a result of our tall stature. What interested him in painting was primarily the values of plasticity; he did not lack a sense of design, as appeared when he did woodcuts for the Press, but his whole emphasis was realistically on volume, his colour was unimportant. I admired the way he had set himself against all modernistic temptations, though I tried to draw him into experiment with colour; and I saw in Elza's friendship with Jeanne a fated road leading us to an essential ally in the field of art.

He had naïve ideas about Jeanne. 'When I first kissed her, she asked me: Will I have a baby now?' In fact her mother had been a prostitute, who sold her at an early age. But despite many harrowing experiences Jeanne remained a most charming and even unspoiled character. Her good nature was genuine, she was easily moved to sympathy, was very kind and never spoke maliciously. She owned a demure steady delight in life despite her deep fears; the smallest and most ordinary things could intoxicate her with pleasure and wonderment. With all her wayward impulses she had a desire for stability which she expressed by paying down deposits of shillings and sixpences on some monstrous Victorian wardrobe or chest of drawers in a junkshop. The more overwhelming and ornate the giants, the better she liked them, though I don't think she ever collected any of these articles. Going down the street with her, as she stepped precariously on high-heeled shoes that always seemed likely to fall off or cave-in sideways, I have seen her dart away to some secondhand furniture-shop with a muttered excuse, then emerge with a warm smile, relieved at having added a few more pence to the deposit. She felt less a waif if she had such heavy and respectable objects weighting her down. Her desire for security by means of mahogany lumber did not however prevent her from a continual series of ill-managed escapades. Some of her adventures I heard of from Elza; others I noted for myself. Thus, a wild Irishman whom I had met at Oxford, a voluble excited talker who was well-off if one could judge by his clothes, somehow met her and had a hectic affair. A worse actress than she was, I have never met. I soon came to tell when she was wrestling with an acute sense of guilt, about to slip out and meet someone. Her voice grew smaller and mincingly-sweeter; she fluttered about, made the most inconsequent remarks, laughed at herself (as no one else could see the joke), and finally managed her exit,

swaying with a special lubricity of the spine. At any time she found it
difficult to look one in the eye. Sometimes she made a strong effort,
braced herself, and turned on one her eyes of tranquil blue in which the
most guileless sincerities were melting; her full lips parted moistly and
her hands made feinting movements.

Suddenly, for no particular reason, she disappeared and was found
to have taken up with a crippled artist, who treated her badly. She was
very fond of Lionel and must have been torn between her need to
restore his self-confidence and her wish not to hurt the cripple; she
may also have had in mind one of the excessively devious plans for
success, wealth and respectability, which obsessed her without ever
getting beyond the first stages of incompetent application. Lionel was
unhappy without her deft and gentle tendings; and after a while he
somehow coaxed her back. They were married. But she spoiled things,
perhaps deliberately, by addressing him with the name of the other
man at one of the crucial moments on their nuptial night. And she
could not stop her philandering. Once I stopped for the night and slept
in the upper gallery of the long studio; Elza had gone into hospital
for some uterine curetting. Lionel had for some time been telling me
about the way Jeanne was talking in her sleep. 'It's wonderful. I know
everything she does. I say to her: I know what you were doing yesterday
at three o'clock. And she says: How can you know? what was I doing?
So I tell her and she's knocked endways.' I guessed that Jeanne was at
one of her tricks; and that night I wondered how she would carry on.
She couldn't stop her night-chatter altogether or Lionel might grow suspicious; but I knew that she'd feel shy with me as eavesdropper. What
she did was to put up a modified performance, indulging mostly in an
unintelligible babble about an old man bearded like Bernard Shaw. This
was the period she was meeting the Irishman, and she knew that I knew.

Ellis said he'd like to paint me. I think the result was a good portrait,
and I was pleased at what seemed a Dostoevskian touch in features and
mood. (Later however the work was offered to the National Portrait
Gallery as a portrait of D. H. Lawrence.[1])

[1] I lost the work, as will be later told here. In 1958 Harry Moore told me
he had been consulted at the National Portrait Gallery about a portrait offered
as of D.H.L.; he recognized that it was of me. The picture, he said, had once
passed through the hands of Bertram Rota. I went to Mr Rota, who did not
know where the work now was, but found and gave me a photo of it, which I
reproduce. He paid me the compliment of saying, 'We always thought it looked
too gentle for Lawrence.'

In the late summer of 1927 the Ellises stayed with us for a fortnight or so at Winchelsea, in a house on the slopes of the north-east approach. At least Jeanne came for a few days, then developed flutterings and pipings, and remembered that she'd promised to pose for some artist and must really return to London; she went, but Lionel stayed on. We had chosen Winchelsea because Elza had stayed some months there once, more or less living with Ellen Terry, Robert's grandmother, in her last days; she had been a favourite of the old lady. And there was a friend she wanted to meet, a girl about whom she showed the same flushed excitement as about Jeanne. The girl however had become stupider, rustically lost, resentfully shy, and at the same time flauntingly painted; the reunion was not a success.

We saw children playing conkers with horse-chestnuts, and Lionel suggested a game. We collected nuts and played, grew exhilarated and looked for more nuts. Lionel stripped to the waist and beat furiously and vainly at my conkers. In the end we must have spoiled the game for the local children by gathering in all the nuts, and I had proved I was good at one sport at least.

Winchelsea was the first country-town I stayed at in England, and I savoured the square with its church-remnant and its broad roads running out, the Georgian New Inn with a spectacled phantom of Thackeray and the Tree nearby under which Wesley preached his last open-air sermon, seeking once more to make smugglers conscious of original sin; the vaulted wine-cellars and the Gate with its drum-towers and portcullised archway where one had a fine view of the sea and also of the huts and coops marring the shingly waste; the ruined castle on the way to Rye. We had the sea to ourselves when we swam, but somehow we were drawn into visiting one of the coop-dwellers, a retired accountant who fervently declared that he kept himself sane by perpetually beating out copperwork.

We walked to Rye over the shingle, the crisply-turfed pastures, the sweeps of sea-gravel, the dunes, and watched the medley of trawlers and coasters in Rye Harbour. And we also walked to Hastings, stupidly taking the dusty main road instead of the coast-tracks. Our beards, rare ornaments in those days, caused quite a traffic-sensation as we entered Hastings. Still, in lounging about on the flats below Winchelsea hill, I got some idea for the first time of the charms of the English countryside; and Elza murmured accounts of it in the spring with a host of larks, with yellow sea-poppies burning on the tawny-red shingle-sweeps and with golden and saffron flashes in the turf-grass.

In a sand-nook I tried to write a verse-parable on Elza as Cinderella, which was also an account of the struggle of concrete and abstract art—the ugly sisters representing both the repressive forces of society and the thingifying death-trend expressed in abstraction. But I got lost in my symbols. Cinderella grew too pathetic, archaically dowdy, and the Ugly Sisters showed sparks of a new vitality. I gave up and considered the moving waters.

At Ellis' studio I met many painters, such as Mark Gertler of the lobster-tinted nudes and lively Whitechapel Jews, who seemed a solid character glowing with many good sensuous warmths, but who ended by committing suicide. Also Edward Bawden, whose humorous drawings I liked and to whom I gave his first commission. A frailly-built painter with a wispy tow-beard, whose name I never caught, kept sniffing catarrhally and once remarked in explanation of his lack of interest in women, 'You see I get rid of so much of it through my nose', imagining that he enjoyed an orgasm with every sneeze. Horace Cole looked in a few times to wink at Jeanne, wrapt pontifically in his huge reputation as a jape-deviser: if he put his hand in his pocket, he was expected to take out a baby or a machine-gun—like Fishey Frank the local snake-merchant who was liable to produce a live eel from his trousers. Cole had once boarded a battleship as an eastern-potentate, had a famous man arrested for stealing his watch, and held up Piccadilly traffic by digging a hole in the road while wearing the trousers of an L.C.C. navvy.

Sometimes it is said that one always accepts the fashions of the time; only in retrospect they appear silly or ugly. But that was certainly not true of the Twenties. Ellis, Elza, myself and the others hated the short tubular dresses with their low waists, which made most women (who have short legs) look impossibly dumpy and clumsy, while the toques and kiss-curls we thought the brightest stroke of the devil to degrade Eve since the scandal of Eden.

Unheralded, Lawrence, my musical friend of Sydney, now turned up to complicate life yet further. Elza didn't like P.R.S., but she did her best to control her feelings, recognizing his indispensability to the Press. But here was Lawrence, another incalculable adventurer, who knew how to warm a woman's midriff with his lordly flattery, yet could not altogether disguise his peculiar streak of chuckling recklessness. She resented the spell he could cast over me: a spell diminished since

Sydney days, but still capable of making me succumb to his mockeries, his dares. For the first time since I had lived with Elza, there were a few bouts of heavy drinking; Lawrence was a whisky-man, a restless quester-out of the odder and more dissolute drinking haunts. However, all this did not last long. I pulled myself together and resisted. Apart from Elza's withdrawn eyes, the responsibility of the Press made me afraid of losing my grip on things. Poetry could find its own devious ways of rebirth; but our financial tightrope-walking demanded a cool head and obedient feet.

P.R.S. and I had now worked out an extensive programme. There was *Aiax*; and we had asked Ellis to illustrate a selection of Herrick made by myself. I was scheduled to translate Theocritos, Catullus, Aristophanes' *Ecclesiazusai*, and many other works of ancient poetry; and we decided to do complete editions of poets whom we considered neglected: Beddoes, Skelton, Wyatt, Webster, Tourneur, Suckling and many others. Some of these we were to succeed in doing; but we were less lucky with a project of contemporary poets (Yeats, Bottomley, Roy Campbell, the Sitwells). We began on Abercrombie's *Phoenix*, for which N.L. did several illustrations. Abercrombie gave a flattered assent; then at the last moment he grew scared of associating with us and said that his publisher would not let him assign the play for a limited edition. S., who knew him well, said that he was afraid of moral censure and had been much upset by Squire's assault on the production of the play, and that this lack of guts was what had inhibited his development as a poet.

One of my ideas was to use N.L.'s pen-and-inks and etching of Tom o'Bedlam to make up a book with the Elizabethan ballad and Francis Thompson's version of it. Browsing in the B.M., I decided to add various 17th-century mad-poems, annotate the whole, and ask Graves to write an introduction. I wrote to Graves, who promptly called on us. A tall rawboned slightly gaunt fellow, with a touch of the wilderness about him, like a mountain-dog trying to keep his tail up among the city-tykes. I liked him at once. He said that he already had ideas about the ballad and would be delighted to write the essay. We had a drink in the Plough and he asked me to go home with him. After I had run upstairs and told Elza, we went off to the flat at Hammersmith he shared with Laura Riding, whom I felt to be a disagreeably self-centred person with a hard discontented face. In reply to her lifted eyebrows, he elucidated his remark that the Press had done Petronius. 'A Roman high-flyer.' She replied, 'Aw.' (I still don't know what a high-flyer is; but I felt an instant dislike for anyone who had to have Petronius explained by such a term. I may add that I am sure she didn't like me either.)

She had been boiling some corn on the cob for us. But when she managed to spear the pieces with a fork and put them on our plates, they turned out to be as hard as the dried corn given parrots to nibble. 'I thought I'd boiled it enough,' she said with a vague helplessness, which I would have found amusing and charming in most women. Robert set about opening various tins that didn't need cooking. After the meal we walked down to see some friends who lived in a houseboat on the Thames. In a comment about some light-effect on faces, as we passed down an ill-lit street, Robert made a sarcastic allusion to Yeats as sentimentally soft; and I wanted to argue. I had been reading Yeats' chamber-plays, his *Vision*, and his more recent lyrics, and had been deeply moved; but I didn't like to admit it in the face of Robert's cocksure contempt for his work.

Laura, I learned, slept always on her back in a definite line of orientation, east-west I think; and she had a number of similarly stern ideas. Robert treated her with the utmost respect and tenderness.

They agreed to come and eat with us; and for a while we were all very friendly. I think Robert liked Elza. He offered to give us his house in Wales, which I should have jumped at if it had not been for the Press; and one day he turned up in a taxi with a pleasant old table for us. He was in a generally rebellious frame of mind, keen for gestures against the establishment; but though his breakaway had its roots in a reaction against the war, where he had been left for dead on the Somme, it had narrowed its scope down to the literary world, and a blow against the powers-that-be now meant a blow against the critics and the rulers-of-taste. He had published a poem through the Hogarth Press under a pseudonym and was overjoyed when critics who praised Graves dispraised the new poet (who was in fact rather a dull dog). At the moment he was quarrelling with various writers or publishers and evolving elaborate plots to trip them up and get them technically in the wrong on some point or other. The plots indeed were so elaborate that I cannot remember the details, only the general effect of a furiously-spun web. Though his methods were not mine, I approved of his distaste for the literary world and its denizens, and was pleased to discuss the fine points of law and discourtesy involved in his feuds. Gradually all his angers had become focused on to a defence of Laura Riding (Gottschalk) against a world that refused to admit her merits; the crusade for truth and independence turned into a crusade for Laura as philosophic poet. But there was a fresh rumbustious element about his proceedings that I liked. Both he and Laura told at length the tale of the break-up of his marriage; and rightly or wrongly I gained the impression that Nancy Nicholson had become fed-up with bringing forth an endless round of children and had encouraged Graves to invite over to England his admiring pen friend, with whom he rapidly discovered a soul-affinity.

One night when Robert was with us, an Australian, my brother Ray's friend rather than mine, turned up with some gramophone records. He had worked his way across to England by serving in the fo'c'sle; and he mingled lurid tales of shipboard with excited discussion of the fine dynamic control of rhythmic pattern in the performance of Beethoven's 5th Symphony on the records (Fechtwanger the conductor). Robert said nothing all the while, and I couldn't make out if he disapproved of the crude Australian jokes or of the passion for Beethoven, though I felt nationalistically proud at the mixture.

I had written another play, *Bussy d'Amboise*, drawing on my boyhood's memory of Dumas' romance for the image of an heroic and foolhardy death. Françoise de Montsoreau I based on Elza; not on her wilful and tormented side as in *Ragnhild*, but on her dreaming hopeful side, melancholy and doomed to betrayal. Bussy betrays his Françoise by an inability to resist the call of various life, the challenge to his male vanity, his bravado. I drew to some extent on P.R.S. and Lawrence for his stormy character, but at root the conflict was that of which I was sharply aware in my relations with Elza; I was trying to wake myself up in time, at the same time evading the issues by glorifying a death in which the unresolved conflict came to a head. We decided to print *Helen, Ragnhild*, and *Bussy* in a single volume; and P.R.S. suggested giving the job to George Roberts, who was acting as a sort of freelance printer. A small sturdy man, who looked like the captain of a tramp-steamer, he was reputed to have sat for the trimly-bearded mariner who appears on Player's cigarettes. He had known Joyce and was an encyclopedia of Joyce's Dublin.

One night, at a period when we were in rather dire straits in the Press, P.R.S. rang the doorbell of 30 Museum Street and told me that George must have £50 down or the book would be indefinitely held up. 'All right, we'll let him have it,' I said, and wrote the cheque. Before the end of the week some accounts that we'd given up were unexpectedly settled, and the Press was saved.

About this time Lawrence came in one evening, looking worried and flurried. He moved about the room uncomfortably, then sat down and said, 'You know they laugh at you, I don't like it.' I laughed back at him. 'Of course, do you think that's news? How could it be otherwise?' All the same, the information wasn't particularly pleasant. So I delivered a lecture on the nature of art-responses. Because a generation or two ago there were important painters ignored, like Cézanne and Van Gogh, nowadays anyone confused, obscure or unconventional is sure of being boomed, because all the advanced critics are afraid of being taken for Philistine frumps. The one thing they can be sure to miss and to slight is Grand Form and the Image of Beauty. That's what is new in our miserable world, so it must seem old and stale and misplaced to the hounds of the modish and the abstractly original. Disintegration alone now looks like form, deadness like life. The only tribute they can pay the upholders of Form and Life is to laugh at them as archaic fanatics, etcetera.

I ended by convincing myself, but Lawrence shook his head sadly. 'One has to fit in somewhere.'

'That's the one thing I refuse to do.'

8. WARLOCK HESELTINE

SOON after the acceptance of *Aiax* I took Lawrence on a visit to Eyns-ford. I wanted to show Heseltine the preface I had written. So far he knew nothing of my work and considered me only an eccentric publisher. He was engaged in rendering on the piano a Victorian oratorio with an ultra-seriousness carried into parody; but stopped and read the essay right through. At once his manner changed and thenceforth for a couple of years I was a close friend of his. He resumed his game of giving an obscene slant to the words of the oratorio, something about opening the doors of heaven.[1] Lawrence was charmed, until his tittering hinnying laugh almost exhausted him; he joined Philip at the piano and tried out his own bawdy variations. We drank up all the beer and hurried across to the Five Bells, where we sat at the back on the garden seats by the rickety table, with the leaves of the trees brushing the sweat from our brows. An old fellow with a white beard full of Kentish vocables helped us to consume the beer, and Darkie, another ancient, came in with his sack on his back. Then we carried a beer-supply home in a huge earthenware jug. (Darkie did not join us this time; but when he did on other occasions he always insisted on eating at a separate table. Swarthy and bushy-bearded, shy and careful-mannered, he lived alone in a small tumbledown hut. Philip once showed a photo of himself. 'Aye, that's you,' Darkie said, then, scratching his head, 'No, it can't be, you're here.')

---

[1] Parody favourites were J. A. Maunder's *Penitence Pardon and Peace Cantata*, in which a passage was given the words of the limerick about the Old Man from Newcastle; a Victorian duet *The Fairy Queen* frilly with trills; Reger (defined as the roaring-drunk of music) played on a pianola with rude comments. Nina comments, 'Moeran and Lambert played together with very serious faces. They generally had an argument in the middle and one would push the other off the end of the piano stool.' A ribald concert was normally held on a Sunday morning to offset the neighbouring chapel; the congregation responded with prayers for lost souls. Philip's passion for parodies led to score a *jeu-d'esprit* on Franck's D Minor Symphony for a jazz band, his piece being played in a West End hotel. (After the first amusement, I grew bored with all this parodying, but didn't like to admit it.)

We were now too thoroughly caught up in the steady crescendo of uproarious laughters which Philip knew so well how to start off and conduct to a staggering blind-drunk conclusion. I sent a wire to Elza and we stayed on a couple of days. We had a bonfire next morning to celebrate our discovery of one another, and moved on to the pub run by Pansy, a lady with a face of brilliant reds and purples. She had been rebuked by her husband for drinking in the bar, and so she kept a soda-water bottle handy, having previously replaced most of the soda-water with gin.

Early the second morning I found out how effective a retainer was Hal Collins (the alias of Te Akau, a half-Maori, who boasted a cannibal grandmother). He was devoted to Philip and watched over him and his interest with a dark and stealthy eye. I had woken early and felt that I would best restore my stomach and head by a cold shower. The house was dead-quiet and I walked into the unlocked bathroom without knocking. Barbara Peach, the small daintily-made and reserved girl who lived with Philip, was sitting naked in the bath. I muttered an apology and withdrew. Turning, I saw that Hal had come up noiselessly behind me, crouched for a leap if it turned out that I was intentionally intruding on Barbara. Seeing that my action had been innocent, he nodded and went off.

Hal could improvise systematic compositions, but not write them down. A song of his, *Forget me not*, was taken down by Philip and published by the O.U.P.; and he had a knack with the pen. One day Philip looked in at Museum Street and produced drawings in old broadsheet-style that Hal had made to some ballads of boozers. I at once suggested that he should illustrate a book I was editing, *The Parlement of Pratlers* by John Eliot. I had struck Eliot's book by chance in my B.M. researches round *Aiax*. I had been thinking of the meagre evidence for any effect of Rabelais on the Elizabethans, and by sheer inspiration turned up Eliot's book on French conversation. In it I found a hitherto unnoted imitation of Panurge-in-the-storm for the use of Channel crossers. The work, though missed by previous researchers, was far livelier than the other French-English dialogues of the period. (Heseltine must have been impressed by such finds of mine. For long after, in 1950, Constant Lambert remarked in a pub when speaking of the fortunate find of some musical MSS in a Cambridge college-library, 'It was Jack Lindsay's luck, as Heseltine used to say about putting out one's hand and unexpectedly finding something you want.')

Through Philip I met van Dieren and Cecil Gray. Gray, heavy and silent in a seat of the Café Royal, smoking his pipe and acutely aware of all that was going on, despite his look of somnolence: a man whose critical judgments I much respected, and who seemed well-balanced till he momently unbared his fierce contempt for women. And van Dieren groaning as he woke in the morning, complaining that he had to put himself together bit by bit—he couldn't get up hastily or he'd leave parts of himself behind; a man with an obviously rich mind, who had long pondered on art and life, but whose music I could not judge, since, despite the reverence in which Gray and Heseltine held it, I had no chance to hear it played. Somehow I felt sceptical about their insistence on van Dieren as the regenerator of musical style. I suspected, with nothing to prove it, that he was too intellectual, too narrow, for such a role, though I was ready to believe his compositions sensitive and valuably exploratory.[1]

On my second visit, Nina was there, living with Jack Moeran. I had seen her often since our meeting in the Plough, but without the intimacy of our first acquaintance. She always had some fresh enthusiasm, such as boxing at Camden Town, to which she liked to lure a crowd, basking in their clamour as if she were the entrepreneur of the event. For a while she was full of the Crystal Palace and her adventures in drawing London Statues for the book she was doing with Osbert Sitwell. Now at Eynsford she fell flat on her face on the flagged kitchen-floor and damaged her nose, so that she had to be carried to bed in a stunned condition. There Hal the handyman washed her nose in gin and restored her. Moeran merely bubbled in red-faced confusion. The household had tales of a fancy-dress protest against the selling-up of a woman who had foundered as a sealyham breeder in a near village. Normally a sealyham breeder would not have attracted Philip's championship;

---

[1] I think I now have some idea of the part played by van Dieren and Heseltine in the development of English music: their enlargement of the spheres of interest by their fine scholarly sense, their return to early national sources and their sense of European developments, including the contemporary ones—though they rejected many of these. They felt Vaughan Williams to take too simple an attitude to folksong; yet, admirers of Delius and Sibelius, they clung still to a direct nature-harmony as an escape from the alienating pressures of the urban (industrial) world, which were reflected in work such as Schoenberg's. (There were thus affinities to our Fanfrolico positions, which however were cruder and more violent, and at the same time tried to bite off more. In the last resort the differences were connected with the differences between the English situation and the Australian, which we imported with us and then tried to adapt to the English.)

but he loathed the house-owner, a woman combining the sins of wealth and religiosity. So he dressed as a magician in his purple Moroccan robe sewn with spangles and bits of glass, and a tall black hat attributed to Augustus John. With a red-lipsticked nose he interrupted the auction with lengthy speeches, backed by Constant in a huge black beard and Nina in a sheet with death's-head mask. Barbara turned up half way through, tricked out as a Tinytot with a bright pink face. A small slight thing, with smooth hair combed in a thick sweep over on to the right side, she must have made an impressively wicked infant. As a detachment of mounted police were announced in the offing, the masqueraders drove off.

I, too, once delivered a speech on the same green. We had driven across to drink at the pub, and some tale of local oppression like that of the sealyham breeder started me off on my anarchist desire to see the rulers and the foolers of the English folk taught a lesson. Several yokels were gathered chatting on the green and I went over to give a John-Ball speech, waving my tankard to prove my points that a free and happy life was possible, advisable, and necessary. I am sure that 14th-century rustics would have applauded me and run for their pitchforks; but their 20th-century descendants merely gaped. Philip listened with an ironical sneer and then carried me back to Eynsford.

He was rather pallid-faced, but his neat gingery beard, added to his dangerous eyes, gave him the effect of a waspish Elizabethan bravo with a courtly air. I argued with him that if one was to grow a beard, one should produce a peasant Tolstoyan beard like mine, and that there was no point in shaving one's cheeks. He told me I was a barbarian and that a beard was a means to an end, not a master given liberty to mat and bush over one's features.

I knew that Coleman, the ranting ravisher of *Antic Hay*, was drawn from him, but I did not yet grasp that he was also Gumbril, the mild and melancholy man beard-transformed to a daring wencher. When in 1918 he grew his beard, he was trying to change his character, to become ruthless and forcible, to dominate women instead of being despised by them.[1] His musical capacity was linked with a fine poetic sense; in a way he remained a frustrated poet finding his lost words in musical

[1] In letters he stated, 'The fungus is cultivated for purely talismanic purposes', and 'it does have a certain psychological effect on me'. 'It is necessary for me to make use of any little magical energy-saving devices that suggest themselves.' Grey cites examples of his verse, and stresses the two sides of his personality, the mild idealist Heseltine and the bitter revengeful Warlock.

sounds. But if he came to set other men's words, he went on using words to mock at all conventional attitudes and to devise obscenities which especially delighted him when blasphemous. The inside of his privy-door was plastered with newspaper cuttings twisted to read lewdly, with bawdy announcements and limericks. He laboured hard to deserve the epitaph he composed (Munn being his landlord):

> *Here lies Warlock the composer*
> *who lived next door to Munn the grocer.*
> *He died of drink and copulation,*
> *a great discredit to the nation.*

The name Warlock had been chosen to baffle the critics and editors who he was convinced would never do justice to Heseltine, but it also reflected the demoniac character he had decided to construct. One can easily compile a list of the manifest opposites in his personality as it developed under the deliberate pressures he put on himself. The gentle, even somewhat feminine, hater of violence, and the compulsive brawler; the fastidious youth, once a vegetarian, who took steak tartare as his favourite dish; the benevolent lover of the humble and harmless, who told himself that he hated children, liked birds and snakes, and wor-shipped cats; the yea-sayer who delighted in finding life 'swish', and the sufferer tormented by what already at Oxford he called 'grisliness'. Gray makes much of the extreme cleavages, but with no effort to explain them, as if Heseltine were simply a schizophrene and the attachment of a label did away with all need to understand.

I think we can get behind the dichotomies; and I feel it is important to understand Heseltine as a typical character of the Twenties—that is, one who drove the characteristic conflicts to their limit. Though drink-ing a lot, there were periods when he shut himself up and worked hard; one has only to glance at the list of his works, and to estimate their quality, to realize that. Yet he had set out to build up a legend, and it steadily swallowed him up. He had created, for the public and for himself, the image of the possessed warlock and he could not run away from it. Whether or not he wanted to, he had to carry on with his drinking-bursts. Fresh admirers as well as old kept surrounding him, expecting him to act up to his legendary role. Enclosed in a limelight he had himself fabricated, he felt a growing strain.

It came out in the tarantelle that was liable to snatch him up, send him racing naked in the street or whirl him in strange acrobatic steps and *pas seuls*, without concern for where he was or what sort of people were round him. Gray tells how he mimed his own funeral in that witchdoctor's robe and black hat of his, intoning the chanty *Walk him along Johnny* in a *danse macabre*. The strain came out too in his way of dropping dead-asleep, in concert-hall or train. The train-slumbers became a problem as they often whisked him beyond his station, and in the end they caused the wild leap that broke his leg. Jestingly he insisted that he must have been sober as no drunk ever hurts himself. I cited Baudelaire's *Litany to Satan* as the corroboration. And he pointed to the fat volumes of a composer: 'At last I have learned the true value of his compositions.'

The mild man came out in his non-smoking. Myself, I never smoked on my own, but could not resist the offer of cigarettes when drinking. I remember how surprised I was one day lunching with him in a Charlotte Street restaurant when he made a grimace at the olives and said they were too sharp for him. As the staple food of ancient Greece they were holy things for me. But his restlessness made him like motor-cycles. Any idea or liking indeed was liable to become obsessional. He had a right-minded objection to the chemical defilement of beer; but once having taken the matter up, he couldn't stop. It not only furnished an inexhaustible theme for fiery or fantastic conversation; it also led to an endless, angry, and remarkably complicated correspondence with Ministries, Brewers, and the Institute of Brewing. Nothing pleased him more than to read out the detailed letters sent or come in reply.

He told me that he had refused to have any truck with his cousin who had done the expurgated version of Petronius for the Loeb. Such an action was not a passing expression of vexation or the excuse for some squib of wit; it usually led to a strong vendetta. At a concert he heard a critic say what a pity to spend a summer afternoon in a stuffy hall instead of open-airing at Lord's; he proceeded to harass the man with a series of postcards and even sent him a pair of bellows with instructions as to how to get a maximum of fresh air. A proper sense of fun and independence of spirit thus became unbalanced, overvaluing the object of attack. Once, scheduled to talk about some Elizabethan songs which Victor Carne was to sing on the air, he went round the BBC staff with a petition for the removal of a musical adviser, unmoved (or rather stimulated) by the fact that the man was in the room. Such tactics could hardly hope to succeed and expressed a wish to be unpleasant

more than a hope of achieving anything. At the same time we must
recognize the sense of persecution and the wish to exact retribution, a
genuine anger at injustice, at the wrong perpetually done to life, and a
courageous refusal to reckon consequences as soon as mind and heart
were convinced.

The same mixture of qualities appeared in his personal relations.
Gray stresses his power of giving himself unreservedly in friendship;
and that is true. The strange magnetism of his character for those he
liked derived from this ability to give himself in a happy fullness. Yet
he could make savage changes in his attitudes to people, the outstanding
example being the way in which his hero-worship of D. H. Lawrence
turned into a ferocious hatred. Understandably he was hurt by the picture
of Halliday in *Women in Love*; but he forfeited my sympathy by having
threatened legal action and extorted £50 from Secker and Lawrence.
And worse even than the action was the vicious self-righteousness
with which he recalled it. Though at the time not sympathetic
to D.H.L.'s outlook, I disliked Philip's account of him as a mere
neurotic scoundrel. (From Gray's book I learn that he behaved even
more badly than I then knew. He wrote to the solicitors urging that
Women in Love was obscene and that Scotland Yard or the National
Council for Public Morals should take action. Gray tries to laugh all
this away as an expression of Philip's too-subtle humour; but clearly
the latter was violently serious and he did all he could to get the book
suppressed.)

D.H.L. saw deeply into him, saw his sexual split. Monogamy, he
says, is only for the whole-man; split men need two women. So Halliday-
Heseltine

wants a pure lily, with a baby face, on the one hand, and on the other, he
must have the Pussum, just to defile himself with her. She is the harlot,
the actual harlot of adultery to him. And he's got a craving to throw himself into the filth of her. Then he gets up and calls on the name of the
lily of purity, the baby-faced girl, and so he enjoys himself all round.
It's the old story—action and reaction, and nothing between.

The linking of the defilement-need with the cat-passion (Pussum) is a
home-thrust. Philip had a graded set of cat-values, ranging from
Pussum to Mog the supreme cat; and he showed more tenderness to
cats than to women. He had a special cult of the self-red cat and obtained
one of the breed near the end. His exasperation with life developed in a

definitely sadistic direction. A girl told me how once at a party he took her aside and tried to whip her, insisting, 'Come on, you know you want it'. Later, sober, he apologized and swore not to repeat the performance; but the next time he got drunk, he made the same attack. After that she avoided him, deciding that he was mad.[1]

His split appears strongly in his attitude to religion. Warlock the ranting boozer was highly blasphemous and rejoiced in nothing so much as a mockery of religion. Yet the mild Heseltine had a weakly superstitious side and dabbled in magic. He had a spiritual guide, 'a model of virtue, uplift, and propriety', comments Douglas Goldring, adding, 'I recall a Ouija-board seance I attended in Dublin at which the "control" ordered him out of the room because he was pursued by "evil influences".' While in Ireland he gave a lecture in the Abbey Theatre, with musical illustrations: he was clad in his witchdoctor's robe and showing a long unruly beard, his first magical growth: a beard-of-nature like mine, not an emblem of defiant dandyism. There were green or amber toplights for the stage, and the performance ended with the Old Man of the Mountains, a commercial-traveller turned hermit, exhorting the audience to go into the hills and live with the Sun and the Fairies.[2]

In his *Delius* Heseltine makes a furious attack on that composer's *Requiem* because of the materialist attitude to death. Augustus John tells how he drove with him from Eynsford to Stalham in Norfolk, where the local folksingers met on a Saturday evening. They called in at the parish church.

Philip had just given a rendering of Harry Cox's beautiful but profane song *Down by the Riverside* upon the organ, and we were about to leave the building, when, moved by a perverse whim, I proposed to revive the rites of a more ancient cult by there and then offering up Miss—[Barbara] on the altar.

[1] Gray admits that about 1920-1 Heseltine experimented with Indian hemp. Philip himself wrote, 'The taking of drugs may exalt a man so that he surpasses himself (i.e. his normal self) and proportionately they enable him to sink to a lower level than his normal self could descend to. Everything depends on a man's nature.' I had a strong suspicion several times that he and his closest friends did have recourse to drugs in the course of long bouts of drinking; and I was not the only one to think so. But I have no proof.

[2] During his year in Ireland he musically found himself; he projected, perhaps wrote, an essay on *Music as Number* and 'the employment of hypnotism for the direct investigation of musical thought-forms'. His lecture was entitled *What Music Is*. In 1917 he had his horoscope cast.

At that moment a thunderbolt struck the building, with a flurry of smoke and dust, electric crackles and charwomen's screeches:

a vivid impression of Hell being opened and its devils loose! Philip with his peculiar beliefs in 'Principalities and Powers' was the most shaken, especially as he was about to mount the tower of which a pinnacle now lay shattered on the ground outside. I believe he composed, at the vicar's request, a hymn tune for the church 'as a thanksoffering for our providential escape'.

If now we look back at the pre-Warlock Heseltine we can begin to understand what the split portended and why it came about. The material in Grey's biography—Philip's early letters and the account of him at Oxford by Robert Nichols—show that he had early arrived at an overpowering need to break with the whole existing set-up. His father had died when he was two years old. 'A moody, vindictive youth,' he calls himself; he hated Eton and Oxford. Intended for the stock exchange, he found himself on a holiday in France, when about sixteen, not far from where Delius lived, and came under the musician's spell. 'Only fit, as I am, for the lethal chamber,' he wrote in February 1913, 'my strongest joy lies in expectation.' Nichols describes him as going through cycles of grisliness and hilarity; a vegetarian pacificist, who admired both Nietzsche and Wagner.

He overflowed with expressions of loathing for Oxford. 'At the age of nineteen, the product of Eton and Oxford is worth a thousand times less than the product of the national board schools.' He repudiated the 'love of empire' and acclaimed 'the things that really matter—which are all the common heritage of humanity, without distinction of race or nationality'. He felt isolated, and, taken away from Oxford in a family financial-panic, he schemed to start a magazine, the *Sackbut*. Then came the meeting with D.H.L., the uprush of hopes for a new life with a small group in 'Florida, Tahiti, anywhere', the passionate admiration for D.H.L., the episode in Cornwall, and the revulsion. Meanwhile he has dreamed of starting a private press for books and music, *The Rainbow*. London he found afresh 'a subtle and deadly poison'.

One still wastes much energy resisting and resisting, saying No to the sausage machine which gulps down human individuality at one end and disgorges at the other a conglomerate mass of units organized for human destruction—though this vortex is an influence rather than an actuality, something intangible—one feels it in the streets, in the strangers who pass one by, but one cannot lay hands on it—all the while one must skirmish, be fighting a shadow.

Schemes for taking over a theatre and putting on opera and concerts, experimenting with mime-drama. He married and fathered a son; he yearned for a new start. 'Write to me about yourself,' he told Nichols, 'not a word, though, about London, not a whiff of the old stench that still hangs over the dead past. Let us cut adrift and start anew!' The Cornish spring inspired him. 'My head is dancing all day long.' He felt that he saw Hy Brasil over the sunset sea, and went to Ireland.

A May letter to Delius expressed his sense of the need for a choice of the whole-man, a breakaway from the entire corrupted scheme of things:

Material and psychological difficulties combined with other things to produce a kind of climax, a decisive point at which it became imperative to break right away from old paths and choose a new direction—or rather pull oneself out of the mud and regain the path one had slipped away from. The English capital, which our countrymen like to call the hub of the universe, is really a great cesspool—more especially where any kind of art is concerned; if one lives in it continuously for a year or so, one sinks deeper and deeper into the mire until one reaches such a pitch of blasphemy that one begins positively to enjoy one's wallowing. Then comes a horrible moment when the truth of one's position rises up against one—and there is nothing to be done except to clear out of all the muck, or else to sell one's soul to Satan for ever and a day.

Ireland gave him a sense of escape from corruption; he began to mature as a musician; and in gratitude he studied all the Celtic languages, including dead Cornish—partly as an 'effective protest against imperialism', and partly through a hope for 'a Celtic rebirth': though he saw Celtic nationalism as anti-nationalism, 'an individualizing movement—a separating one, at any rate'. He still felt a horror at 'the filthiness of the world at large', at 'the Cimmerian darkness which for most of our race constitutes life', and he still believed he could achieve his regeneration:

If only one has the courage to make no compromise and to be ready at any moment to chuck anything and everything that becomes a nuisance overboard, then not much harm can happen to one. And it is surprising, after a little practice at clearing the decks, what strength and dexterity one acquires in the art of throwing overboard lumber—people, things,

ideas, superstitions, fears, fetishes—the whole cargo, lastly perhaps the
old creaking ship itself! then one develops wings!

Both the strength and the weakness of his position appear in his formulations about art. He sees the creative image as born from 'instantaneous
vision', and he realizes that life and art are perpetually in movement.
The theory of art as 'self-expression' is for him a proof of the failure of
the art-impulse:

The self is carefully partitioned, and when the surface portion has become
absolutely static and completely cut off from its own roots and from
everything that, in its drunken diplobia, it considers the not-self, it pro-
ceeds to strut about before a mirror and call its vain reflections works of
art. The true self can never be static . . .

He sees the true artist as always oscillating between 'the pure mystic
and the artisan', but does not arrive at the notion of the dialectical unity
of opposites. He denies the divisions of life (into Being and Doing,
Known and Unknown, Conscious and Sub- or Super-conscious), and
says there is no sharp transition from darkness to light, from the unknown to the known, 'but a ceaseless becoming and intermingling of the
one with the other—which is the unity we call mystical—why, God
only knows. It is this free passage through the *whole* of our being, this
being-*not*-divided-up-into-compartments, this being open to the
infinite (which is within, not outside ourselves) that alone can make us
'ενθεos a term grossly and almost universally misunderstood thanks to
the dichotomizers.' The aim is then 'the realization of the central peace
subsisting at the heart of endless agitations'.

There he comes very close to a dialectical grasp of unity, but slides
away from it at the crucial moment; the conflicts and the variety are
lost, not resolved, in the unity; the agitations are overcome by the
central-peace, they do not earn it. There is thus a flaw of passivity and
resignation at the heart of the rebellion's effort to throw off the rags of
the old man and find a new birth, an uncompromising clue to the resolutions of art. Philip rightly claims to have arrived at 'a purely mystical
conception of the nature of art'. The whole of his *Delius* is based on this
conception.

Here then is the weakness that perverted his rebellion and inverted
the adventure of the whole-man into a satanic defiance, a Warlockian
foray. The defiance was entirely handed over to personal living; no

attempt whatever was made to attack or change the world through art. Philip gave up trying to understand what was wrong with the world and sought his refuge in the peace that was given, not created from conflicts faced out to the limits of endurance—to the confines of truth where unity is grasped as the innermost core of married opposites. And so the peace in fact was phoney, merely a faked counter used to deceive himself and to escape from struggle. But the struggle went on, between the two sides of his split self. The Heseltine dream of oneness-with-nature fought to the death with the Warlockian masquerade, in which the defiance of the world shaded off into an acceptance of evil and violence. Instead of fighting violence he took it into himself; and there it tore him to pieces.

9. FRONTIERS OF FANFROLICO

CONSTANT LAMBERT had rooms not far off, in Lower Oxford Street. When I called on him, it was mostly with Philip; and we seem always to have discussed poetry, not music. 'Your father is the best realistic Australian artist,' I said, rather straining the term *realism* to be friendly, 'and mine is the most romantic.' I repeated the phrases a couple of times in the hopes of evoking some response, some admission of our both sharing an Australian element; but he kept on ignoring the remark. Neither he nor his sculptor brother, whose studio I visited, seemed to want to mention their father.

Constant asked Elza and me along to one of the melodramas performed at Collins' Music Hall, where he had taken two stage-boxes. After drinks at the Plough, we piled into taxis and drove out. Nina has recorded the event. 'The play was *The Executioner's Daughter*, and it was a masterpiece of horror. It was played by a stock company and the executioner's daughter was supposed to be sixteen and have a lame leg. She was in reality about forty-five. The villain was a splendid specimen. He had black bushy eyebrows, fiery eyes, and a large black moustache. He seemed fascinated by Constant and in the intervals of murdering people he would pop his head into the box and glare into Constant's face. In the play nine people were bumped off and the General Post Office blown up.' We were near enough to inspect all the dints in the heroine's pudgy knees and hear the hoarse voice of the overworked prompter.

We had drunk copiously in the long bar during the intervals. After, we hurried to a nightclub and the party broke up. Elza and I ended in an underground joint with green lights and a barman dressed as a Hottentot, with an assegai to threaten the rowdy. A girl with big purple circles painted round her eyes was weeping into a gramophone; the scratched record sounded as though hiccuping through a jazz-moan. Bits of ceiling-plaster fell into the whisky that tasted of methylated spirits and rust. A snub-nosed girl was proving that she could fit her left breast into a champagne-glass pressed against it. I felt wonderfully happy and at home; but Elza was complaining of the bad air and wanting to go home. Generally I was loath to drink more than a pint at the start; but, proud of my Australian stamina and my desire to push all things to their extremities, I found it hard to stop after the sixth round and impossible after the twelfth. However, after scowling at Elza's complaints, I went with a bad grace and never found out if the girl could get a glass to stick on each breast without any support.

We went once again to Collins' with Constant, this time with a less noisy group. Eating first at a Soho restaurant, I asked another of the guests, an old friend of Oscar Wilde, what he thought Oscar's opinion of Norman's art would have been. 'It would have confirmed his worst suspicions, I think,' he said. In the play the seduced heroine trailed round with a doll which now and then leaked sawdust as she rocked it to sleep.

It was in the stuffy cellar of the first night, I think, that we met Basil Bunting, poet. Anyway he called on us soon after, and for a while often looked in. Elza was the point of interest, which may have increased his shyness. Once when I remarked on a letter of his in the *Nation* learnedly commenting on Dante's icy layers in hell, he blushed and stammered that he had only done it because he was after some academic job and wanted to impress. Perhaps he got the job, for he suddenly disappeared.

Among my own friends was Philip Henderson, who later edited Morris' Letters as well as working on Marlowe, Skelton, Samuel Butler. In recalling those days he says:

To me Elza always seemed an elusive watery Ondine-like creature in a long green dress who seldom spoke and smiled with a wry twist of the lips. Perhaps she appeared to your friends rather as Janey Morris appeared to Morris' friends—beautiful, remote and cold. But I used to love coming to your rooms in Museum Street, just to listen to you and the whirl of ideas about Blake, Wagner, Nietzsche, Rubens, and talk about Elizabethan drama and fine printing and stories of your father Norman capering faun-like in the wake of Bacchus and his pards through Australia. I found it all exhilarating and delightful, and lived at that time in a state of intoxication between writing poems and making love and bathing in long evenings of Wagner and Strauss in Covent Garden, thinking nothing of standing for anything up to five hours outside the opera house for a gallery seat. This period was for me the time of discovery of everything that was to matter most to me in life.

Elza was aware of her coldness, her watery element. She often used to say to me, 'I'm a fish. I live cold and deep down like a fish.' And her favourite picture was Botticelli's *Venus*; she had the head with its blown snaky tresses in a full-size reproduction over the bed, the only picture she ever had. And rising up into the waking day, she seemed indeed that Venus, sea-pure and only that moment sprung from the foam, her flesh made marble with the cold beating of the wind on all its pores.

Roy Campbell was another poet who showed up now and then in the Plough with his wife and who was keen on Nina's boxing parties. I admired his verses for the stark images and explosive colour-virtues that marked him as a fellow-colonial in grey England; and I wanted to do a book of his in the Press. Nothing came of it and before long he went south. I remember him lamenting, 'Give me a theme.' Which rather sapped my admiration. He felt a strong poetic force, but in something of an emotional vacuum; he didn't know what to exert his sinews against. His efforts to live a tough life, or at least the appearance of one, I always felt, came from an inner void—the Africa which he had left without understanding and which had become a vast spiritual desert that he wanted to colonize single-handed, a small-boy with an epical dream.

Round the corner in Great Russell Street was the Poetry Bookshop under Harold Monro. I went several times to hear him read poems; and though I was anti-Miltonic, I especially liked the way in which he brought out the full rolling reach and the local vortices of rhythm in *Paradise Lost*. A soft-voiced wistful-eyed Irish lad, Mike, a Plough-frequenter, had taken up with Nora, a well-built wench of amiably accessible body. They lived together, pleasantly squabbling and using devious tricks of money-making, until some beady-eyed rogue in the Plough, afraid of a police-hand on his shoulder, deposited with Mike his stock of Paris-printed books which described perversions in the flowery prurient way of such stodgy commodities. Nora read them avidly, though one would have thought she needed no further education in such matters; and her anxiety to try every detail of the advocated acrobatics led to a strain in her relations with Mike, who, though totally lacking in scruples of any kind, was a lazy fellow. Nora grew resentful and accused him of cheating her in various ways. He tried his blarneying voice in vain; and one night, worked up by a commiserating tart-friend, she stabbed him in the back with a carving-knife as the Plough was emptying. I had passed them about a minute before, as she stood pushing at him, shrouded in a heavy cloak, and he leaned against the doorpost,

The Eynsford pub-garden: Locals with Barbara
and Nina Hamnett.

Aleister Crowley with his second wife.

Two studies of Betty May

giving the soft answer that stirs up wrath, when he turned away, she stabbed him. Carried to hospital, he told an improbable story of falling on a knife when trying a circus trick, and no prosecution ensued. But instead of returning to Nora he took up with Harold and acted as his shop assistant. Several times we had drinks there after pub-closing. One night, with Mike sitting on his lap, Harold told us shamefacedly how he'd once managed to embrace his wife. He had been out riding, and came in heated and exhilarated, saw her lying half-asleep on a couch with disarranged clothes, and was moved to mount her as if she were still the mare he'd been riding. He considered the event remarkable and disgraceful, needing an elaborate psychological explanation, and insisted it had happened only once.

Not long after Mike went to stay with the crippled artist who had lured Jeanne off: in Highgate, I think. There was a press for printing etchings there and he wheedled out of me the set of small plates etched by Norman for Sappho's poems. I knew it was rash to hand them over but I liked his handsome guileless guile. He never printed the plates, and when we needed them for our edition, I had to push my way into the house and forcibly collect them.

Among the Plough dwellers was a tall very flexible Welshman whom we called Sexton Blake, as he was the main ghoster for the periodical devoted to that detective. He smoked a huge pipe, perhaps to keep in character, and was always groaning at being behind with his instalments. Indeed he lived the life of a hunted criminal rather than of a masterly detective; he often had to flee or hide from his editor's emissaries. Once he lurked in the Plough privy till I came to tell him the hunter had retired. At times he worked out the adventures to go into his next instalment, drawing plans on the table with beer-dipped finger and puffing energetically at his pipe as he spoke in his squeaky excited voice. When not in the pub he lived at the Post Office Social Club, where the counter of a dismantled post office on the ground floor served neatly as the bar. At times he gave up being Sexton Blake and impersonated other characters in the endless saga which he both lived and wrote about, slinking in with a Cockney accent or pounding in the bar as he squandered ill-gotten gains. His mania for dressing-up infected the other denizens of his odd club, which Nina knew better than I. She thus describes the goings-on. 'In the morning all the inhabitants appeared in fancy dress when the bar opened. They crept down the almost completely dark staircase early in the morning and sat in the dark on the

D

stairs drinking beer. At eleven o'clock they would all come into the daylight of the bar. A Frenchman appeared dressed as an Arab. He wore a face-towel round his head for a turban and his wife's purple dressing-gown. His wife would appear dressed and painted up like a ghost, which was not very encouraging for the rest of the guests, who frequently were not feeling any too good themselves. Sexton Blake would appear about every ten minutes in another disguise: as a criminal, as an effeminate young man, and as a dope-fiend. The latter was the best as he painted his face greenish white and put black rims round his eyes and made terrifying faces.' Never have I known any writer so possessed and engulfed by his material. In Paris he would have been a leading surreal-ist; in London he was a poverty-stricken improviser of sixpenny-dreadfuls.

A character as tall, as assiduous in his Plough attendances, as addicted to a pipe, but giving an effect of bluff sanity, was Hanchant, in charge of some art-and-crafts society, the magazine of which he edited. His passion was the collection of street-ballads. I contributed several articles to his magazine (one on Ellis, one entitled *The Artist as Goya*) as well as a series of verse-parodies; and began to feel the need of a periodical of our own. Arts-and-Crafts was not prosperous, and Hanchant was a man of infinite resource and sagacity, with shifts that were obviously too good to be true. Sweeping his hair back and nodding at one with his pipe, he explained hoarsely how a fortune waited just round the corner; but somehow the corner was never turned.

Another haunt lay near St Martin's Lane, a club where Hal Collins, familiarly Collie, had served as a barman and where he painted the walls with vast nudes, lumbering or snoozing, against a tropical fury of greens, blues, reds. The speciality as advocaat, made of methylated spirits mixed with sugar and custard-powder. (An equally fiery drink was purveyed at the Fitzroy, called Jerusalem Brandy; but what its throat-rasping ingredients were I never found out.) From a piano on a platform the club-owner used to sing *Old Mrs Dyer the wretched baby-farmer*, with the drinkers joining in the chorus—among them a rubicund priest with a bellowing belching voice that would have wrecked any Gregorian chant. Nina was proud of having sung *The Servant Girl in Drury Lane* there. Like many of the clubs, it went down in a police-raid and the elephantine nudes scaled off from the walls. Most of our drinking was done in a space bounded by the Café Royal, the Fitzroy and the Plough, but there were a few visits to outlying sites like the Prospect of

Whitby, where one could gaze out at the passing ships over tankards of meditative beer.

On the street floor of 30 Museum Street was a bookshop, Davis and Orioli, which only later I found had been started off by Norman Douglas' friend, Orioli, in 1913. It was now run by a man with an imperial beard and a calm, capable and desirable daughter, with a Russian husband. I rarely looked into the shop as I couldn't afford to buy the tempting books. But in the basement, amid tottering book-piles, there were occasional drinking-parties at which Mike sang in his fruity Irish voice, emotion-throbbing, and the mad-eyed Russian in his hard metallic voice, cutting with the sharp edge of aggressive melody and the beat of indefatigable folk-feet dancing. Though I did not much like the Russian, his singing woke something deep in me and I wanted to dance, on a table, a mountain-top, the axis of a star spinning out of chaos.

Tommy Earp often looked into our office in the later afternoon, bringing us news in his scratchy scrannel-pipe of a voice about the latest French verse. He gave me poems by Valéry, Aragon, and others; Éluard I knew from *Transition*. I set out to translate the *Cimitière Marin*, but stopped half way. With Tommy I also discussed Hegel, Croce, Gentile, with rumours of Husserl and Heidigger. Liam O'Flaherty, too, had become a close friend of ours. In the Plough or the teashop close to the office he sat and discoursed, telling long tales of the Troubles in his persuasive voice, with his blue eyes flashing. These tales were better in the hearing than they ever were when written down. He wrote with sweat and pain, and in addition was having much argument with his wife at home. Keen on horses, he often asked me to go over to Ireland and see some of the smalltown races; we even got as far as planning a trip. But lack of funds, the need to stick daily to the work of the Press, and a disinclination to leave Elza for more than a few hours, came together to prevent the carrying-out of any such ideas, however overwhelming and necessary they had seemed in discussion over the pintpot. Liam himself was never a drinker; he found enough inspiration for his tales in cups of tea. Such a hypnotic talker also had less distractions to cope with in holding his audience in a café than in a bar.

I had also come to know Dennis Bradley, the tailor of Bond Street, who put eccentric advertisements (common enough now, but then very unusual) in the *English Review* and who had written the best-selling book on clothes, *The Eternal Masquerade*. He was also a spiritualist. At one dinner at his place Austin Harrison talked about the old days of the

Review, with Norman Douglas on the staff and works like Masefield's *Everlasting Mercy* appearing in the pages, and made *double entendres* to embarrass his young daughter. Oliver Baldwin delivered a pacifist tirade and declared that if the Old Men dared to launch another of their wars he would launch a movement of passive resistance. 'You can enrol me,' I said. Mrs Bradley was worried about the effects of spiritualism on Dennis and consulted me about it—presumably I was considered an expert on account of my father's interest in spirits. She expected a breakdown and thought she'd get him away on a Mediterranean boat-trip. That night a strapping girl with a horse-face drove me home, as the whisky had gone on till the late hours. As she chatted in her hard breezy voice and wondered whether or not she'd ask me into her flat for a final drink and a hasty rape, I asked myself why I hadn't taken Elza along. It wasn't that she lacked presentability, being beautiful and much better-mannered than myself; it wasn't that I was scheming for a life of my own, with culminations in the wooden arms of horse-faced girls. Rather, it was a feeling I had no real place in such a world as Bradley's and was myself there on sufferance, so that I didn't want to include a second person in an invitation which I felt had come my way by some accident. But it was also an admission that my emotions about her were still unsettled, pulling in different directions. And I was afraid of the criticisms implied in the aloofness I knew she would assume, the spirit-damping question readable in her eyes: Why waste time in such pointless activities?

And why indeed waste it? what was I looking for?

I felt Elza as a sort of poetic conscience, which made me feel stupid in my unaccompanied sallies, so that I seldom went to the same place twice. Through Bradley I met a capable but uninspired sculptor Sykes and dined at his flat, which seemed to consist of large rambling stairs and corridors. And I went once to the Belgravia house of a retired Australian governor who had bought one of N.L.'s water-colours of Pavlova. Mentioning to P.R.S. that I had met there a vague young man with the name (I am sure) of Lord Smith, he jeered loudly, 'What, your first Lord! Oxford's lousy with 'em.'

I had written to Norman Douglas saying that I wanted to dedicate the *Satiricon* to him. He replied affably. 'Many thanks: I'll find living up to it *uphill* work.' As a result a steady correspondence developed and I must have had some fifty or more letters of his, many of them long, when I destroyed my MSS in 1931. Through our project of a complete edition of Beddoes I met Sir Edmund Gosse. He was old and tired, but charming. He assured me on his word as a scholar that every possible effort had been made to find anything of Beddoes in German publications and that the texts in his editions were carefully collated. Nothing would ever be found that wasn't in those editions. Except the Juvenilia in the Charterhouse Library, I said. Yes, except the Juvenilia; he hadn't thought them worth mentioning. Then he remarked, 'As one gentleman to another, can you assure me that you have enough money in your firm to carry your scheme through?' Staring him straight in the eye, I said, 'Yes.' But then, as I didn't consider myself a gentleman, the oath was not as religious a matter to me as Gosse had supposed. In any event I felt sure that by hook or by crook we'd get the two volumes out. A few weeks later Gosse gave us a good review of the Herrick book and *Loving Mad Tom* in the *Sunday Times*.

We had the texts set from Gosse's editions—by the Crypt House Press: the right sort of name for Beddoes, we thought. But when I came to correct the proofs by the first editions in the B.M., I found that Gosse had had no respect whatever for their punctuation, capitalization, and so on. I did what I could to repair the texts without running us into ruinous costs; but I had lost my faith in Gosse as an editor. I added extracts from the Juvenilia for which I went down to the library of Charterhouse School at Godalming one hot day, lunching on beer and cheese at a pub not far off; but it was now too late to go chasing for any possible MSS of the later work or letters. However, after the edition appeared, with the Holbein Dance of Death cuts as decorations, I was invited to talk to an Oxford club about the poet. A member of the club was a Beddoes who was descended from a close relation of Thomas Lovell; I was put up at Worcester College and next day the Provost showed me some copies of Beddoes' letters, including the famous last one, in which I recognized at a glance many different readings from those in Gosse's texts. It was my final lesson as to the reliability of genteel Victorian scholarship. However, our edition revived interest in Beddoes and thus led to the correctly edited texts of Donner.

Before the lecturing visit I had gone up to Oxford at the request of the University printer, whom we had asked to print the Beddoes. To my surprise I was asked to stay the night and was shown over the works, which seemed to me ramshackle in their organization—though I enjoyed seeing the 17th-century Fell type still being hand-cast from its original matrices. In our after-dinner conversation it became clear that the reason for asking me up was to plumb the delicate matter of Fanfrolico finances. The printer did not have Gosse's downright method of gentlemanly appeal, and asked me many questions. In talking about Kirtley (who in any event was no longer connected with the Press) I casually remarked that he had been on the Sydney stock exchange. I saw that the information was being carefully tabulated in my questioner's mind; and only then did I ask myself exactly what had been K.'s office-position. I hadn't meant to infer that he was a full-blown Member of the Exchange, but that, I saw, was the way in which my remark was being taken; and obviously on my departure the lists of Members would be consulted—and no K. would be there. I could easily have retrieved my words by saying something about K. having been chief-clerk, or manager, or something of the sort, in the firm for which he worked; but the longer I put off doing it, and the more clearly I foresaw the process by which I was going to be nailed down as an unreliable boaster with forged credentials, the less capable was I of saving my face. Naturally, about a week later we received a letter from the O.U.P. regretting that owing to pressure of work they could not undertake our Beddoes. And who can blame them?

Eric Partridge, whom I had known well at Queensland University, got in touch with me. He was keen to have a try at publishing, and for a while we discussed the possibility of his coming into the firm. But without a considerable increase in capital there was no room for a third person with full rights; and I at last reluctantly had to say so. However we agreed to publish on commission his biography and selection of the writings of Robert Landor, brother of Walter Savage; he had done a thorough job of research, though overvaluing Robert. But in his determined way he proceeded to organize his own press, the *Scholartis* (for which he later took over our rooms in Museum Street).

P.R.S. used to do a day's work for the *Sunday Worker*. I told him, 'I'm financing your party, since you take off a workday to help the paper; but don't think I'm complaining.' The anti-socialist positions I'd accepted from Norman were being corroded, by my anarchist reactions to the English scene and by P.R.S.'s political enthusiasms. Not that he ever tried to convert me. But through him I came to know Charles Ashleigh who, though English, had been in the American I.W.W. and who therefore had a good supply of rebel songs. One night, in the week Elza was in hospital, he and a dozen others came up to our rooms and sang folk or working-class songs till the early hours. Some of the latter

I felt sure had never seen print and I wanted them written down so that
the Press might issue broadsheets; but I never got the words.[1] In the
moment's excitement I told Charles I was going to join his Communist
Party.

Next day P.R.S. disapproved. 'It's all right for a man of action like
me, but you're a poet and you mustn't belong to any party.' Yet he knew
the poetry of Mayakovsky, which he introduced to me. I made a slight
effort at some translations, but could not carry them through. However,
with P.R.S. I worked on *The Scythians* of Blok, which we later printed
in the *Aphrodite*. I also translated many Essenin poems on my own,
putting one into our periodical.

In a small book, *Kookaburras and Satyrs* (1954), and elsewhere, P.R.S.
has stated that:

I explored Marxian Communism, having joined the Communist Party in
Brisbane in 1921, but discarded it in 1926, when I discovered that it was
only banditry disguised as a political philosophy, based on resentment and
hatred, and completely lacking in human kindliness, toleration and
humour.

This statement seems to have compressed a development which in fact
took several more years to mature. In 1926, however, P.R.S. did leave
the Party. He remarks, 'The circumstances of my resignation were,
though unimportant in themselves, widely publicized by a question in
the House of Lords, a debate in the Oxford Union, and even a leader in
the *Times*. My room-mate in The Queen's College, Oxford, at that time,
Tom Inglis Moore, is one of several, in Australia, who know the circum-
stance.' In that year he got into trouble for distributing Gandhi pamphlets to Indian students; and in a letter to me in 1961 he confirms that this
event was what made him resign from the Party.

You might also remember that I was actually sent down from Oxford for
twenty-four hours by the Vice-Chancellor's Court for spreading Communist propaganda among Indian students. This on the complaint of the

---

[1] I responded to these, given straight, as I never did to the parodied versions
of popular culture so characteristic of the decade—whether Elsa Lanchester was
singing *Sell no more drink to my father*, or Gwen Otter at one of her Sunday
parties at Chelsea was reciting Ella Wheeler Wilcox's *The woman is stoned but
the man may go*. Huxley might lament the passing of the last stages of a lively
popular culture; the intellectuals revived its songs in order to jape them or made
slumming visits like those to Collins'. My impulse was always *not* to laugh.

Earl of Birkenhead who revealed it in the House of Lords. There was big
excitement about this when the Oxford Union carried a vote of censure on
the Vice-Chancellor's Court for sending me down. The story made head-
lines in the London press and a sub-leader in the *Times*. Anyway, as usual,
I was right, and where is the British Empire now?

The dispute was then with the University authorities and *not* with the
Party. In fact P.R.S. mentions in this letter that he 'wrote many book-
reviews in the *Sunday Worker*, applying the Marxist basis to evaluation
of bourgeois works'. And in 1929 he was declaring:

Anarchism in immediate working-class politics has long been put on ice,
first by Marx in Bakunin's day, and still more recently by Lenin in *The
State and Revolution*. The modern anarchists (if any) are a mere handful
of die-hard syndicalists with a flavour of Tolstoyan watery 'non-resistance'
theory which washes them out from the field of action entirely. The
revolutionary working-class movement of the 20th century is and will be
Communist. . . . Exit the Bakunin principle, exit Trotsky. Enter Stalin,
up-stage, sits at desk quietly, works.

Strange words for someone who three years previously had decided
that Communists were bandits.[1] In a note in *Biblionews* (Sydney,
February 1959) P.R.S. fills out the account of his earlier literary activities on behalf of the Party:

My Oxford vacations, before I had resigned from the Communist Party,
were spent chiefly in Paris, in company with other students. Tom Inglis
Moore was one of my companions on some of these expeditions. We spent
most of our time blowing froth in the Café du Panthéon. I had friends

---

[1] My brother Philip had the same impression as I had; in 1939, in *I'd Live
the Same Life Over*, he wrote: in autumn 1929 'Inky was a volatile Communist,
with spasms of anarchism, during which he would drink noisily to the memory
of the great Bakunin, while he boasted of donnish cabals at Oxford, due to his
socially heretical soapbox speeches; therefore it is most difficult for me to
realize the change that has evidently swept over him. He is now back in Sydney,
having launched into publishing there, and were it not that Lionel occasionally
sends Peter, and Peter passes on to me, his monthly, *The Publicist*, I would
refuse to believe that that light-hearted, generous Communist, Inky, could
have become a vehement cheer-leader for Japan and German political philosophy: pro-Nazi, pro-Fascist, at least in theory. But whatever faith Inky might
accept, he would accept it with such zealous excitement that it would temporarily blind him to everything else. Such was his nature, such was his charm.
You heard him approaching a pub many, many minutes before he flung wide
the door and entered bellowing for drinks all round. Then there would be
back-slapping, laughter, excitement that seemed to tinkle thrillingly along the
very glasses on the shelves. He stirred a pub to life.'

there among the students from the Sorbonne. Two of these were Communists—one a Frenchman, and the other a Russian Jew [Michel Zipine]. That was in 1925 and early 1926. . . . While I was in Paris, I was busy translating (from the French) two books by V. I. Lenin. These books, *Imperialism* and *On the Road to Insurrection* were published by the Communist Party in London in 1925 and 1926. They were the first works of V. I. Lenin published in English translations. While I was in Paris, I also learned a little Russian from my Jewish Communist Russian student friend. With his aid I translated into English Alexander Blok's poem, The Scythians, which was later published in *The London Aphrodite*. I also translated Mayakovsky's poem *The Death of Lenin*, which was published in *The Communist Review* (London). These were the first works by Blok and Mayakovsky to appear in English translations.

The two Lenin works were in fact published in 1926, with no translator named; and though they were not the first writings of Lenin done into English, P.R.S. might justly feel proud of being responsible for the version of such an important work as *Imperialism*.[1] 'With these and other efforts, during my five years membership of the Communist Party, I earned a little niche in the Communist Hall of Literary Fame.'

One of the singers I had met with Ashleigh was a coarsely handsome Cockney girl who lived round the corner in a flat she shared with a Canadian nurse. She was a Communist and worked for Arcos, the Russian trade-delegation. And she was having an affair with the representative of an American publishing house: which worried her a lot. Was it right to accept the embraces of someone who was not only no comrade but was also the envoy of a capitalist firm? Her qualms did not stop her from the affair, but spoiled things between the embraces. The nurse had worked during the war with my uncle Daryl, who had turned the family art-knack to account by making surgical drawings in a military hospital.

The compressed account of people and events in this chapter may give the impression that we were gadding about and drinking all the time. In fact it covers about eighteen months, most of which was spent in hard work, as a glance at the list of things we turned out will prove. P.R.S. and myself took £5 each a week from the earnings, and never

---

[1] *State and Revolution* appeared 1919 (Allen & Unwin): *Left-Wing Communism* 1920 (C.P.) a couple of pamphlets 1919: *Will the Bolsheviks Maintain Power?* 1922. The passage from Mayakovsky's *Lenin* (7 pages) was printed in the *C.R.* January 1926 as by P.R.S. and M.Z.

D*

once during this period did we exceed that sum. When things had become more stable, we employed a typist, a plain but efficient girl, so that P.R.S. would be more free to concentrate on sales. At publication times the three of us got down to making up the packages and carrying them to the near P.O. P.R.S. was also working on Nietzsche's *Antichrist*. We wanted to do new translations of all Nietzsche's major works, and began with the *Antichrist* because there were several of Norman's pen-and-inks that went excellently with it. P.R.S. made a fine job of the text, and we had what we thought the brilliant idea of printing it entirely in Poliphilus capitals, to give it the monumental effect of a Roman Inscription—though it was not easy to read except in small bits. At the same time I was working over my *Dionysos*, mainly revising passages where I could bring in diagrams derived in idea, though different in application, from those in Yeats' *A Vision*. We issued the book with illustrations from Titian, Rubens, N.L., Turner, Blake, Goya. My Blake book we had printed earlier; it at once sold out and we issued a second edition with a new chapter. This was the only book, apart from a collection of my lyrics, which we did not publish in a limited edition.

All the while I was doing research at the B.M., mainly into 17th-century poetry on the popular level. Only a small portion of this work went into *Loving Mad Tom*. Among other things I was hoping to produce a critical edition of Rochester, to follow the rather haphazard omnibus issued by the Nonesuch Press; and had sketched translations of several dialogues by Plato, to go with our Nietzsche series. As a preliminary work I collected and published *Inspiration*, an anthology of comments on the creative process by poets, artists, musicians. I was also working Donne and the Metaphysicals, and hoped to produce a series of selections. I had almost lost touch with contemporary writing, and joined Mudie's Library, which was close at hand. The first book I took out was the first volume of *Scrutinies*, which excited me very much, especially the long essay by D.H.L. on Galsworthy. Almost all the essays woke my hearty assent and for the first time since I landed I felt that I was not alone; somewhere there was developing a body of critical opinion with which I felt a considerable kinship. I wanted to get in touch with the editors, but we were so busy I postponed the matter.

In a prospectus P.R.S. outlined our policy, saying that we wanted effects neither 'showy nor stodgy', but 'adequate to express the individuality of each book (not, be it noted, of the typographer, who should be much more in the background concealed in his beauty-parlour, than are several too-shining contemporaries)'. He added that 'in fine book production the question is not merely how to print finely, but what to print finely', and defended the use of illustrations. I contributed a credo in verse, which began:

> *Disguised as publishers, perhaps,*
> *We, the last simple trustful chaps,*
> *believing poetry has power*
> *to clap wild heaven for an hour*
> *upon a new earth glittering*
> *with rhythm lacing everything—*
> *we have essayed, the best we can,*
> *to temper prophecy to man;*
> *to tune our trumpets till their rage*
> *fills the advertising page . . .*

P.R.S. had pushed me into writing a novel, *Face of Poetry*, with the aim of entering it for an Historical Novel Competition by Chatto and Windus; but the result was poor, an attempt to translate some of my Elza-problems into an Elizabethan setting. However, in pressing me to do the work, P.R.S. showed a good sense of the direction in which lay such talent as I owned—though I was still too far from the everyday world to do much with the genre or to get anywhere near my aim of 'bringing a Dostoevskian tension into the picture of the past'. I unwarily mentioned the MS to Bennett Cerf, a pleasant American, who gallantly insisted on taking it off to New York in the hopes of getting it done there. At a lunch at his flat I met a well-built silken-legged woman who had once been Dreiser's secretary. She insisted that Dreiser's 'bad style' was deliberate. Once a friend revised a whole novel for him, but Dreiser threw out every single one of the corrections; he felt that the 'clumsinesses' of his style were necessary for the psychological effects he wanted.

Foyle's asked me to take the chair at a lecture and reading by Osbert Sitwell; so I went along to the preceding lecture in order to see how things were done there. The speaker was Coppard, who made the excellent point that the short story had a quite different origin from the novel, so that the techniques were not comparable. I liked his lean dark simplicity and later became a friend of his. Osbert after his lecture asked me to print a poem in a set of contrasted types to match the variety of its ingredients; I drew up a specimen layout, but nothing came of the project. Another friend made around this time was John Gough, Australian musician, disciple of Delius, a large-bodied vulnerable chap whom Lawrence with his superior sophistication found pleasure in baiting. One night he took advantage of John's imbibing an unwonted amount of beer to carry off all his records, which he handed to me. I thought they were a loan till John tracked them down and reclaimed them. But he was too good-natured to bear any malice, though he was rather short of money and the loss of the records would have been a sore loss.

With Lawrence I had gone to sell all the ballets staged by the Diaghilev Company. As I never went to the theatre, I should have missed the ballets if he had not dragged me into the gallery to see one of the performances. After that I needed no push. The ballets opened a new dimension of art for me; they seemed a verification of all I had ever dreamed of the image of beauty. Together with Yeats' symbolic chamber-plays they made me discontented with all the forms which had been satisfying me in poetry; they opened up a myriad new possibilities in my thought; but I could not find how to develop in words the emotions and impulses they stirred. In the hope that by direct collaboration in a ballet I might come closer to what I was after, I suggested to Heseltine that we should compose a ballet of Elizabethan Drunks—I doing the libretto and he the music. He at once vehemently turned the idea down, saying that he despised the Diaghilev ballet as an impure form and the performers as a pack of perverts and exhibitionists. It was true that he, like Gray, was an opponent of the Diaghilev Ballet (though he had once written a potboiling Chinese ballet which was never performed, as well as a Pierrot mime-drama with Rodker); but I think the vehemence of his recoil had more in it than a dislike of the artificial ecstasy of the dancers. I had not yet realized the split between his life and his art. Thus, he hated Christmas, yet set many carols and Christmas songs; the last thing he wanted to do was to express in music the life he lived.

One night when we had tickets for the stalls at the ballet, we went to have a drink during an interval. As we stood by the bar counter, I had a sudden panicked conviction of being stared at by a host of hostile eyes, looked round and saw that I was in fact surrounded by several bulky men with their ugly gaze upon me. Then I noticed that I was standing next to King Alfonso of Spain. With my ragged beard I had seemed to his guard a menacing anarchist. Hastily I moved away.

10. ELZA AND ESSEX

ELZA had introduced me to an elderly benevolent man who, she said, had befriended her years before. She insisted there had never been anything except pure patronage on his part, and I believed her. He had all the characteristics of a middle-class eccentric wanting to save the world but without any idea how to struggle against evil except by helping young women and by proving that Bacon composed the works of Shakespeare and heaven knows what else. All his strong sense of the world's evil, its omnipresent cheat and lie, had been absorbed by his hope of vindicating Bacon and unmasking the paltry actor Shakespeare. He had written several books on the subject, which he backed with his own money. His edition of the Sonnets with an elaborate exegesis was a remarkable work, which I kept for long with me. One had only to read its analysis for a few pages to feel all one's own most cherished and ingenious ideas undermined; he showed so clearly how strangely convincing a fixed idea could be in picking up clues and exposing hidden relationships—even when one knew quite well the premises were hopelessly unsound.

But he was a likeable and solemn man, with whom we lunched several times. He told me how happy he was that Elza had found the protector she had always needed. I winced at such praise, but tried to repay him by saying nice things about Bacon while keeping off the subject of the plays.

Elza had begun writing poems. One day I came in with P.R.S. and she handed me a sheet of paper on which a quatrain was scrawled. I typed the poem out and handed it to P.R.S. We were both impressed. One of the lines—'or the toning of a tear'—seemed to have an odd echo in my thoughts, and next day I recognized that it was stolen from Herrick. I did not say anything to P.R.S., but I included the Herrick poem in our *Delighted Earth*, and he there noticed how Elza had borrowed the phrase which gave distinction to her scrap of verse.

However she went on writing; and she did not again steal any phrases. She had gained in confidence and let her inner self overflow on to paper.

But P.R.S. was unconvinced; he plainly believed that I was writing the poems for her. And so when I put one of them into *The London Aphrodite*, he cut it out of the proofs; I put it back again, he cut it out again; I finally managed to get it back in time for the printed text. This odd duel was carried on without either of us saying anything to the other.

I did not write the poems for her. Clearly she was much influenced by my work, especially by *Ragnhild* which she must have read far more than I guessed. And at first I helped her by discussing what she had written, trying to make her more conscious of what she wanted to say, encouraging her to rewrite, sometimes several times. She found such revision difficult and fatiguing; her natural bent was to 'express herself' and say that the result however inadequate was all she could do. Gradually however she came to build up her own kind of technique. And the result was so palpably a revelation of her own character that no one could have written the poem but herself.

I bound up a little book from paper-samples in the office and copied out the poems, adding small decorative drawings. The book opened with the second poem she had written:

> *This is my loneliness, and here*
> *amid the frightened voices hid,*
> *I see the earth, as in a maze*
> *jewelled lamps hung from my mind.*

Certainly a large part of her initial impulse had been to tell me about herself as she could not tell me in daily speech—and by the quality of the things said to make me have faith in her spirit, to make me love her as she wanted to be loved. But after she had started, she found a satisfaction in the writing itself, a happiness that came out of what she proved, not to me, but to herself. For the first time in her life, I think, she had a certain peace and security.

Thus runs *Before I met you*:

> *I see a sky of faces*
> *blown out on the clouds*
> *and bubbles of the wind.*
> *Their plump white mouths are lapping up the skies,*
> *always thirsty, for my tears are so salt,*
> *and they find no rest. Tumultuous are the heavens*

and the faces angrily fade across each other,
coming out the other side like anguished moons.
They press their knotted hands upon the wind
and hem me round, beating cloudily,
seeking to tear the kisses from my mouth
and slake their thirst in the immortal sun.
They do not see the gods drifting by
through my tossing hair
which suddenly is filled with wings,
and I am carried far away
while wailings fill the dark forest
where the shadows fade back through their own eyes
and I die.
And I escape the blood of earthly kings.

That is one of the easier ones. Others were direct transcriptions of
dreams, written down in the early morning. The world of the poems is
one of elemental change and dissolution, with her lonely spirit pursued
and tormented, finding release only in momentary identifications with
the bright life of nature

> *trees kissed by the passionate sun,*
> *fountains playing everywhere*
> *between the birdsongs and the gold*
> *and the clouds of my own hair—*

and in momentary raptures of the embrace:

> *Little sprites tripped up the ladder of my spine*
> *to peep at beauty awakening;*
> *from my burning eyes they saw him*
> *leap the skies and moonlight swarming*
> *round his scarcely breathing nostrils.*

> *My body stood inside my soul*
> *as in a fountain, and through each fingertip*
> *dripped rubies and drops of gold.*

Both releases are steadily linked with her discovery of me, with the
point of difficult safety that discovery had given her.

The poems moved me deeply, intensifying the impotent pity I felt
and yet confirming me in my still-reluctant conviction that we were
bound together for life and that my task was to help her towards an
increasingly full happiness. Graves saw several of the poems and liked
them. That his liking was genuine and penetrating was shown by the
fact that he criticized some in detail, disapproving only of the lines
where my influence was strongest. Gordon Bottomley, with whom I
was now in touch, also liked them very much. I had written to him
about his work, and soon a strong bond developed. I met him several
times during his visits to London and breakfasted or lunched with him
at his hotel opposite the British Museum.

My friendly relations with Graves did not last long. I sent him a
copy of *Helen Comes of Age* with a rash request for a frank opinion. He
wrote back at courteous length, but his comments boiled down to the
statement, 'I have never been able to bear the scent of hawthorn and
these works are heavy with that scent. No doubt the best kind of
hawthorn scent, but not for me.' A sensible judgment. I should agree
now that the style is clogged with that sort of sweetness, the imagery of
the fused senses, though I think still there is more to be said of the total
effect. But, for all my request for a frank opinion, I was hoping for a
more sympathetic response. I had enjoyed Graves's own work very
much, though I disliked the intellectualizing attitudes that had come
with Laura; his opinion was one of the few I valued.[1]

Thereafter our relations worsened. I was the one mainly to blame;
for I had tried to extort from Graves more than I had the right to ask.
But I think it was something about Laura that caused the final break.
Oddly, I can't remember. Clearly the reason is that the break was
blurred in my own mind by the disappointment I had brought on
myself.

From Bottomley on the other hand I got as strong a response as I
could have hoped. In his generous way he stressed the positive aspects,
insisted that I was on the right path for the reinvigoration of drama;
and when I pointed out that I had unintentionally stolen a line of his

---

[1] In the *London Aphrodite* I wrote that 'instead of purging a tendency to
prettiness by persisting till it turned to emotional depth, he has succumbed
to the temptations of the "Intellect" '. I did not take into consideration that the
intellectualization might in time help him towards emotional depth and complexity of structure. What seems to me the real weakness in Graves I shall
discuss later in this book: his refusal to see the social implications of a revolt
that was essentially social in origin. Hence the limitation of his world of ideas.

('I love you and I love you and I love you'), he replied. 'I forgive you.
Let the omen stand. Marlowe once provided a line for a greater man'—
referring to the line: 'Who ever loved that loved not at first sight.' I
had many long letters in his clear fine script on the problems of verse-
drama, which were burned in 1931. One phrase I recall, about T. S.
Eliot, 'He is very talented, but no man can create poetry out of his
inhibitions, and that is what he has set himself to do.'

Suddenly Elza mentioned that her child was coming over from Paris
and that we should have to collect her at the boat-train. The news
threw me into confusion; for in my efforts to escape thinking concretely
about the situation, I had taken 'child in Paris' to be a sort of remote
counter in our relations, like 'husband in Paris' and 'wife in Australia'. I
had never faced the fact that sooner or later Elza would want to see
and be with her child. I had no objections, except that I could not
conceive our relations carrying on with a child in the household. For
those relations were so strangely removed from anything domestic,
everyday, ordinary; they existed at the level of silence or of Elza's
poems.

Robinetta proved to be a plump little thing, very quiet and reserved,
seven or eight years old. No child could have been less trouble. I took
her for walks and through the British Museum, and liked her in my
timid way. I was afraid of children. I was afraid of all the child represented in the way of family and social responsibility. Our idea of art
had in it too much of the play-element abstracted from social function;
the child in his or her blitheness was a rival who showed up what was
false and highfalutin in our claims. Also I think my fear masked an
intense but repressed wish to become a father; the fear was that I
would repeat my own father's irresponsibility and desertion.

Suddenly Elza announced that she wanted to go to the country.
Behind her decision there lay a slowly mounting tension, which the
arrival of Robinetta had brought to a head. She made no complaints
about me or our way of life; she merely said that she could not bear to
live in London any longer, that she needed country air and fare; and it
would be better for the child. I talked things over with P.R.S. and we
decided that it would be sufficient if I spent three days a week in town;
much of the editorial, translating and other work could be quite well
done in the country. Elza found a cheap top-floor room for me in
Gilbert Street opposite us, and read through *Dalton's Weekly*. I think
it was the first house we looked at that we took: at Alphamstone on the

Essex-Suffolk border, overlooking the Stour Valley in Constable country, between Sudbury and Bures. The owners of the cottage (or rather bungalow with one room raised at the end) were two elderly tweedy spinsters with a horde of dogs; all their conversation was on the problems of mating bitches.

Elza was deeply excited; and I too looked forward to the change. Elza I think had a hope of some idyllic situation in which all her difficulties would vanish; I felt that the tension between us would end through my being half the week at home entirely at her call and the other half out of her sight, unworried-about, free to spend my time as I liked. Things worked out like that for a short while.

We moved and had the happily-occupied time that settling into new pleasant surroundings always is. There was a large untended garden, which I dug up. We had bought a bicycle before we left London. I had never ridden and now began to practise. After falling over a few times I more or less mastered the machine, but was never at ease when a car or lorry came at me down one of the lanes or winding roads. I preferred to stop and if necessary to fall off sideways into the hedge. What were a few scratches as long as one wasn't run over? I used to ride into Bures for the train and leave the bike there, to be picked up on my homecoming. The road between the cottage and the station was about as unsatisfactory for cycling as could well be found—all twists and steep ups-and-downs. There was a sharp downhill on the way back, just before I reached home, and almost every time I crashed in the dusk at the bottom into a large stone—one of the glacial deposits, eaten with pockmarks that look like the cup-holes of prehistoric sacrificial rites, which are almost the only rocks found in that part of the world. I became an expert at mending punctures. During my days at home I rode about the neighbourhood, which at that time had little traffic, though there must be few stretches of hedge where into which I didn't plunge some time or other. Parts of the Stour valley were delightful and I spent hours lying at fine vista-point, now at last absorbing in leisurely happiness the earth of the English poets and landscape artists.

Elza, with more time to spare in the scattered village, made several friends. An old couple used to call us in to chat over parsnip-wine; otherwise I never touched a drink. My Stour musings increased my dissatisfaction with my London life. The Press was flourishing, but I felt myself as poet standing still. In August 1928 I wrote a longish poem *Time Torn to Stars*, which attempted to define what I took as the linked but opposed trends of disintegration—intellectualism and primitivism—to show how the way-forward lay in a resolution of their conflict by a new synthesis of the colour-image: the image using the fused senses of *symbolisme* with a deepened human content. I wanted to work through a series of broken forms to the triumphant recreation of the Cleopatra-image ('burned on the waters, etc.'): to reveal the Shakespearean image enriched by the resolution of the poetic conflicts intervening between 1600 and 1928. In this sense the poem was an anti-*Waste Land*. I was attacking Eliot's use of the Cleopatra-image for a flat contrast with the dead present of depressed naturalism, of which his religious formulations were the ghostly reflection; his blank ignoring of the fact that in ritual-myth the Waste Land existed in order to become the Earth of Plenty through the generative energies, through the creative act of transformation. But my protest against intellectualism was itself far too aridly intellectual; my protest against expressionist hastes, itself far too hasty.

Next to us was a countrywoman, whom a stumpy naval petty-officer had married as a widow with several children. She told Elza that the P.O. had never consummated the marriage. 'I dunno what's wrong with him. Many the time I've tried to strike a light or make a lucky grab and find out if he's got anything there, but he always beats me to it. I got an idea it was shot off.' She wanted to leave the useless man; but he baffled her by never straying beyond the vegetable-patch save at erratic moments for a quick one at the pub. As a result she couldn't arrange to smuggle the furniture out; and without the furniture she couldn't go. Almost every time I came home there would be a new story about some effort of the woman to find out just what the P.O.'s physical condition was or to diddle him about the furniture; but he was always too smart for her. The struggle was still going on when we departed.

About this time I read D.H.L.'s *Fox* and *Captain's Doll*, the first of his fiction I had looked at since *Women in Love* in Australia. Though I still felt hostile to what I thought his general positions, I had been much shaken by the essay on Galsworthy, and I found these two tales stimulating. In our Fanfroliconian ethic, the woman had the right, indeed the duty, to mock at her man; *The Captain's Doll* made me begin to doubt such attitudes (based as they were on the idea of the spiritual segregation of the sexes, of primary differences between man and woman which necessitated a perpetual sex-war)—though at the same time I could not accept D.H.L.'s position that the male as male must be respected.

I had heard nothing of Janet for some time, and therefore had myself ceased to write to her. Nothing definite had happened and I was able to shut the matter out of thought without coming to any decisions. I could not visualize an end of my marriage with Janet (which implied a decision not to return to Australia); I could not visualize an end of my relations with Elza (which implied a turning-back from the path on which I had now set my feet).

11. THE LONDON APHRODITE

BOTH P.R.S. and myself, having got the Press stable, could not feel satisfied with limited editions alone. We decided that we were now able to launch a magazine without wrecking the firm; and we began preparations for *The London Aphrodite*. The name was a joke, though a serious one. If there was room for a *London Mercury*, why not for a London Goddess of Beauty? (Mercury, we recalled, was a patron of businessmen and a guide of the dead; we wanted a deity who damned all profitable prudences and who guided the quick.) The publicist work of Wyndham Lewis, which was having a considerable success, also spurred us on. A. L. Morton called lankily in at the office, travelling for adverts for Lewis, and we merrily concocted one in which we set out our positions and called Lewis various forthright names. Needless to say, he did not print it. However Morton gave us some poems, which we used.

The first issue of *Aphrodite* announced that only six numbers would appear. In it, as in all the numbers, P.R.S. composed the commentaries:

This periodical may even be epoch-marking because it has nothing whatever to do with the *zeitgeist*. Therefore the Editors invite contributions from the world at large outside the lunatic asylums of the abstract and other official cliques. . . . Each number will contain a series of exercises in the forgotten art of lyrical poetry. . . . Do not subscribe, please, if you are quite satisfied with the prevailing standards in literary periodical journalism.

And underwriting my generalities, he added his credo (in a series of his best puns):

that it is amusing to be alive, but that it is a question of blood in the arteries and you cannot get blood from a Stein: that the emptiest moderns make most noise, owing to the Decline of the Best: that modernity, like maternity, is already out of date, owing to correspondence from France and American specialities: that the Transcendental Unity of Apperception (Kant) has been overcome by the Trans-Atlantic Disunity of Introspection (cant); but that Freud means Joy not Joyce; and that consequently there is No Sale for Poetry because there is no poetry for sale, the nigger being in the woodpile of (musical) Time and (middle) Western Man when he (she or it) comes to Europe with a literary aspiration: that the gods whelp those who whelp themselves, which means instead of Cummings, They Went, because Beauty is (see page opposite *et seq.*) possible.

(*They Went* was the title of a book by Norman Douglas; otherwise I think the jokes wear well.) The contents included poems by Slessor, McCrae, Robert Nichols,[1] Powys Mathers, and others; a verse-play by myself as well as a long essay *The Modern Consciousness* and an instalment of the *Dung of Pegasus*; a tale *Patsa* sent from Ireland by Liam; P.R.S.'s satirical verse, *Bullets and Ballots*, ridiculing the Fabianism of Shaw and Wells ('Lenin and Trotsky were Up and Doing, and what about Shaw and Wells? They are up and doing some more new books, for Socialism Sells.')

My essay began by stating that one could not discover the Nature of the Modern Consciousness by abstracting some main point from the position of each of the various competing groups. One must judge the totality of the material 'as partisan', seeking 'to be true to one's deepest experience of life and art in every passing criticism. That is to judge the material, not as isolated completed things, but as imperfect aspirations into the whole human future, the eternity of myself.' (The last phrase shows how I still brought down my method in the final resort to an existential idealism; but now there was the emerging conflict with the 'human future'.) 'I therefore take as my criterion the concrete universal, the human dynamic.' I went on to define Nietzsche as the great fore-runner of the new synthesis, the new creative adventure:

[After the Renaissance] philosophy marched from abstraction to abstraction, the only conclusion of which could be Hume's pertinent use of logic to sever all the knots of divine law, with the Scotch Commonsense Philosophers tying them up again with penny bits of string. Kant, a great destroyer with a disguise of infinitely tortuous terminology, destroyed metaphysics by carrying to a logical precision far ahead of any predecessor the proofs for the existence of God and then calmly annihilating them.

[1] Nichols had become very friendly. After the third issue he recognized who Peter Meadows was and wrote to me, 'I feel sure that this person looking back on his life has a big future ahead of him.' Mathers also had become a friend: more of him later. Among the poets was Stanley Snaith, a protégé of Bottomley, who called in several times.

Frightened at this vast god-slaughter, he resuscitated the deity with a salve of moral proof; but even then found himself floundering back into danger in *The Critique of Judgment* (which consequently nobody reads) and gave up the task. However his work remained, its stimulus, behind the deadening veils of style, vitally destructive.

Hegel carried on this work, supplanting for the first time since the Hellenes the abstract universal with the human complex: his dialectic bored down into the human process as significance. His limitations do not matter here. Enough that he saw human activity as real.

On to this scene arrived Neitzsche. Absorbing the whole philosophical tradition at a gulp, he intuitively completed the cycle of Plato—Aristotle—Kant—Hegel, and saw in what direction the new cycle must face. He formulated a Dionysian philosophy: a return to the Platonic knowledge of man as the measure of all things, with a new passionate sense of the constructive essences of man himself.

He fused the opposites of the ceaseless flux and of eternal recurrence (which I defined as the liberated judgment), Dionysos and Apollo. Here, I claimed, were the sources of value by which we might illuminate and criticize the modern world. By the criterion of the Nietschean dialectic I then examined Wyndham Lewis, Bergson, Freud, Einstein, Blake and 19th-century poetry, Goya and Delacroix, and the development of art from Cézanne (seen as mainly disintegrative), Mozart, Beethoven, Wagner, and the development of music from Scriabin and Schönberg (again seen as mainly disintegrative). Returning to modern literature, I praised the Sitwells, Turner, Roy Campbell, Yeats and Bottomley, and attacked Eliot; saw Stein and Joyce as mainly disintegrative; tried again to pull Lewis to pieces and then turned on D.H.L. and Shaw (as opposed but equally-partial types). And ended with a fresh attempt at defining the necessary synthesis:

Yeats, drawing on I know not what astrological mysteries, prophesied some years back that the turning-point, the arrival of the third kingdom of the spirit, was to occur in 1928.

The signs of the Third Kingdom are a liberation of irrational Dionysian force and, simultaneously, a strengthening of the antithetical symbols of the intellect.

We have seen, under the stress of Music's conquest of Time, all expressions wearing through their old garments till, growing more and more skeletal, they became inert. That was in order that we might have as clear a sense as possible of our tools.

We have seen, side by side with this, the storm of nervous sensibility tear minds to rags or send them seeking refuge in the hot primitive mud. That was to make clear for us the dramatic potentialities of the struggle into self-consciousness.

It now remains for us to make this effort, legionaries of the new Roman determination to stabilize spirit—defining a new faith in life and the eternality of self, and at the same time washing our hands, Pilate-fashion, in the coolest of ironical despairs.

It remains for the Third Kingdom—ignoring the efforts to return to the primitive slime or to make life a psychological abstraction—to define this freedom of self-motive energy, deepening from consciousness to consciousness, and, with the imageries of all the modes whereby the human spirit redeems itself from death, constructing the fluid concretions of its love.

I proclaim the Third Kingdom.

Needless to say, the essay was full of wild and indefensible generalizations, but at the same time it was a serious effort to grasp in a comprehensive vision what was implied by art in the post-Cézanne, post-Wagner world. Compared with the simple denunciations of *modernismus* we indulged in in Australia, it showed a real sense of what the criticized persons were getting at, even if it summed up their limitations or one-sidedness in too lordly a fashion. To this extent I was breaking away from N.L. abstractions; and the preoccupation with 'the human future' showed an even deeper divergence, derived partly from my whole experience in England, partly from the impact of P.R.S. and his politics.

I had written several small verse-dramas. *Love*, printed in *Aphrodite*, took a theme from Norse saga. A poet meets a priestess wandering with her goddess in a waggon, makes love to her, fights and breaks up the intruding goddess, puts the bits of the idol together, and joins the girl in going round for alms, singing the goddess' praises. Under Yeats' influence I was simplifying, or flattening, rhythm, and rationing my thick image-clusters. Rhythm had been conceived as a series of long shelving (Wagnerian) sweeps full of local recoils and eddies; now I sought a single clear curve equably sustained. I was in fact in search of a form that discarded *ecstasis* for a disciplined purpose, and *Love* made fun of the N.L. gods, though my only course still seemed to hymn them before the world. In attempting to deepen irony I was beginning to rebel.

Aphrodite One did well. A steady support flowed in, though the critics ignored us or jeered. Our staunch partisans included such diverse types as the Hon. Evan Morgan, an American business-man A. P. Sachs (who wrote us an essay on Heisenbergian Indeterminacy), and a bank-clerk who lived at Bromley and bought all our books. Sachs, a large beaming fellow, visited London periodically and took us out to dine. One night we were at the Eiffel Tower run by the Viennese Rudolf Stulik, where the charges were high but one was liable to meet persons like Augustus John or Matthew Smith at its small tables with pink-shaded lights. Sachs took up the theme of a terrible disaster coming on mankind. P.R.S. argued that the spread of literacy made a decline into barbarism impossible. 'But that's just why it *is* possible, and likely,' I protested; 'the next barbarism will be the worst ever.' Sachs seconded me. I argued, 'It's the mixture of literacy plus the degraded level of life that's becoming more and more general; there's the danger. People can be got at as never before.'

We went to the Eiffel too with Aldous Huxley. He had heard of us (as a passage in *Point Counter Point* shows); and came into the office in response to a note from me. Tall, willowy, with lavish brown hair and loose red mouth, with a large hat and strongly-lensed spectacles. He was then badly short-sighted and held a book close up against his face. I liked him. He was living near Paris, but was on a visit to London, rather pessimistic about England and its vulgarized dulled ways of life, the pervasive jazzband burbling away and the old kind of music-hall dead. He listened attentively and politely to our expositions, perhaps wondering if we might add some new horror-types to his fiction—though I think he was responsive to much in our attitudes even if he could not accept many of our point-blank positions. He had been fascinated by D.H.L. and wanted to find how to break thoroughly from the negative positions on which he had built himself up. Something more easily hoped-for than done. Anyhow I think he was pleased by our strong admiration of the lively elements in his work, which had come out most playfully in *Antic Hay*.

He asked me to stay with him in Paris. I would dearly have liked to go; but the same reasons as had held me back from visiting Ireland with Liam still tied me down. He sent me two sonnets for the magazine and a copy of *Point Counter Point*. I replied, 'I think you are expelling your rationalist devils. . . .' And tried to analyse helpfully the struggle inside his work. He didn't seem to resent my remarks. Perhaps our bull-roaring Dionysiac declarations had some effect in drawing him on to works like *Do what you will*. But if you have been possessed by rationalist devils and drive them out, the void is more likely to be filled with the angels of systematic mysticism than with reckless maenads. And so it was with Huxley.

P.R.S. in *Aphrodite Three*, in a dialogue between Point and Counterpoint, worked out these positions:

Counterpoint: . . . Thus the opinion of the critics will merely confirm Huxley's main thesis that Intellectuals frustrate themselves in a centrifugally developing futility and hopelessness.

Point: Huxley himself being *a priori* included; which he at least, confound his self-honesty, recognizes.

Counterpoint: Well, recognition of this particular kind is generally indicative of the desire to get out of the bag's bottom; and perhaps *P.C.P.* has now cleared the way in Huxley's own mind for an affirmatory human synthesis, in which case it will be more than a flash of lightning on a dunghill.

Point: Does he really hate his characters? Are these futile people photographs, caricatures, or sheer fantasy-projections? Why need he concern himself with the dull world of Michael Arlen grown more culpable because a little more self-conscious and erudite?

Counterpoint: Because these are all he knows. He has been round the world without quitting the stateroom of his own mind . . .

Point: Then raise the Scarlet Standard high.

Counterpoint: But he abhors Communism.

Point: Then let him espouse Fascism.

Counterpoint: But equally he abhors Fascism.

Point: Then let him leave the Political Illusion alone. We already have Mr Wells. . . . Need he go via D. H. Lawrence to Dostoevsky? Need he succumb to the modern evil and itch when he, with a few, can conquer it?

P.R.S.'s polemics were among the best things we published. His *J. C. Squire (Etc)* in *Aphrodite Two*, taking up our quarrel on behalf of *Pheonix*, was a first-rate piece of clear-sighted uncompromising attack. It opened the fight in defence of free expression against the dominant Philistine puritans represented by Squire among the intellectuals and James Douglas among the journalists. D.H.L. in a short while was to pick up the theme and carry on his duel with the Home Secretary Joynson-Hicks. But he was abroad, and we were in London. We initiated and bore the brunt, and we were in a very vulnerable situation. We received many anonymous letters saying that Informations were being laid against us with the Police, that our Wicked Activities were being

Watched, etc. And the least police action against us would have brought the Press down with a crash. Eric Partridge had no sooner been installed in our Museum Street rooms with his new firm than a reviewer informed against him before his book *The Sleeveless Errand* by N. James was published; the police seized the entire edition. And there was nothing in the least obscene in the book, only the word 'buggers' used casually in conversation. Those who did not live through the period would find it hard to realize the oppressive atmosphere or to understand the power wielded by windy neurotics like James Douglas of the *Sunday Express* who denounced *Antic Hay* as 'ordure and blasphemy', coupled Crowley's *Diary of a Drugfiend*, a luridly moralistic work, with Joyce's *Ulysses*, and called for its banning. He attacked the seriously dull novel on female inverts, Radclyffe-Hall's *Well of Loneliness*, saying he'd rather his daughter took prussic acid than read such a book, and managed to get it suppressed. 'Squire has approvingly commented that the whole nature, objects, and sanctities of morality are involved. There is a solid block between these two field-preachers. Must the struggle for free expression be fought all over again?' asked P.R.S. In making direct and violent assaults on such puffed-up characters we did what no one else of the period did, and we did it in the most exposed position possible. Nor did we leave the matter at the *Aphrodite* articles.

A young artist, Beresford Egan, who imitated Beardsley's *Salome* drawings, had come into the office with some caricatures. We did not think highly enough of his work to put the Fanfrolico imprint on it; but P.R.S. got together with him and turned out a poem satirizing Douglas, with another prose diatribe in his most trenchant style. The result was published by P.R.S. as from the Hermes Press:

The Sink of Solitude. Being a *series of Satirical Drawings* occasioned by some *Recent Events* performed by Beresford Beresford Egan, *Gent.* to which is added a *Preface* by P. R. Stephensen, *Gent.*, and a *Verse Lampoon* composed by SEVERAL HANDS and now set forth for the first time, the whole being very proper to be read both on *Family* and *Public Occasions.*

The poem was mainly P.R.S.'s work, though others of us added bits in noisy discussions in the pub, the last seven couplets being by myself. We had the difficult task of defending *The Well of Loneliness* from moral attack, while admitting the mediocre nature of its achievement. *The Sink* sold very well, and P.R.S. was stimulated into three other pamphlets: *Policeman of the Lord* (an attack on the Home Secretary) with drawings by Egan; *Leave the Well Alone,* with short poems and a lampoon in couplets; *The Well of Sleevelessness,* decorated by Hal Collins, for the Scholartis Press. Though these had some amusing hits, they did not keep the high standard of *The Sink.* 'A moral tripe-hound like James Douglas can say what he likes about almost anything because he has the millionaires backing him in any possible action for libel. That gives him the courage to libel people like Radclyffe Hall and to get away with it, gloating.'

Contributors to the *Aphrodite* included T.F. and Llewellyn Powys, Rhys Davies, Earp, Sacheverell Sitwell, Ivan Goll, Sherard Vines, Edgell Rickword, Norman Douglas, Karel Capek, Frederick Carter, Albert Highet, Edward Marsh—also Philip Owens and Brian Penton, of whom more anon. Robert Nichols gave us an elaborately worked-out libretto for a Hogarth ballet, which may be said to have prophesied the lines on which the best elements of English ballet would develop. I did translations from La Forgue and Essenin, as well as from Blok (with P.R.S.). In a final essay I discussed at length the kind of dramatic blank verse adequate to express the life of our day, and ended by switching into the conclusion of a verse-play I had just written, in which a poet and a girl have taken refuge in a temple of Venus during the eruption destroying Pompeii; Venus appears and they argue about love, life on earth, poetry, as doom gathers. (I chose this setting to express once more my conviction that Science would in the near future develop means of destroying the earth: I arrived at this conviction from an analysis of its mechanistic and disintegrative trends—the trends we have seen in our own day arrive at nuclear fission.)

One point worth making is that *The London Aphrodite,* for all its eclectic furies, was the first intellectual effort made in England to affirm a faith in the Russian revolution, while attempting a comprehensive critique of modern art developments (most of which we saw as floundering away from the concrete image of art into the deaths of abstraction or primitivism). P.R.S. in his essay on Bakunin uttered our lament that Anarchism was Not Enough, and proceeded to affirm his belief in the Leninist revolution. I did not have his clear grounding; but I had come round to this viewpoint sufficiently by the sixth number to write:

With the arrival of the proletarian revolution the human horizon has so far extended that we are forced back insistently upon individuality as the sole universal principle (*i.e.* in the sphere of experience of course, not of cheating). The political variation between Henry Ford and Nicolai Lenin is not the most important one—the chasm in intellect between the two does not need stressing: no one is likely to mistake Ford for even a human being. The true conflict, which however must express itself in the struggle for the control of the instrument of production and distribution, narrows itself down to the question: Which party will centralize its organization on the needs of the individual, his right to experience . . .

The *bolsheviki* are in my opinion a genuine expression of the Roman constructiveness. In any case the Russian revolution displays a huge and happy uprush of the human spirit; and this brimming worldtide of new energy is to be seen even in the reactionary military dictatorships among the Latins and the commercial dictatorship of the United States. England, bogged in the products of its own cunning and so now its own dupe, remains outside this hurry of energy, whether of the constructive Russian kind or the sporadic American. It is among this international expansion that the poet must find his vindication of Force.

The statement is confused. I did not have at my disposal the terms needed for what I wanted to say. I meant I had now come to believe that capitalism could only thwart and cripple the deepened individuations it had once helped into existence, and that the communal control of production and distribution was now the only way to release new individualities. I then went on to argue that the breakdown of the old kind of democracy into dictatorships and monopolies inside capitalism was a symptom of the necessary fundamental changes, which had been carried out in the right way in Russia. By finding his unity with the proletarian revolution, the poet could find the way to harmonize his creative energies with the Force operating through the workers and breaking down the bourgeois system.

I only imperfectly understood what I was saying; hence the muddled terms. Otherwise I would have gone ahead to build coherently on the new-found basis. In a sense my development in the next eight years was a struggle to clarify what I had here said. All the same, I had said it, and I was to be haunted by the problems thus raised, and I had raised them before anyone else in Britain. My debt to P.R.S. does not need stressing.

Both in the final essay and in *Aphrodite Three* I attacked T. S. Eliot as the supreme example of the dessicating trends, the surrender to the fear of death which Wagner had called the source of all love-lessness. I pointed out that in his picture of Baudelaire the Classicist he simply inverted Symons' picture of Baudelaire the Romantic and produced an equally false image of the poet. 'Both points of view of course are unaware of Baudelaire the Individual, or his genuine creative conflict.' Re-reading the Eliot essay with its bad jokes—'more efficiently spectral . . . in a phrase from Joyce, Imperthnthnthnthnthn . . . absolute pu(er)ility'—I feel how much closer we were to the Continental Dadaists than to anything in England (apart from the early Sitwells). Our irreverences and puns did have something of an intention of expressing a chaos, of being a shocking reflection of the dead-end bourgeois world, as the first step towards the striking-out of a dancing star: even if we prematurely announced the star-advent.

As an offshoot of the *Aphrodite* we published a book of my lyrics, *The Passionate Neatherd*, at the low price of 1/6d, and promptly sold out a couple of thousand. This time we had one defender. A long review of the *New Age* welcomed a work of adult verse in a world of beastly adolescents. I forget how many we printed of the magazine, but it must have been round 3,500; and after the last issue P.R.S. told me that he had raised the money for a full reprint of some 1,500 copies, which we sold bound. Clearly, despite the critics and the trade, we were building up a strong support, and it is a pity we did not decide to carry on. However, we had announced that all magazines soon got into a rut and that we'd stop with the sixth issue. So we stopped and P.R.S. wrote in the advert in the last (July 1929) number:

Having demonstrated by publishing the London Aphrodite successfully for six numbers without any concessions, literary competitions, politics, advertisements, or poems by Humbert Wolfe, that there is no reason at all why most of the Reviews should exist, the Fanfrolico Press abandons this diversion of its long summer evenings and prepares to assault another popular misconception—that poetry cannot be produced cheaply and profitably in a handsome format for a large public.

We were therefore going to produce *Hereward*, music and all, at 6/-, and *Marlowe* at 5/-.

One meeting around this time surprised and excited me. A wire arrived out of the blue from Yeats asking me to lunch at the Savile Club. We were joined at our table by some uninvited others—W. J. Turner and an Irishman who had worked at the Abbey Theatre. The latter told tales of the poet Darrell Figgis whose famed beard was cut off by his opponents in the Irish Troubles and who gassed himself in

October 1925. It was my beard that started the discussion, and Figgis' was voted a grander spectacle. According to the stories, he was addicted to Piccadilly tarts, who made derogatory comments on the beard and were always beaten by his quick wit. Turner with a rather smug grin remarked that all men of rich creative power were much given to copulation; Yeats gravely agreed. After lunch he politely dismissed the others and we spent the whole afternoon together, apart from an interruption when Wilenski interviewed him about the controversy on the Lane bequest of paintings. During the interview he was very much Senator Yeats, keeping the art critic quietly in his place. Unfortunately we discussed, not so much poetic drama, as spiritualism and neo-platonism. I told him of N.L.'s experiences with Rose, which interested him a lot, and he told me of similar experiences with his wife, which at that time he had not written about. He seemed pleased at the seriousness with which I took *A Vision*, and we parted with a general agreement about further discussions. But in the difficult time ahead I forgot all such matters.[1]

By covering in this chapter the whole career of the *Aphrodite* (July 1928 to July 1929) I have hurried on, and must now return to pick up the thread of my personal narrative.

---

[1] Other *Aphrodite* contacts were W. J. Turner who used to lunch with us at the pub near the office and argue about music; Sherard Vines; Edward Marsh, who gave me two of his La Fontaine translations and a lunch in his flat with its interesting collection of pictures; Anna Wickham, a roaring-girl (literally so, with her great booming voice) and a plague to solicitor husband, who lived in a grimy Hampstead den, steadily darning socks and sleeping with a dusty floor-rug for blanket. She became attached to P.R.S. and wrote him a poem which began something like 'I've made a bond with Bundaberg', he'd liked to repeat it and gave me the incorrect idea he was born in that town.

A. J. Symonds once proposed to me that I should do an unpublished work of Corvo's he had found, binding-in with each copy one sheet of the original MS; but he wanted too much money down. With his club he inhabited a large room at the back of St George's church not far from us.

12. BETTY MAY

One day in the Plough, not long after our removal to the country, I encountered a strange woman, who spoke to me. We drank a few beers. There was a merry calm about her. She had a broad face, with some grey streaks in her hair, and wore a long tweed coat and a sort of robin-hood cap of green. She was Betty May, who had just left her fifth husband to carry on with his genteel breeding of dogs in the country. Her frank clear fearless face, with its strong sculptural force, had an unsettling effect upon me. As we were walking out, she took up the hand of a whore who sat near the window and held it a moment. 'You're sick,' she said with a friendly sternness, 'you'd better do something about it.' The whore started and stared back, wanting to say something rude and violent, but quelled by a superstitious fear and Betty's calm eyes. She stammered and finally hid her hands under the table.

There was something barbaric and yet gentle about her, a peculiar emanation of beauty and strength which was all the more powerful because she did not use the least cosmetics or show the least element of coquettishness. Her face with its simple breadth of modelling owned a deep self-confidence that had nothing trivial about it. Although we had exchanged only ordinary remarks, I left her with shaken senses and mind. Despite the extreme difference in effect, she seemed like Elza to possess her body, her own piece of space-time, with a dangerous and serene completeness. I have never known other women with quite this fullness, this presence—though in Elza the energies were turned in, in Betty they were turned out. I wanted to meet her again, and was afraid of meeting her.

I knew I would meet her again. Next evening she came into the pub and walked straight up to me as if we had arranged to meet. She hardly smiled. We had known one another a long time; there was no need to say anything. With a mixture of despair and reckless abandon I knew that I could not escape; she had come to me as much a part of my poetry as Elza. We drank quietly and then went back to her room off Charlotte Street.

Constant Lambert
From the portrait by Michael Ayrton

Edgell Rickword at Halstead, 1961, with a bronze head of him
made in the late 1920's by an American sculptress

Norman Douglas with Orioli

Philip Heseltine

I soon heard lots of things about her. Betty the Tiger Woman, the Epstein model, drug-taker, nympholept, man-eater. But she remained to me someone I had always known, known through and through, who was as true as my own images were to me. But the time I lived through with her was a nightmare, haunted with guilt like a horrible *leitmotiv* of music thudding up from deep in my mind, and yet in a way as simple and innocent as a game of children. She accepted me as I accepted her, but without the guilt. She knew all about my divided state; I told her at the outset about Elza; she looked on at me from outside as if a little rueful, but not really concerned. While I was ready to be with her, she felt herself to be mine and left wholly to me the problems raised by our relations.

No doubt I idealized her. But not much. I feel sure there was in her a strange sort of integrity, directed by an image of herself as a *femme fatale* (but without any glorying in tragic roles). She dominated me by making no effort whatever to dominate. She was quite 'unfeminine' in the usual meanings of that word; she hardly made up, she dressed neatly but carelessly; she had not the least touch of coyness, of fluttering invitation; she never laid herself out to attract. In all respects she seemed the active counterpart of Elza, taking what she wanted instead of being taken, resolute mistress of herself instead of being a victim.

Till this moment I had always felt that all details of the Press were under my fingers and that I controlled the situation. Now it all slipped away. I left everything to P.R.S. and for the first time cashed cheques for drinking purposes. The days at Alphamstone were a dull dragging misery, in which I tried to hide my distraction from Elza by pleas of illness, of business-strain. She was worried, but did not seem to suspect. The small girl was thriving and I found a certain dogged release in digging hard, in pedalling fast along the lanes. Rats got into the roof and rattled thunderously like great dogs, waking me early for the ride across to Bures. Though I dreaded facing Elza, it was a great relief to escape London and the calm ruthless face of Betty. At least I felt happy in the passage between Bures and the cottage, as I wheeled my bike up and down the hills or strolled across the sweltering fields.

P.R.S. encouraged me. Not by words, but by taking over the complete charge of the Press without complaint, slapping me on the back and assuming that all was well. No doubt I should have resented it if he had asked me what I thought I was doing; but deep down I resented even

E

more that he did not try to pull me up. The seeds of our disunion were sown.

Strange driven nights. In various pubs or the Café Royal which still had for Betty pre-war memories. Mostly there was nothing much to show the deep satisfaction I felt, despite my fears, at simply being with her. She never made any pretentious remarks but seemed to understand anything I said. Always with that dark and generous emanation of strength and beauty. I felt it even if we merely sat and sipped beer on a Monday evening in the Fitzroy when the old women and men of the Loan Club filed down the long saloon bar to where the daughter of the house waited to take their sixpennies (which would turn into a magically large sum at Christmas): shawled and bonneted old women, and old men with every sort of bushy moustache, exhaling the hard dry soda-smell of a desperately clean poverty. If we lounged in the White Hart, run by small dark Daisy with her husband Albert, who had once done a turn of acrobatic dancing mixed up with soapsuds and who now basked in the reflected lights of the mahogany bar with its signed photos of forlorn theatrical celebrities and its barrels on high over the bottles. Or if we strayed through Luna Park at the corner of Tottenham Court Road and Oxford Street, among the snorting merry-go-rounds, coconut-shies, peep-shows, slot-machines, shooting galleries, booths of Madame X. A woman wrapt herself in cottonwool, which was set alight; flaring, she dived into a tank and emerged gasping, the devouring red coat of death changed into a soppy mess of dirty black. Her daughter the Seal also dived, glittering only with spangles, and stayed underwater so long that everyone felt sure she was dead or a cheat, flapping her long thin legs or sinking in a lump to the bottom. It's done with mirrors. She lived in the Post Office Club and we knew her, knew the clammy touch of her hand. In ragged lights the clown-faces grimaced, the hurdygurdy tune wheezed ever more hoarsely, and young girls licking coned ice-creams fell over tent-ropes or stood in the niches of shadow flicking up their skirts to show they wore nothing underneath; whimpered with a sweaty fist clutched full of pennies, an ear bleeding where the ear-ring had been torn off, or screeched as the monkey jumped. Kiss-curls elaborately drawn out and plastered across the cheek to the corner of the eye. Ebony page-cuts under ugly cloche-hats. Cellars in Soho cobwebbed with smoke, dice clicking and a girl peeing in the corner: 'Sorry, but the Ladies stinks.' Beer in Covent Garden pubs among brawny tender-hearted porters and broken tomatoes, five o'clock A.M.

One night at the Café Royal, as I was talking to someone across the table, she held some ethyl nitrate under my nose so that I inhaled it before I knew what was happening. I was very angry. That was the only time I had any experience of a drug; and I felt nothing from it at all. Another time, in her room, I suddenly woke up in the early hours with a clear image of elephants surrounding me, all standing upright in a sort of hieratic pose. For the moment I did not feel anything strange or frightening or ridiculous in the sight. Then the whole thing vanished. I went to sleep again. But next morning I told her. She said that she had been drawing blood from me to use in a 'white spell' for the help of friends in trouble; the elephants had had some connection with the words of the spell. I could only surmise that there had been a case of thought-transference and that in my semi-drunken state I had projected the image. Anyhow, I had learned that Betty was a witch.

In her way she was as typical a character of the period as Heseltine. That is, she showed certain key-tendencies in an extreme form. And because of this, and because of the crucial part she played in my life, I shall give here a summary of the tale she told of herself. On the whole I feel it was true. She may have omitted much, and heightened a few points, yet the effect was true enough to her personality.

She was born in the Tidal Basin of coster-folk, one of four kids. Her half-French mother was left by her husband while Betty was still an infant. One day Betty rebelled by throwing her brother's shoes, the only pair in the family, into the Thames; and she was sent to her father, who was then living with 'a huge dark Jewess'. Betty recalled that 'his right eyebrow was almost obliterated by a scar which kept the eye beneath it perpetually open. He looked absolutely devilish.' They lived in Limehouse, amid bugs and stench. He had been a gasworks-fitter, but now only boozed. Naturally cruel, he was a fiend when drunk, set dogs fighting or swung cats to bash out their brains. One day he was arrested by his own father, a police-inspector, whose wife took Betty in, then sent her to an uncle and aunt who lived in a barge. Betty stayed in the barge a couple of years, learning to dance for sailors. Then she was sent to another aunt, on a Somerset farm. Here she at last went to school, in the village. She became much attached to the schoolmaster, who gave her her first idea of the things of the mind. But people made a scandal out of it and she ran away to London, ending up in Commercial Road where she bought some grown-up clothes and roamed about looking for a job. A woman in a pub took her home.

She drifted into a pick-up life, helped by a girl named Rosie. Still in long plaits, she encountered a Cambridge student Gerald outside the Holborn Empire and came to know lots of clubs and the Café Royal. She posed for artists. At a club in Endell Street she met the Cherub or Pretty Pet who lured her to Bordeaux with offers of a dancing job. She did some dancing there in a *café chantant*, singing ballads like *The Raggle-taggle Gypsies* or *The Bonny Earl of Murray*, fought the Cherub, and got a place as a professional dancer. Going to Paris, she took up with the White Panther, leader of an apache gang in the Glacière district, and had a fight with the jealous Hortense who tried to knife her, thus gaining her name of *Tigre*. Trouble came when she lured an English undergraduate into the gang's den, where he was robbed. A police-raid was made and she was told that she must find the student. After much searching she found him and managed to get him into a taxi with an accomplice driver; she took him to the gang, and, to save him from a worse fate, branded him on the chest with a hot knife. However another raid followed and she retreated to London. (Her account of her life in Paris has a melodramatic air, but may well be true.)

Now she haunted again the Café Royal and the Crabtree Club in Greek Street. She became engaged to Dick a barrister, who tried to reform and educate her by sending her to his father's rectory in Cornwall. She soon rushed back to London, met Dick by chance in the Café Royal, but turned instead to an Arthur, who also wanted to marry her. At an eve-of-marriage party, however, she decided she loved a drug-addict, Bunny, who was a Cambridge blue, On the way to their Oban honeymoon he introduced her to cocaine.

Returning, they lived in the house of Stewart Gray, who led a back-to-the-land movement. The place was a warren of similar couples, and Betty drugged a lot. When the 1914 war broke out, Bunny put her in a Richmond flat and enlisted. Bored, she found a job in a hairdresser-tobacconist's shop in Buckingham Palace Road, drinking and drugging heavily. She took up with an Australian major, who married her when Bunny was killed. With much devoted care he broke her of the drug-habit. She sat for Epstein, who did his *Savage* from her.

She next took up with Raoul (really Frederick Charles) Loveday, an undergraduate of Oxford, whom she married in the summer of 1925. A photo on the afternoon of the marriage in St John's gardens showed an ectoplasmic figure lying above his head. (Before this, he had dragged her to the Egyptian galleries of the B.M. and introduced her to the mummy of a royal priestess of Amon-Re. When he talked of the baleful power of the god to destroy those who offended him, she put out her tongue at the mummy. He hustled her away, then came back alone to prostrate himself with a prayer for the curse to fall wholly on him.) Raoul gained a First in History and they came to London.

One night at a Soho café, the Harlequin, a Mrs E.Z. said she had the magician Crowley with her at 31 Wellington Square. Raoul, already fascinated by Crowley's ideas, went to her house; but Betty, who had seen him at the Café in 1914, refused. After two days and nights away, Raoul returned by climbing up the drainpipe, stinking of ether. Crowley felt that he had found his ideal pupil, his magical heir. Betty moved lodgings, but Crowley turned up in a kilt and a black curly wig, with a snake-coiled wand—a mad-eyed sallow-skinned man with very full red lips.

He decided to return to his Abbey in Sicily, and from there wrote asking Raoul to join him. Despite Betty's protests Raoul set off, and Betty went at the last moment with him. 'One of you will never come back again,' Epstein prophesied. They arrived at the Abbey on 26 November. Crowley refused at first to let Betty in, as she wouldn't make the ritual reply, 'Love is the law, love under will,' to his, 'Do what thou wilt shall be the whole of the Law.' However, she forced her way in and continued her resistance, using even fists and a revolver—though she had to agree to sign the Oath of Affiliates. Raoul was admitted as Pro-bationer of the order of A∴A∴, with the name Aud (magical light). He enjoyed climbing daily a blind buttress of sheer rock to a spot where he considered an ancient town had been; then he intoned the names of God and the Archangels at the four cardinal points to exclude evil in-fluences; read the Gnostic Collects; and spent the rest of the day in talk, chess, and mandoline-strumming. On wet days a sort of Rugby Fives was played with a football. Also sex-magic (sex-acts) were carried out to the accompaniment of hymns, prayers, and symbolic per-formances. Betty settled down to doing the housework and looking after two children of Crowley's, one of whom had been a cigarette-fiend from the age of five and threatened people, 'I am Beast Number Two' with magical powers of shattering.

On arrival, all inhabitants of the Abbey were given a razor with which they were expected to cut their arm every time they said 'I'—a word permitted only to Crowley; they were commanded to say only 'one'. Betty threw her razor away, but Raoul covered his arms with nicks.

The men shaved their heads save for a symbolic curl on the forehead; the women dyed their hair red or yellow with henna (a sun-aureole) and wore loose robes of bright blue with scarlet linings, hood, and golden girdle. In the refectory Crowley broke food with his fingers while Betty stood by with towel and basin. One day she poured the water over him, but he simply ignored the action. Another day he decided to sacrifice a cat that had scratched him. Betty smuggled the animal away, but it came back and was caught.

The Bloody Sacrifice was supposed to release terrific energy, in a sort of Black Mass adapted from the Gnostics. Raoul was in charge. He failed to slash hard enough. The bleeding cat rushed round the room till chloroformed. Then Raoul completed the sacrifice and drank the blood. Both Crowley and Raoul proceeded to fall ill; the local physician diagnosed an infection of liver and spleen, but Betty thought their condition due to drugs and cat's blood. Crowley cast Frater Aud's horoscope and said that he would die at four o'clock on 16 February (1923). Five days before that a violent brawl broke out. Newspapers were forbidden and Betty had been found reading one by Raoul's bedside; in the struggle bottles, glasses, furniture were smashed. Betty packed up and went down to Cefalu below, writing a complaint to the British consul at Palermo. Next day the Chinese Oracle told Crowley to be charming and forgiving, but to make it clear he'd stand no nonsense. A letter from Raoul persuaded Betty to change her mind; she wrote to the consul rescinding her complaints, and went back to the Abbey. But on the 16th Raoul died. Betty thought he lay in bed in the exact pose of the wraith floating over his head in the marriage-day photo. Crowley conducted the funeral rites.

Betty went straight back to London. The *Sunday Express* of 25 February headlined 'New Sinister Revelations of Aleister Crowley', and *John Bull* followed with accounts of the wizard of Wickedness. Crowley was ordered by the Italian Ministry of the Interior to leave Italian territory.[1]

---

[1] Betty's account was authentic, as is shown by Crowley's diary (used by J. Symonds in *The Great Beast* 1951). Crowley was born in 1875 at Leamington of very strict Plymouth Brethren. His brewer father dinned into him and everyone else the Imminence of Death and the menacing Face of God, indefatigably posted tracts and travelled round preaching. When he died of cancer of the tongue, his wife carried on the work—Crowley then being eleven. The boy loathed his mother ('a brainless bigot of the most narrow, logical, and inhuman type'), but tried awhile to tread in his father's footsteps. When he rebelled, his

Betty felt relief at being back in the Fitzroy: 'It seems more of a café than a public house, or at least more like a café than anything I know in England.' She took up for a while with the artist Jacob Kramer. Then, after a wild interlude in Yorkshire, she was back in a Soho attic with only one dress, which she washed and wore wet. A journalist wrote up her life-story and got her £500. An odd fortune-teller calling herself Princess Walatka took her to the U.S.A. and Canada, then gave her £100 and the boat-ticket when she wanted to leave. Through the journalist she met Carol, assistant editor of a sporting paper, a country-type obsessed with hunting and shooting, who married her in the end despite his mother, 'one of those cold drooping ladies who seem more to live because "one must" than for any other reason. Her only hold on life was her fierce love of her son, which amounted almost to mania.' After a quarrel that drove Betty to London, Carol gave up his job to have more time watching over her and they lived in a bungalow by the family-house. To have something to do, she set up a cake-and-sweet shop in a tent, but grew bored with the routine. One day Carol slaughtered a number of rooks and made her wring the necks of the wounded birds; he ate the rookpie, which she refused, and fell ill. She tended him till his mother accused her of trying to murder him. She left for London and I met her with the robin-hood hat that was a survival from her life with Carol. 'I believe enormously in the overpowering influence of Fate,' she said, 'which seems to haunt me equally in good or bad fortune.'

I had expressed no claim on her and she made no bones about going with others while I was in the country. She pointed to a large bedstead in a shop-window at the corner of Bloomsbury and Great Russell Street, 'I spent last Wednesday night in that. Y. had the keys of the shop and we pulled down the blinds.' She told me many amusing tales of her adventures. One of them about a commercial-traveller I wrote down straight after hearing it: he mistook her for an ordinary trollop and she led him into several undignified situations before she dropped him with a bump. She was not herself a passionate person, though she was reputed to have violent tempers when she let go. I never saw her anything but calm, with a certain ironic insight into the

mother called him the Beast of *Revelation* and he believed her words. In a mystical experience of visionary rapture (31 Dec. 1895, in a Stockholm hotel) he was convinced of his spiritual power, developing as a Satanist to oppose his parents as fully as possible. (His real name was Edward Alexander Crowley.)

false and pretentious, and with much warmth towards the genuine of any kind. Her driving-force was a complete belief in her Fate—which in effect meant 'being herself', living in the dead-centre of herself.

I had met her almost simultaneously with the appearance of *The London Aphrodite*; for in the second issue P.R.S. wrote up a stag-party held in a cellar in Coptic Street, and I remember dodging off every short while to see her in the Plough. I think I remember that so clearly because it exemplified the way in which at a pinch I was always ready to sacrifice the male companionship I vaunted as the poetic and philosophic bond, and to turn to a woman in whom the values I most admired were incarnated. In the same way, despite the strong pull, I turned down not only Liam O'Flaherty's invitation to smalltown races in Ireland, but also his suggestion that I should go to Soviet Russia with him—the journey that he wrote up as *I went to Russia*, 1931. I also turned down the invitation from Heseltine to go across to Normandy with him on a visit to Delius. (Perhaps he did not go; I do not know.) This invitation was one of his last friendly acts. In October 1928 he moved to Wales, unable to stand any longer the strain of Eynsford; and after that our relations grew ever more difficult.

Thus P.R.S. described the party:

Upon the appearance of *Aphrodite* No 1, a titled lady cancelled her subscription, one reviewer said he had thrown his copy into a garbage-tin out of consideration for his waste-paper basket, another duly said he was not amused, another said he could not understand Jack Lindsay's article, the *Nation* said 'no artistic value', several women tried with no success to cut Liam O'Flaherty dead; however several minor reviewers welcomed the rash venture, kind friends did not hesitate to backslap, and for instance Charley Lahrs sold 60 copies in his sentry-box bookshop in Red Lion Street. Whereupon the Editors and Liam and Charley Lahrs got drunk in a cellar kept by Louis XVII, other guests being Rhys Davies, who couldn't find the cellar at all; Tommy Earp, who tried to sing *Rule Britannia* at 3 a.m. on a beer barrel (empty); but overbalanced and broke Louis's collarbone; a calm German scholar who had to go early; an Oxford Don who passed out; an ex-member of the I.W.W. with good intentions but a too-small stomach; a bald and cheerful Australian cartoonist; two roaring Irish bhoys covered in tap-room sawdust; two great policemen; and other Bloomsbury intellectuals. At dawn Charley Lahrs and the Editors took Liam home where he irrationally began swallowing raw eggs. Then Charley vanished in a mist, and the Editors sat down in the gutter, together with a pint of (salvaged) whisky to reflect upon the Universe. Hence *The London Aphrodite* No 2, a sincere production, if somewhat melancholy in places.

A footnote in No 1 announced that this periodical is being produced 'not for profit, but for the fun of the thing'. A wondering old gentleman wrote in to ask what Jack Lindsay does when he is serious if he wrote *The Modern Consciousness* for fun? The answer would get us into trouble, we feel sure.

Will Farrow, Australian artist, was one of the guests; and as I was at work on this chapter he wrote to me after some thirty years' gap in our acquaintance and referred to the party, so it must have left a mark. 'I always think of you when I hark back to the wild party we had in a cellar in Bloomsbury with Liam O'Flaherty as the guest of honour. First we lured in the unsuspecting Constable, then finished up with a rather ponderous Sergeant who came looking for him. I still have a broken thumb, the after-effects of a wild dance we had when I was unlucky enough to slip with 15 stone of Metropolitan Policeman on top of me.' And even now, when I meet Charley Lahrs, he chuckles and makes comments on that night, convinced that he then begot his daughter.

Among new friends was Powys Mathers, whom Betty was very fond of: a tubby chap of jovial and learned wit, with a pointed beard and a vast black brimmed hat. Somehow I acquired this hat and wore it with a red neckerchief which Betty had given me; my beard was now more-than-Tolstoyan. Betty once mentioned having gone to bed with Powys; and when I commented on his rotundity, she said, 'Oh, it's just a matter of patience and mountain-climbing.'

One night in the Fitzroy we met Edgell Rickword, quiet and solidly built. He had lost one eye in the war, where he gained the Military Medal. Ever since I read *Scrutinies*, which he edited, I had wanted very much to meet him. I remember going over to Betty, who did not know him, and saying, 'It's Edgell Rickword, the person I most wanted to meet in England.' Through him I met his friends Douglas Garman, handsomely tall and large, and Bertram Higgins, an Irish-Australian with considerable poetic capacity, which he was too acidly sceptical to develop. Garman had started a publishing firm with his Cambridge friend Wishart, who put up the money (he had married one of the impressively handsome Garman girls—Roy Campbell married another). Edgell came into the Wishart picture through Roy. 'We wanted to

E*

publish all the good literature that was being rejected by commercial firms,' said D.G. to me, 'but we found that meant we wanted to do D.H.L. who already had a publisher.' However, they were building up a small but distinguished list, and had issued the *Calendar*, which had recently been wound up.

I now got hold of Edgell's poetry and admired it very much. He had published the first book in English on Rimbaud, and was strongly influenced by Baudelaire and Rimbaud, by the true *symboliste* tradition, but had organically absorbed what he needed, making it all warmly his own. He had a profound sense of the city-desert, the pleasure-lash, the alienation of man from man in our world of the cash nexus; and in a sense was trying to live out a Baudelairean life.

> *And the I retreating down familiar paths*
> *creates defences from the terrible sun*
> *and in its figurative way rebuilds*
> *the altar and brothel of legitimate state*
> *adjacent, with mean fanes darkening our streets:*
> *the silver-swimming gutters blench and fade*
> *to sinks and sewers where tarnished spirits lap,*
> *obscenely supine, the stale brink of day.*

In the Baudelairean ethic the whore has a key-place, for by reducing love openly to the cash-nexus she strips the pretences with which society covers up the bargain of marriage, covers up its whole attempt to reduce people to things, bought-and-sold things. By accepting the whore one accepts her exposure of the respectable and the self-righteous; her degradation becomes the accusation of the degrading powers, who are the real polluters of life. So on, goes the logic, which I thought theoretically inexpugnable; but in actuality I felt only repugnance and fear for this 'symbol'.

About the same time as the *Aphrodite* appeared I also met Philip and Molly Owens. In Philip I felt that I had encountered at long last the fellow-poet I had been seeking, the poet who would work with me in refounding a vital and tumultuous verse-drama. His play *Marlowe* was a work vividly intoxicated with words—intoxicated as Marlowe himself and the Elizabethan audiences were. As he and Molly were hard up, with no fixed residence, I handed over to them my room in Gilbert Street, first warning them that it was rich in bugs. They said that in view of the low rent (5/- a week), they wouldn't mind the bugs at all. Indeed, they managed somehow to keep them at bay or wipe them out, and were soon comfortably installed. Thus Phil a little later described the place:

His room, inevitably, was at the very top of the stairs, and it was a minute room with, on the landing outside, a tap and bucket for washing, tea-making, etc. The room itself was very small indeed, with space only for the double-bed and a table under the window, against which Blasco could usually be found wedged tightly in, writing furiously, while he tugged at his pipe, being in truth almost unable to get up again, once jammed into position. A kitchen-range made both a fire for heating and a stove for cooking. 'Molly,' was Blasco's invariable command at the sight of a visitor, 'tea.'

Philip Owens, a slightly-built chap with a roundish face and an eager look of ceaselessly-excited youth, was said to have gained his nickname, Blasco, through a long argument with a Dutchman in Antwerp, during which the latter kept trying to shut him up with the shout, 'Blast-you-Owens!' For some years he had been on the Continent, having gone first to Hamburg to study chemistry. The inflation of the mark made living easy, and he wandered round, staying in Vienna with a German artist Gungoff (eating orange-peel collected from the gutter and washed with Condy's fluid) and then in Paris, where he fared better by teaching English at Berlitz and doing translations. He had become a Communist. In Paris he met Molly Matthews, a young art-student from Manchester, and married her.[1]

Phil, who became his closest friend, remarks of him at this time, 'He had a passionate choler, swiftly roused and as swiftly doused; there was always half a laugh even in his rage, an impish cock to his head, as if he acted the part of temperamental genius, and not being a particularly good actor, he very soon forgot his part, and the next moment would be argu-

[1] It was probably of an earlier stay that he told me an anecdote in which P.R.S. figured. The local party-office asked him to call in and take an unobtrusive seat at one side when an odd Englishman called. Blasco did as asked and found the Englishman to be P.R.S. with his flamboyant manner. When I published this tale in an Australian periodical, P.R.S. took me to mean that I was accusing him of having been an *agent provocateur*. Of course I didn't mean anything of the sort; I always considered him to be one of the most loyal, open and frank persons I have known. I was merely paying a tribute to his breezy magnificence of manner, his unfailing panache, which had quite incorrectly stirred the suspicions of the dull officials.

ing volubly about Lenin or Trotsky, for at this period he was often quite a solemn Communist.'

Just before I handed my room over to the Owens I had the excellent but impracticable idea of getting some capital into the firm, and talked things over with Dennis Bradley. He offered me a letter of introduction to his bank-manager, who was good about overdrafts and loans; and so I transferred our account to a bank in Bond Street. To my horror as I was chatting with the manager and doing my best to impress him with our solvency and prospects, I saw a bug crawling over my shirt-cuff. I hastily put my hand under the table and shook the bug off. I hope that it wasn't a female and the bank didn't soon find itself infested. Either the manager was extremely poker-faced or he didn't notice the creature.

Meanwhile I was being carried along on my dark tide of submission to Betty. There were times when I seemed to be riding with miraculous poise on the crest of the wild wave; then came the floundering and panicked fall into the trough of confusion. One high moment came when there was an explosion of a gas main near St Giles Circus. The area was left in a dusty and smouldering disorder, with a stinking sense of world-end. A line from Aeschylus' *Agamemnon* came to my mind: 'This very day the Achaians enter Troy.' I said it aloud several times with a sort of ecstasy.

Then one day, as I felt quite sober, I went to sign some cheques in the office to meet accounts, and found that my hand trembled so much the signature was illegible. That frightened me. And not long afterwards Betty came to me and said, 'Do you mind if I go and live with Edgell? Do you say I mustn't?' I was startled, as I hadn't noticed that Edgell was particularly interested in her. Sorry to lose her and glad to be free from entanglements, I said that of course she must do as she wished and that I had no claim on her. And so my relations with her ended.

13. A NEW START

ELZA must have guessed something of what was happening. Suddenly one week, after I had been in London a day or two, she turned up early in the office and wanted to know where I had slept the night before. I took her to the room round the corner which I had borrowed from the Davis-and-Orioli bookseller. I had then broken from Betty for over a week, and managed to convince Elza nothing was wrong. However, I felt a hard and resistant fibre in her—for the first time since the day when she forced me to have a showdown with Kirtley. And she remained restless. She decided to move, and found a small house at Takeley, further west. Then the agitations of removal took up her mind. The house was of brick, but with lichened apple trees and with shady lanes of hazel-nuts running into the Rodings. I took Robinetta for walks, now more at ease with her silence. I had plunged afresh into work and was translating Theocritos. The period of dereliction had taken up between two and three months, and I was back in my normal relations to the firm; but something had happened, a break that couldn't be mended; the first impetus and its innocences had gone.

A bad public speaker, I gave three lectures. The first was on the nature of poetry, before a literary society of London University in rooms off the Strand. All I recall is that when I used the phrase 'the hell of childhood' (coupled antithetically with *paradis enfantins*), a beautiful slender girl got up and went slowly out, staring at me all the while with eyes of burning accusation; and I watched her with such love that for a while afterwards I spoke with eloquence as well as passion. The theme of the second lecture was Greek Attitudes to Sex for some sex-reform society. Garman tried to encourage me with several whiskies beforehand, in vain; and he, Edgell and some others came in near the end, as they had threatened, to make me lose the thread of my discourse, but I had already lost it. I had been talking about the Platonic Concept of Desire and not the homosexualities which the emancipated audience, behind their serious spectacles, had come to hear me defend in learned detail. The

141

theme of the third lecture was Christ in Blake's poetry, delivered to the Blake Society from Wesley's pulpit near Bunhill Fields where Blake's neglected grave lay. I was rather put off by the serried ranks of parsons smiling with benevolent teeth to show their broadmindedness as I spoke of the rival religions of Christ and Dionysos. However, I was pleased to meet old Wright, a patriarchal-looking figure like one of Blake's old men with the wind of eternity flowing through his silken beard—but with a mild distrait aspect, as of a prophet who had stood up to denounce the world and embarrassingly at the last moment had forgotten what he wanted to say. President of the Blake and Cowper Societies (and later the first revealer of the truth about Dickens and Ellen Ternan), he had liked my book on Blake and written to me about it. We met a few times and talked of Blake and Cowper, and got on well together, though his deprecatory cough seemed now and then to rebuke God for failing to prompt him at the moments when he was about to rise to the prophetic status.

Norman Douglas had more than once mooted the project of a visit to Florence; but I should never have gone if it had not been for an accident—the arrival of an Italian artist from that town, the protégé of a rich Australian woman who fluttered in a portly way round our office. The rich woman wanted me to publish a book of his drawings; but though they were excellent in their way, I did not feel they fitted into our Fanfrolico universe. So, though I would rather have liked to gain access for the Press to the rich woman's bank-account, I handed the scheme over to Hanchant, who finally produced the book—not very well. I was present as umpire at the depressed meeting, in some arts-and-crafts dim-lit basement, where the annoyed artist denounced print after print as inadequate, and I had no course but to agree with him, though Hanchant with reproachful eyes moaned that the cost of the book was going to be prohibitive. The cost went up, and the book was still not all it should have been. And despite my visiting the patroness' lavish flat for tea once or twice, I was further off than ever from the moment when it would be tactful to suggest an investment in the Press. The artist, disillusioned as to English art-books, decided to return to Florence with his wife and patroness. They suggested that I should go with them. P.R.S. supported them, saying that it would do me good to have a holiday; and after some doubts I decided to go. I was feeling out of sorts and my under-the-weather condition had been worsened by my lying out under the apple trees to read Greek poets and catching a cold in the bladder from the damp earth (the same trouble as I contracted from my one night in the dripping Sydney jail).

With a wrench I went. We stayed for the night in Paris, where, left to my own resources, I wandered round some of the haunts I knew from my stay with P.R.S. two-and-a-half years before. Then we went on. I remember the unpleasant feeling when, after we had passed the Italian frontier, I made some comment about Mussolini, which reduced the artist to abject terror. He begged me not to mention the name again. I found that Douglas and other English folk in Florence had their various pseudonyms for the dictator, such as Mr Smith.

Douglas met me at the station, tall stiff and straight-backed, but carrying his heavy build lightly; with his close-set ears, strong jaw, expressive eyebrows, large nose, and silver hair parted in the middle, he had a very Scottish look, but more sanguine and overpowering than I had expected. From the back his head had a Highlander's oblong height; and in his tweeds made up by an Italian he had an indefinable air of masquerading as himself, testy and benevolent, impatiently waiting for some enemy to materialize and be knocked down by his lairdly stick. He carried me off to his spacious flat, where the boy of the moment was pettishly doing housework with the pert air of a spoilt favourite, barked at by Douglas in his sarcastic indulgent way. After lunch he took me to a near hotel, where I threw my bag under the bed and lay wondering why I had come.

For a fortnight of fine weather I roamed about Florence, often with Douglas, or sat in Pino Orioli's cramped shop on the Arno looking out on the Ponte Santa Trinità with a window full of books, engravings, parchment-bindings, bits of medieval music. Pino with his easy, chattering malice was good company, his tales of the foibles of D.H.L., Frieda, and scores of English inhabitants of Florence made all the more amusing by his odd pronunciation of *v* and *w*, *z* and *s*. An excellent mimic, he enjoyed his imitations so much that he was both performer and audience, and imagined his renderings to be so much more exact than they were, that in the end one did not know if one was laughing at the mimings or at Pino's ecstatic ideas of them.

I visited the artist's studio out in the open countryside and admired the cool charm of his fine-toned paintings of women; and had tea with his patroness at Doney's on the Tornabuoni, fashionably filled with hordes of rich useless women, their strident chatter pitched to drown the jingling of teaspoons, their scandal-mongering glances avidly registering anything to anyone else's disadvantage. To shut one's eyes was to imagine oneself in an aristophanic bog on the verge of hell crammed with sex-starved female frogs. Mrs D. pointed out Miss Pincher, the mean old maid whom Pino loved to pillory, withering himself into the meanest of all old maids and turning his shop with a wave of the hand into her apartments in a palazzo, her terrace-garden stocked with flowers wheedled out of other rich old useless women. 'That flower? O it's Buggarvilliar——' Miss P. staring with a new respect at the bougainvillia and saying gratefully purse-lipped, 'Where's a pencil? I must write the name down before I forget. How do you spell it?' while N.D. drinks up her show-bottle of sham Strega and grumbles with twitching eyebrows at its vile taste.

We ate, Norman, Pino and myself, at Ristorante Bianca with its trolley of boiled meats, or at Fusi's, where N.D. grunted that the place was at least foul enough to scare off tourists. For a couple of days Faith Compton-Mackenzie joined us. Norman had a special tenderness for her; he told me that she was the only woman who stuck up for him when he had the London trouble that led to his exile. A generously warm person. I could never take seriously N.D.'s squabbles about food or his grave comments on grey truffles, his ritual with the cheap hard-twisted Toscano cigars stuck in the upper pocket of his coat, which never drew however much he cut them or broke them in half, or his topsyturvying of accepted notions: 'Come on, close the windows and let's have some good healthy nitrogen.'

One day Pino, expatiating at his flat on the trials of dealing with a suppressed homosexual like D.H.L., showed me some of his paintings. (Pino's world was composed of homosexuals, suppressed or unsuppressed.) I found the pictures interesting and said there ought to be an exhibition. Pino shrugged. I said we'd do anything to help, and he said he'd raise the matter with Frieda. I had just missed the Lawrence period at the Villa Miranda; and Frieda had looked in at Florence a few days before I came.

Theoretically I approved of N.D.'s hedonism, but in practice found it humourless and tediously amoral; when I came to write of it in the *Aphrodite*, I clothed it in an existentialist thesis of Desire that had little to do with it. I myself had never kept a review or any of my journalism, and I was shaken to find that N.D. had everything gummed-up in big books. True, he was now building up an industry out of his trivia, reprinting them through Orioli. Again in theory I approved of the cynical things he said about making a living out of his American collectors; but the paltry details of the procedure seemed beneath the dignity of the man who had written *South Wind*.

Thus I spent my fortnight in a mixture of pleasant idling and enjoyment of N.D.'s sharp comments, and of disquiet and uncertainty, which prevented me from more than cursory glances at Florence, its buildings and galleries. I wrote to Elza saying I felt it had been wrong to come without her; in the future I wanted to live my life out in companionship with her in all matters. Only once, late at night, as we drank in a small squalid hostelry along the Arno, in ragged lights and amid croaks of song from a malevolently-tipsy boatman, did I feel N.D. in the flesh coincide with the sort of person I had built up in my mind out of *South Wind* and the early travel-books.

On my return I found Elza ill in bed. Later I learned that she had been sure of my departure for Australia. An old woman from a near cottage had been brought in to attend to the house, and though she was doing her best, things were in confusion and Robinetta rather untended. However Elza was soon up when she realized that I had not gone off. For my part, the mood in which I had written from Florence about our achieving a fuller companionship did not dissipate itself. Looking back, I can see that the effect of my change-of-heart was not however to make Elza any happier; from this period she became more demanding and at moments dictatorial. The more I gave in to her, the more this side of her character came up. My yielding to her stimulated her jealousy of me; it did not pacify it. I suppose that her fear of my going off had previously stifled her other fears; now, as that fear gradually went, the others grew stronger and more domineering. If at times I resented her attitude, I told myself that I was to blame for the stress I had put on her during my gadding-about with Betty. I believed that forbearance and gentleness on my part would make amends and bring her to a better balance.

Eric Partridge had happened on a visit at Museum Street to pick up the little book in which I had transcribed Elza's poems. As soon as he started his press, he asked if he could print the poems with my decorations. When *I Saw the Earth* appeared, it was selected as one of the Best 50 Books of the year. I also did a preface for an edition of Blake's *Poetical Sketches* for the Scholartis Press.

About this time I met someone else who had been in the Cefalu Abbey. Mary Butts had been married to Rodker, then had turned to

Cecil Maitland, who was interested in abnormal psychology. They met Crowley in Paris in February 1921 and were invited to Sicily, arriving in time to take part in the rite of the Cakes of Light, which seems to have consisted of the sacrifice of a young cock by Cecil—the cock being baptized Peter-Paul to represent the Christian Church. 'Alostrael [Leah Faesi, Crowley's mistress] then dances against the will of Mary, on my swearing to give to her the half of my Kingdom. She demands P.P.'s head on the Disk. I behead him and the blood is caught in the silver "charger" on the Disk.' Later, Mary (whom Crowley described as 'a fat, bold, red-headed slut . . . pompous, pretentious, and stupid') seems to have taken part in the rite of the Goat's copulation with the Scarlet Woman (Leah), during which Crowley cut the beast's throat and its blood spilled over Leah's back. Now Crowley praised her clairvoyant powers; she saw blue lights and once 'a huge Assyrian bull demon'. Still, after some three months, she and Cecil left the Abbey. According to Goldring, they said their health was permanently injured and they had acquired the habit of drugs.[1]

I met Mary in the Fitzroy, where she had come, I think, to see Edgell. She was then about thirty-five. Careless of herself, she was still impressive with her red-gold hair, her white skin and rich blue eyes, her large naked face. In build she was rather stocky. We talked about Theocritos. She had a passionate interest in the Greeks, and every time we met we spoke of nothing else, apart from a few words about her Butts ancestor who had been Blake's patron; she considered that she had an intuitive understanding of the Eleusinian Mysteries. (Cecil had died in 1927 and I never met Gabriel Atkin, an artist, with whom she went to Cornwall.)

Edgell was now living in some rooms near Bedford Square. I saw a fair amount of him and Garman, though after a few drinks I generally had some strong disagreement with the latter, who was liable to suffer from colic. His tight belt was blamed. Once Edgell, Bertram and myself carried him home at a late hour on our shoulders and handed him over to his sleepily irate wife. Cecil Rickword asked me to write the

---

[1] It is surprising how many people were affected by Crowley. He crops up early in *Laughing Torso*; and Nina introduced Mary to him. W. J. Sullivan, who wrote on Maths and Music, was won over at the same time; he signed an oath 'to discover my own True Will and to do it'. Next day the Beast, sending W.J.S. south after his True Will, carried out an act of sex-magic with his wife Sylvia. A man met at Austin Harrison's paid Crowley's fare back to Cefalu as well as the fares of Raoul and Betty. See also Calder-Marshall's *The Magic of my Youth*.

essay on Joyce for the second volume of *Scrutinies*. I recall the moment as several of us were packed in a taxi and squinting out of the window I caught the eye of Eros aiming his bow at some all-too-easy Piccadilly breast. Not long after Cecil was killed in a motor-car accident.

About this time the Nonesuch Press advertised a coming complete translation of Plato. After writing to mention our plan of doing several of the dialogues, I called on the Meynells at their suggestion. I remember the vexed silence that fell when Meynell carelessly mentioned he lived in north Essex, and I broke in enthusiastically, 'So do I.' I had also met Pearl Binder who did drawings for our Skelton's *Tunning of Eleanour Rumming*, which we bound in sacking with XXXs on it; we meant the book to be a try-out for a full text of Skelton. Through Pearl I met Tom Driberg's bearded elder brother, who had much of interest to say on anthropology. And it was perhaps about this time or earlier that I met Gordon Craig, with Elza, and was shown his woodcuts; characteristically the book of ours he most liked by far was my little book on Blake. Elza also went with me to lunch at Compton-Mackenzie's flat; but was very offhand and rude. I remonstrated with her on the stairs and she went back with a perfunctory return-invitation; but nothing more came of the acquaintance.

One day in the B.M. I had what I thought was an inspiration: to produce a fine edition of Byron's *Manfred* with an introduction giving the facts about Augusta Leigh. Frederick Carter was often in the office, a likeable but melancholy man, who was in correspondence with D.H.L. about *Revelation*. I asked him to do the foreword and make illustrations; but somehow the book didn't come out as effective and lavish as I had hoped the purple-printed drawings would make it.

I had written to Orioli repeating my remarks about D.H.L.'s paintings. At first I had the idea of getting the rights for a book of them; but D.H.L.'s conflict with Joynson-Hicks was increasing and the customs were doing their utmost to find and burn copies of *Lady Chatterley's Lover*. For our Press to print an edition of D.H.L.'s paintings would have been to invite trouble. Meanwhile a certain strain had grown up between P.R.S. and myself. He was not in the least to blame. At root I think I had lost interest in the Press as it had been originally constituted. In *The London Aphrodite* we had turned from the fine-book market and in the process had begun to develop ideas that broke away from the Fanfrolico aesthetic. P.R.S. was in a large part himself responsible for my growing pangs; but in turning away from the Press as we had together built it up, I found myself turning away from him. I really wanted to escape the Press, but had no alternative economic basis.

These changes in my attitude were also helped by the arrival of a young Australian, Brian Penton, who had been at the Brisbane Grammar School like myself. As a junior contemporary there, he had known me by sight though I had not known him. He was a boarder and once ran away, he told me, because he grew scared at the excessive mutual masturbation. An odd-looking fellow with a thin hatchet-face, as though his skull had been pressed in by someone putting hands on either side of his temple, he had dark wiry hair and piercing dark eyes; a terrific talker, very ambitious and amorous. He had brought over the MS of a novel and many letters of introduction into the world of journalism. He disliked P.R.S. and used all his considerable powers of biting sarcasm to belittle him. Not that I consciously took much notice of what Brian said; for I had the feeling that he'd be as biting about myself to P.R.S. or anyone else behind my back. Yet, despite my distrust of his urbanely stinging tongue, I liked him and no doubt his witticisms had a certain effect on me.

14. D. H. LAWRENCE

As the end of 1928 was nearing, P.R.S. suggested that he should take a business holiday in the South of France, calling in at Nice and such places to sell copies of our books. I was sceptical about the likelihood of Nice buying our books, but thought P.R.S. deserved a holiday, especially after my fortnight in Florence. He went south and took the opportunity to call in on D.H.L. at Bandol. At this time I thought I was the first person to have suggested an exhibition and book of the paintings; much later I learned that the idea had already been mooted by Dorothy Warren. However P.R.S. now stepped in and really got things moving. On 19 December 1928 D.H.L. wrote to Frieda's mother that Rhys Davies had been staying with them.

We also had a young Australian here for two days, this afternoon he left for Nice. He makes those beautiful expensive books that people collect nowadays—he says he will make a book next year of my paintings—of all my paintings, with a foreword by me, to be sold at ten guineas each. It seems madness to me, but it's his money and he will pay me well—if he does it. [Translated from the German.]

D.H.L. had been much agitated during Rhys Davies' visit about the attitude of the young. Rhys records that D.H.L. told him, 'Kick, kick all the time, make them feel you know what they are. Because you *do* know, you're intelligent enough. The young know, they *know*, and yet they let be. Oh dear, it drives me to despair when I see them holding back, letting be. Because your chance is now, the world is all wobbling and wants a new direction.' P.R.S. told me that at lunch D.H.L. got worked up and attacked Rhys for deserting his class, the workers. He bade him stick to them at all costs. 'Don't desert your class! Don't run away from your class!' It seemed to me a case where the speaker was attacking himself and regretting that he had not himself carried out the good advice he gave.

P.R.S. has stated in print:

Penton and Philip [Lindsay] were very anxious to join the Fanfrolico
Press, and easily persuaded Jack that they had a stimulus to impart. I left
them to it, and stepped out in about March, 1929, Penton then becoming
my successor as manager. I had other plans. In January, on a visit to the
south of France, I had met D. H. Lawrence and offered to publish a
book of reproductions of his paintings; but Lawrence did not want to be
associated with the Fanfrolico Press, as he disagreed with the Lindsay
Aesthetic. (*Kookaburras and Satyrs*)

  I visited Lawrence at Bandol, in the south of France, and stayed several
days with him. . . . Lawrence did not like Jack Lindsay's writings or ideas.
He would never have consented to the publication of any of his works in
the Lindsay-dominated Fanfrolico Press. But Lawrence took a liking to
me, and gave me his paintings to take to London. The agreement for
publication of the paintings was made by me with Lawrence's agent in
London, L. E. Pollinger, of Curtis Brown Ltd. All this is on documentary
record in *The Letters of D. H. Lawrence*, edited by Aldous Huxley.
(*Biblionews*)

But in fact, so far from D.H.L. rejecting the Fanfrolico Press, the
initial project put up to him was for his pictures to be done by that
press, and he accepted. Also most of the paintings were with Dorothy
Warren, to whom he wrote on 19 December 1928.

I think you've been a bit cool, keeping my pictures there all the time and
merely doing nothing. However, now the men of the Fanfrolico Press,
Jack Lindsay and P. R. Stephensen, say they want to do a book of reproductions of my paintings as early as possible in the New Year. So they want to
have the pictures photographed at once. . . . But if you still want to show
them, perhaps you could arrange with Mr Lindsay to have the show at
about the same time as their book is ready: perhaps in February.

That letter shows conclusively what the original idea was. The objection
to having D.H.L. in the Fanfrolico Press came from me, not from
D.H.L. at all.

  P.R.S. arrived back from Bandol and Nice jubilant, though I think he
had sold only one book: however that was one more than I expected.
We discussed the matter at length. Finally I had what I thought a good
idea. There was a bookseller, Edward Goldston, in Museum Street, on
the corner opposite the Plough; I had often had a casual beer with him
and he had more than hinted that he would like to put some money
into our Press. I had been keeping him up my sleeve in case our needs

ever became urgent. It now struck me that Goldston might well be interested in forming a new press to produce the D.H.L. paintings, which, in view of the publicity gained through *Lady Chatterley* and D.H.L.'s pamphlet against Joynson-Hicks (which I saw on sale in large quantities in Selfridges), could not fail to make a large sum of money. I suggested that he and P.R.S. should float the company and brought the two of them together for this purpose.[1]

There was as yet no suggestion that P.R.S. and myself should part; but since he now had his own firm, it was inevitable we should go different ways. He gives March as the time of his going-off; but he also adds that Phil's desire to get into the Press was one of the reasons for his going—and Phil did not arrive till September! Also, the last issue of the *Aphrodite* did not appear till July, and we were in close contact until then.

P.R.S. gives January as the date of his visit to Bandol; in fact it was then, after our discussion, that he rushed over for a second visit. D.H.L. mentions his arrival in a letter to Rhys of the 11th, saying how P.R.S. 'stirred us all up as usual'. On April 18, D.H.L. wrote to Pino from Palma de Majorca, during a visit to Spain, 'The Fanfrolico Press has more or less dissolved. The *working* partner was always Stephensen—Lindsay was the literary side of it. Stephensen has joined with Edward Goldston the Jew bookseller of Museum Street, to make the Mandrake Press, of which my pictures are the first thing done—The reproduction. of *Moses* seemed very dim to me.' He was handing on the news that P.R.S. had given him; in fact the Press was far from dissolution yet. (It would seem from this letter that April was the actual date when P.R.S.'s direct association with the firm was severed. I cannot myself recall the exact time, as we continued working together to some extent till July-August, as I have mentioned.)

For one reason or another the production of the book of paintings kept on being delayed; and in the end the result was not very good. ('Oh, that Mandrake—vegetable of ill omen!' D.H.L. wrote in one of his last letters.) Nehls remarks, in connection with some criticisms by Earp,

---

[1] P.R.S. must have notified Lawrence promptly; for whereas the latter on 19 December writes of the F.P. as doing his book, by 25 Dec. he speaks of the Mandrake Press. (The name was chosen by P.R.S.) It was about mid-January that P.R.S. collected the paintings from the Warren Gallery (Nehls iii 299). About that time the *Daily News* reported, 'My friend is Mr Jack Stephensen (*sic*) of the Fan Frolico Press (*sic*), and he is arranging a special spring show of Mr Lawrence's work at the Warren galleries.'

'Alternately muddy and garish' as a description of Lawrence's colour will not do. But it *will* do admirably—in fact there is not much else that will—for the 'colour-work' carried out for the Mandrake Press 'under the supervision of William Dieper'. The inference seems clear: While reviewing the 'Introduction to These Paintings' Mr Earp sought to refresh his memory out of the Mandrake pictures—and blurred it.

From early April the Gallery was waiting for the Mandrake to return the paintings and deliver the copies of the book. During this period I exchanged several letters with Lawrence. On his December return P.R.S. had hopes of converting him and asked me to send him a copy of my *Dionysos*; I objected that D.H.L. would detest it, but gave in. In a letter of his to Huxley dated Christmas Day 1928 he wrote, 'Lindsay sent me this morning *another* copy of his Dionysos book!' The only inference is that P.R.S. had already given him a copy out of his portmanteau of books, but had forgotten. D.H.L. wrote asking me to read the proofs of his Introduction and to check up about his statement of Henry VIII having suffered from syphilis. (He had got this from the book, *Post Mortem*, by an Australian doctor C. MacLaurin.) He added, 'Now don't say you'll do all this and then do nothing about it!' He also sent us some *Pansies* for the *Aphrodite*, but I turned them down; they were among the weaker ones, unless my memory deceives me. In one letter he suddenly burst out: 'Give up writing all this muck about love. Leave it to the Sashy Sitwells. You're right in what you hate. Stick to that and you'll get somewhere. Stop the love slush. Stick to your hate. That's what's real and good and creative in you.' (I quote from memory, but as I re-read the letter a considerable number of times I can be sure of having the sense right. Why he dragged Sacheverell in I do not know, unless he had been annoyed by my praising him in the magazine.) He also asked me to have a look over the hanged pictures at the Warren Galleries on a second floor in Maddox Street. Despite the concealed lighting and the silver-grey velvet on the walls of one room, I thought the place didn't look enough like a professional gallery; but the pictures were visible enough. P.R.S. came along, and with us was Barbara, one of Frieda's daughters, an Englishly-nice but rather bewildered girl. We had tea together, but my efforts to draw her out only made her more nicely bewildered.

The show opened on 15 June and the attacks began. The police raid was made on 5 July. But by that time I was taken up with the problems of reorganizing the Press.

15. BACK TO LONDON

ELZA was fretting at Takeley and I asked her why she didn't come back to London. Now that the burden of the firm was falling more on my shoulders, it was difficult to divide my time between London and Takeley. Rupert Atkinson, a rich Australian, was in London. A talented writer of verse and of plays in which he tried to define his own tormented split-up being, his sense of living several lives at the same moment, he was a restless disappointed man, printing his own work hastily and unable to settle to anything definite—poetry or whisky or travel, an intellectual or a playboy role. Generous and kind-hearted, he had done much to help the perennially-penniless Hugh McCrae, who responded with a vast fund of malicious stories which mainly dealt with ridiculous escapades with Rupert's wife, Marie. She was a dark-haired woman whom Rupert had met as a barmaid and who still bore the signs of a remarkable beauty. I slept a few times at their large flat in Bloomsbury, and now and then Rupert swept into the office. 'What, never been into Westminster Abbey! Come along at once. I've got a taxi waiting.'

One evening the artist Nevinson came into the Plough on the quest for guests for a large party. He asked a small gracefully-wriggling model with a slight cast in one eye, whose capacious bottom he pinched and complimented in a loud whisper; and then he included me. Rupert was out of town, so I took Marie along. The Nevinson house was madly crowded, and I chiefly remember a group of students teasing the pianist Mark Hambourg, whose ponderous German manners could not compete with their guerilla tactics of insult. Marie was annoyed that I couldn't recognize most of the important artists and introduce her to them. She was sure that she only needed to be introduced to Epstein to be asked to sit for a bust. But there were too many drunken young beauties kissing between hiccups and charlestoning with lean legs and agilely out-thrust rumps. She had no hope of being a success, even though she kept to the worst-lighted room. I met the model with her black hair braided over her broad brow several times on the stairs, her

squint steadily growing stronger as she complained of her headache
and her inability to find our thick-set host with his dark resentfully-
challenging eyes. Marie complained all the way back to her flat near
Marble Arch at having been trodden-on and elbow-jabbed as well as
innocently involved in a soda-squirting battle of the students. 'And
where were you all the while?' I told her that I'd been listening to old
Nevinson talk.

I had written to Freud asking him if he would write an introduction
to an edition of *Thus Spake Zarathustra*; at the same time I sent him my
book on Nietzsche, *Dionysos*. He replied that he felt too deeply about
Nietzsche and owed him too great a debt ever to write about him, and
referred me to Ernest Jones. He also added that he thought I was quite
wrong in what I had written about Frau Salome and suggested that as
she was still alive I should visit her in Germany. This comment of his
struck me hard. I re-read the passages in my book about Nietzsche and
Frau S., and felt how frivolously cocksure they were, how easily I had
assumed an understanding of a complex situation, reducing the relationship to a simple pattern suitable for the Fanfrolico universe. (I had forgotten she became one of Freud's early disciples.)

D.H.L.'s upbraiding exhortation and Freud's polite snub had a
decisive effect in re-orienting my mind. They continued slowly but
steadily working in the depths of my being, though I lost both letters
on the same night. I carried them around in my pocket-book: the sort
of thing I hadn't done since I received Norman's first letters in 1919.
We were drinking at Edgell's rooms and in some argument I produced
D.H.L.'s letter. Freud's came out with it and I showed both of them
round. Either someone stole them or they were lost in the confusion.
That night I also met a strong reprimand which left a lasting effect. I
had been talking about Aristophanes. (We were doing his *Ecclesiazusai*
in the same format as the *Lysistrata*, with an introduction by Edgell.)
Trying to formulate what I felt about the poet's allegiance to life (which
in Fanfroliconean terms meant Girls and Wine), I said something about
Aristophanes not really caring what happened to Athens. I meant that
his care for Athens was poetically his care for the freedoms that begat
poetry, not for the city in an abstract political sense; but Edgell said
gravely, 'I think he cared a great deal,' and suddenly I felt that
the opposition I was making between the city of poetry and the
city of political actuality was a false one. So, if I lost my precious
letters that night, I gained something of self-knowledge which

was in line with the letters' message, helping to bring me down to earth.

Shortly afterwards, Edgell called on me at the office, and suggested he might be paid for his preface, if we could afford it. We happened to be short at the moment. But Edgell had just handed over his poem on the Lousy Astrologer for the *Aphrodite*. So I went down with him for a cup of tea in the Express below with Betty, and said, 'While we have any money, what's the use of it except for friends?' And wrote out the cheque. About this time Hart Crane was in London; he called on Edgell, who found him very anti-*Aphrodite* and argued with him; I don't know if he convinced him.

Not long afterwards Edgell and Betty moved to a cottage in the south. I paid them one week-end visit. After some games of shove ha'penny in a long shadowy pub at Lewes, we went by bus to a small cottage lost in a ragged rural nook. Betty looked so like a hardworking gypsy in the rough conditions that the place survives in memory rather as a caravan camping-site, smudged with the floating smoke-wreaths of a rich wood-fire, while the crackle of broken-up twigs punctuates the conversation and Betty flinging back the hair from her sweaty face bares her house-wifely elbows.

Elza found a sort of flat somewhere in the direction of Hammersmith, and we moved to London. We had had for some months a mongrel dog Whiskers, and as soon as we arrived he lost himself. A couple of days later I found him in a police-lair for lost dogs, and rescued him. The performance went on being repeated. The back-section of our flat, which housed a huge jingling brass-bedstead as well as a wardrobe that fell over if one let the doors swing open, was roofed with glass; and we had no sooner moved in than a window-cleaner fell through the glass from an upper-storey and had to be removed in an ambulance. Brian Penton found rooms nearby. He was suffering from the frosty chastity of English maidens, or pretending to suffer; for one never knew if he wasn't putting on an act as part of his disinterested belief that life should be as dramatic and exciting as possible. If it was in fact humdrum, one was justified in throwing various bombs of irony or abuse into its midst, simply to enliven it and bring the temperature up to the point of simmer-ing merriment. So his sarcasms often had a purely comic aim and were meant, not to belittle their object, but to blow life up into oversize caricature-dimensions. He acted the fool, charitably, to amuse others and woo them out of the boredom he accounted a sin, and to keep himself up to the level of intense enjoyment of the spectacle of existence, the serious mask slipping from the always absurd face of fact, the gap between profession and actuality in which was expressed the human condition, its idiot ambiguity.

And so his insistence on being a frustrated wooer of all the lovelies of an embarrassingly lavish world was perhaps in part an expression of a genuine uncertainty and modesty, as it was also certainly in part a game that he was playing with himself in order to enhance the rather dull everyday facts. At the same time he found a certain satisfaction in trying to live up to his fabricated role as chief actor in an endless *conte drola-tique*: not so much out of any impulse of venery as out of a wish to see how things went, how a gambler's tosses worked out, how often he could actually bluff life into taking him seriously at his jesting word. He didn't really give a damn, but he foamed at the mouth as he blamed the stringent economic conditions of England that made women conscious of the marriage ring as their blither loose-foot sisters of Australia never were. It was a rhetorical exercise, a sketch of vituperation in the Roman style, with the force behind the outpouring and elaborated phrases coming from his fear of failure, his fierce resolve to cut a figure in the mocked-at world.

One day as we were homing by bus, he winked at me and gave a nod. I realized that he was on petting terms with the gravely-aloof girl beside him, and left him to it. About an hour later he turned up at the flat, in a ferocious rage against English virgins. The girl had grown scared when he got out at her stop, and had threatened to call a policeman. One needed to know Brian well to realize that the affair had gone exactly according to schedule, and that the anti-climax was just what he wanted, since it released him from the need for further action and at the same time proved his point, giving him the desired text for a denunciation. The satisfaction lay in the words, in the clowning, in the social excitement that had been generated, with Brian gesticulating at its heart.

However not long after he picked up in the Plough the wife of a well-known painter, who liked listening to his tirades and who gave him a different set of variants in his exposition of the inferiority of the English female to the Australian. She was a little kittenish ball of a thing, who did not bother to wear pants, at least when visiting gentlemen, as I unavoidably noted one day when she sat waiting for Brian in our front room, yawning wide-and-brawny-kneed on the sofa under a photogravure of Watts' Hope blindfolded on a spinning world. Brian arrived an hour late, voluble in his spattering way with excuses, and gave an uproarious imitation of the editor whom he had been interviewing.

With his capacity to be extremely charming, he won Elza's affection and spent much of his time at our flat while I was at the office or the B.M. Once, however, we went down the street to his lodgings, where the dyspeptic landlady had one of those rare and outlandish things, a radio-set, to hear John Gough's *Wallaby Track* being broadcast. During this period Elza was more uninhibitedly blithe and easy-going than I had ever known her; and I felt that Brian's attentions, blustering, wheedling, and flatteringly docile, had much to do with this change of mood. The three of us generally went out together; and she even found a certain pleasure in having a couple of drinks at a pub with us. She grew excited and flushed when we discussed the plans in which now Brian had his place; and even gave me an unsolicited kiss after emerging from the big tin bath with sunflowers knocking against the glass-windows—a bath that made a thunderous noise when one stepped in or out of it.

She had temporarily left Robinetta with the neighbours at Takeley. The intention was to bring her to London as soon as we had found some large premises. These arrangements had been entirely Elza's. But we had not been long in London when a letter arrived to say that Miss Edith Craig, motoring in the Rodings, had called in at Takeley and carried her grand-niece off. I still do not know who had notified her about Robinetta. Perhaps it was the neighbours who were keeping the child for a weekly fee; perhaps we had some enemy in the area of whom I knew nothing and who had decided the child was being neglected. Elza was normally a capable enough housekeeper in her quiet way; but during my absence in Florence and for a short while after, before she regained her health, things had certainly been in a mess, presided over by the friendly but hag-looking old woman. (In any event, how had anyone known of Edith Craig?)

Elza did not seem at all perturbed. She went to see Edith Craig and told her that she had no objection to Robinetta being kept till we were suitably settled. No doubt she had been so used to temporary residences for herself, Robert, or the child, with friends or relations, that she did not attach any particular importance to Edith Craig's actions. The latter said nothing about being determined to hold on to Robinetta. I was not present at the discussion; but Elza returned in a good humour.

Brian told us that his wife Olga was arriving. With his fervent imagination he drew a picture of an incredibly dainty and petite creature, which he supported with the only photo of Olga he possessed; in it she showed up as a small white summer-blur. On the day of her ship's arrival he had an appointment with Lloyd George—one of his important appointments which he never quite explained and which never came to anything. So I agreed to meet the train and take Olga to our flat. For some hours she waited there as patiently as she could; then the door crashed open and Brian rushed impetuously in. He at once recoiled, stuttered, and advanced again at a more sober pace. I now knew him well enough to understand what had happened. He had so impressed himself with his dream-pictures of Olga that no earthly actuality, however charming, could be identical with the fabulous sylph of his prolonged conjurations.

We decided to set up house together, Lindsays and Pentons, and Elza found a large house in Woodchurch Road, West Hampstead, with a fair-sized strip of back-garden. We moved in and I bought two presses, one of the old screw-type and one a more modern platen. I had decided to start printing as many of our books as possible myself. I had in hand a complete Catullus on which I had been working, with a long and hastily compiled introduction, and for which, as for the Theocritos, Ellis did woodcuts at a small fee. I bought some Cloister type for main jobs, and, at Oliver Simon's advice, Weiss Antiqua— another type which we were the first to use in Britain. (We had been the first to use Koch Kursiv, in *Delighted Earth*.)

I had written telling Phil and Ray that we now had a big house, and inviting them over. Phil decided to come. In early September he arrived. I cannot do better than cite his account. He says that I was late to meet him at Waterloo; probably I was, though I did not know at the time I had given him such an excruciating time of waiting. He describes his anguish as the friends of the voyage streamed past and he clutched the borrowed two-shilling piece that was all his wealth. 'I had received a cable in reply to mine merely demanding to know whether I was a myth, and telling me not to be a damned fool and ask for money, as he didn't have any. This statement I put down to the usual base subterfuge to avoid paying someone else's beer bill, and all the voyage over I had ranted boastfully of my Genius of a Brother and of the mighty Fanfrolico Press; but now I stood alone in that colossal roosting barn for trains, with no sign of a brother, millionaire or otherwise, to meet me on a London Sunday.' He says that he had only the office address, which was no use on a Sunday, and remembered reading of down-and-outs in

St Martin's crypt, so decided to go there if need be. At last our uncle
Jack Elkington, who was holidaying in England, turned up.

Then the other Jack, the villain, my brother, appeared. He bounded
towards me over the platform, and instinctively I paled and stepped back.
Behind him trotted Brian Penton, lean-faced under the dark upstanding
mop of hair, grinning, with his wife, dark slim Olga, at his side: I recognized them immediately, of course, but I scarcely knew my brother. I
could but gape and stare at him. He had left Australia in perfectly tailored
garments, with oil on his hair and a stick in his hand, a man-about-town
who blanched at a speck of dust on his waistcoat, and who carried his
cigarettes in a gold case for fear they spoil with a little crushing; but, now!
his trousers slumped to his ankles, like a tramp's; his shoes had never
known polish, and were cracked; his coat looked as though he had slept in
it for weeks, as indeed he probably had; while instead of a collar or tie,
around his neck was knotted a huge red bandana such as cowboys are
alleged to have worn.[1] From under the black wide-brimmed shapeless
felt hat, wisps of hair shot in every direction, and all were of different
lengths; but more than such details, what froze the smile on my lips and
kept my hands as if paralysed with horror at my side, was Jack's face.
Rasputin boasted no beard such as his: I have never seen one quite like it
before, and hope never to see one like it again.

This was no carefully clipped adornment such as Jack Elkington had
once sported, like Conrad's, or any sailorman's. It was but a beard, a
beard that had grown with a beard's will, haphazardly, in sportive riot,
over cheeks, upperlip, and chin: thick and woolly here, wispy there,
tangled, matted: a confusion of darkish hair that would have made an
early Christian saint bilious with envy. Why did he keep it?

I could but groan and mutter—why?

'Couldn't afford razor-blades,' he explained, gripping my arms, and
grinning through the jungle.

'A drink,' I croaked, 'let's have a drink.'

In a body we thundered down some steps into a street, and in the public
bar of a nearby little house we crowded. There I saw my stoker pal sitting
with a group, and I shuddered in the company of Jack. The stoker whispered: Could I give him the price of a drink? and I slipped the priest's
two bob into his hand, eager to be rid of him with my crushing sense of

---

[1] In his satiric exaggeration Phil here goes too far. I have never in my whole
life oiled my hair or owned a gold case; my ill-starred silver cane I have mentioned early in this book. True, I had left Sydney with a new suit, a good one
paid for by Norman; that is all. (In Ellis's portrait I am wearing the artist's
worn velvet coat, not my own shabby tweeds; and the white cravat was devised
by him to show up the beard.)

shame. To appreciate my feelings you must remember that I am an Australian and was then, as yet, unused to sartorial and, in particular, barbered unconventionality. Badly dressed though I always was, and always am, and undoubtedly always will be, there is nothing unusual in my garments, apart grease-spots, cigarette-burns, beer and ink-stains, and lack of creases.

I have, however, the normal Australian phobia of wishing to be one of a mob. . . . I suffer from this inferiority-phobia to this day, although naturally not in the extreme condition of my first arrival, for London's tolerance has taught me many a lesson; but it was months before I could walk the street beside my brother without wanting to run for my life when anybody looked at us, as everybody inevitably did at sight of such a Bolshy beard. My worship for him naturally remained, and I was therefore unable to tell him my horror as I would have done with Ray or any other friend. I was shocked, embarrassed, and tormented by his company in public.

'What are London beers?' I asked—a vital question.

Penton, who had never cared for drinking, suggested Burton. It was the real English drink, he explained, the working man's tipple, something I'd never tasted before. He was right. I never had tasted it before and swore then never to taste it again. So we ordered bitter; and I didn't like that greatly either, although it was a slight improvement; then we essayed brown ale, like burnt sugar; and lastly, a light ale, which I considered too thin and gassy.

Then truly did the prospect of England darken before me. . . .

In fact, what Phil did say as soon as he tasted the beer, was, 'Christ, take me straight back to Australia!'

In *I'd Live* he tells of his excited journey through London to our house, which he scanned wrathfully:

If he were so broke as he said, how could he afford this mansion? I demanded the truth indignantly, but Jack's reply was quite unanswerable. He couldn't afford it, he told me, with that bland smile of his from somewhere in his beard, his light blue eyes seeming as innocent as any babe's, while he pulled on some ragged strings of hair as if he plucked Pan's music from them.

Whatever might have been my surprise at the exterior of the mansion, it turned to amazement when an obsequious rather-handsome young man opened the door, bowing faintly, and offered to take our hats and coats, even calling me *Sir*! I could but gape at Jack who calmly, as if it were the most ordinary thing in the world, whispered: 'Our butler!' while we were ushered through a door to the right.

This led us into a long room that was, in fact, two rooms, with dividing doors, now open. Great windows opened on to Woodchurch Road, and french-windows at the back revealed a garden which looked, with its thigh-high weeds, that if it weren't haunted by satyrs, it should have been. The furnishings were simple to poverty: a table, a few chairs, an arm-chair, book-cases, and various paintings—mostly by Lionel Ellis—unframed on the walls, with a few of Norman's etchings.

'This is Elza,' said Jack, and I turned to greet a pale pre-Raphaelitish girl, with very fair hair parted in the centre, and drawn tightly back from the forehead; round china-blue eyes; and a pale rosebud mouth; her complexion being of such transparency that it was as if a soft candle glowed inside her skull, diffusing the veins with golden ichor rather than blood. She was dressed in pre-Raphaelitish fashion, to enhance her Burne Jones features, wearing a high-breasted simple white gown, reaching to her ankles, the stockingless feet being encased in sandals.

I forget what the house's rent was; but it was not so much when halved between Brian and myself. And when one considered that it was also a workshop, with the printing machines in the basement, it was quite cheap. The man-servant, whom we jokingly called a butler, was a brief experiment. Elza, who had grown tired of cooking for two families, found him somehow in Kilburn; he was an unpleasant homosexual, intensely genteel, who loathed us as much as we disliked him; and he soon went. He did his best to act in a butlerish way, serving our meals with extreme decorum, and Brian, expecially if there were any guests, tried to disconcert him by saying the most obscene or blasphemous things in his best upperclass accents. I will say for the butler that he never gave away the disgust he felt, though behind the scenes he com-plained bitterly to Elza. I was glad to see him go, not merely because I disliked him, but because the presence of any servant in the house has always given me a sense of humiliation.

Phil was installed in the topmost room and we settled down to live a happy united life. Brian had slid into P.R.S.'s managerial position. He worked hard and did his best; but he came into the firm after the first burst of energy had gone, and he lacked P.R.S.'s enkindling flairs. I left the office almost entirely to him and mainly stayed at home, writing or printing. Phil did any odd jobs and lent a hand in the basement, damping the handmade paper and so on.

I had a large number of projects on hand: the translations of Ausonius which Bawden illustrated; a version of the *Mimes* of Herondas for which

F

Brian wrote an introduction; a selection of the Letters of the first Earl of Chesterfield, which I had come on in my Rochester researches. Finding that the scheme of printing our own books was going successfully, I managed to get a capable printer, W. J. Hatton, whom I paid union-rates for full employment. Among the books we printed were *Guenevere*, poems by William Morris with an introduction by Bottomley and some unpublished drawings by Rossetti; *Festival Preludes* by Bottomley; *Fleas in Amber*, an anthology of poems on vermin, for which I used the paper cut off one of the larger jobs—hence the odd shape of the book. I was also doing a lot of writing for myself. *Hereward*, in which I tried to define my divided condition between Betty and Elza, was finished in June; I asked Gough to devise some simple drum-rhythms to go between the scenes (which were linked by spoken lyrics), but he composed complex musical backgrounds, which were printed with the text. I also wrote a full-length play on Wycherley's marriage; and shorter plays on Rembrandt and Paracelsus, which were, I think, among my best things— as well as an experimental play based on Tuareg traditional songs. At the same time I had a shot at prose in a surrealist novel, which began with an episode based on a tale that Owens told of his first stay in Paris. The hero arrives at his hotel, then goes out wandering in the streets of the Parisian night, expecting some romantic adventure; nothing happens; he goes back disconsolate to the hotel, rings the bell by acci-dent, a servant-girl comes in, and he suddenly recognizes the light of invitation in her eyes. The novel proper opened as he went to sleep in the girl's arms, entering into the dream-world of his desires.

I had written to Alan Odle asking if he would illustrate the *Herondas*. He at once called on us, and both Phil and I were struck by his likeness to Norman. With his long yellowish hair, his dead-white face and large bright eyes, his long nails and slender hands, he was a sort of Beardsley-ish caricature of Norman, yet a caricature that had a haunting aspect of the original: we felt that we had met our father in his youth, in an off-moment when he was trying for a joke to be aesthetical. We also found Odle most likeable, and he quickly produced his splendid baroque designs. I felt that he was extremely shy and modest, somehow lost and very grateful at our calling him out of a dungeon or Gothic cave in which he had gone to sleep.

In *Hereward* I carried on with the method of *Love*, adding a rapid kaleidescopic effect of short scenes organized on a cinematic system, with snatches of song in darkness between. Thus, a scene that ends with

Alftruda (Betty) and Osulf embracing is followed by another which opens with Hereward embracing her; he has hastened in and Osulf has dodged off in the between-dark. And this second scene breaks through the dark of another sudden and contrasted song into a scene of argument between Hereward and Torfrida (Elza). Thus a nightmare effect of the divided self was built up, reaching a sustained climax in the battle for Ely, where battle-effects, babbling-voices, counter-songs are mingled, and Hereward is shown in a paralysed state, with a repeated action and distracted meditations in the dark. The cinematic devices recur throughout, mainly in the sharp juxtaposition of linked but opposed scenes and in conflicting relationships. My aim was to depict a man struggling to carry on a great emprise while torn in different directions by unresolved contradictions. (Bottomley, praising the work, added that my Hereward was far from the hero of history.)

I felt the Fanfrolico days were drawing to an end, and discussed with Garman the possibility of our starting an experimental theatre which specialized in verse-drama.[1] Bottomley sent his blessing and I felt sure we could draw Yeats in. Garman and I went to shows at small theatres. I best recall a Toller play at the Gate under snorting Charing Cross station, a play about the frustrated German revolution after the war, with film-passages on a screen at the side. We did not doubt that the moment we decided to act we would find our theatre and begin work.

---

[1] Garman had written a book of verse, *The Jaded Hero*; he had spent some time in Moscow as an English-teacher and I asked him many questions about the Soviet Union, but at that time he was not very political-minded. When I printed in the *L.A.* something about a better poet than T. S. Eliot (meaning Edgell) saying that the great need was a symbol for Hell, Garman surprised me by remarking that the comment had been his, not Edgell's. (I had sent some parts of *Between Two Kisses*—a section trying to put the *Liebestod* into words—to *Calendar* and had it promptly rejected. It must have been in relation to this that D.G. once said, 'People should call in with their contributions; only then can an editor quickly get a sense of someone with something new'.) He later had a chequered career: husband of the millionairess Peggy Guggenheim and then a functionary of the C.P. (after the amalgamation of Wishart's and Martin Lawrence's), retiring with stomach trouble to pig-accountancy in Dorset.

16. BREAKDOWN

OUR united family did not last long. As soon as Olga arrived, Elza began to lose her liking for Brian. Perhaps he ceased to pay her such flattering attentions. Anyway her brief period of easy expansiveness came to an end. And for no reason at all she grew jealous of Olga and me. Once Olga came into my workroom half-way up the stairs to chat for a quarter-of-an-hour, and Elza was in a furious state. There were many episodes of chafed tempers, which Brian's spluttering efforts at humour and chaffing could not dispel. Before long Elza made things impossible for the Pentons, who moved out into a Bloomsbury room, in Brunswick Square.

Still, we had now and then some junketings. Once Alec Brown, whose poems we had printed in *Aphrodite*, turned up in a huge ramshackle car full of strange delicacies, goat-cheese from Sicily and the like, to celebrate the acceptance of his first novel: a slightly diabolonian character in looks, with his fair pointed beard and his air of having been whisked away from archaeological excavations on the Danube on a journey to some world of lost elegances, full of subtleties that one couldn't decipher. Thus, some thirty years later, he recalls the moment:

My impression was one of surprise, after the more comfort-loving ways of Yugoslavia, to find you in a big, spacious dark, dank, indeed gloomy house. I was dismayed by the chilliness. I wondered if I really should have come then, and not in the morning. Elza appeared, looking like a poetess arriving from a Parthenon situated somewhere in Finland, and I felt unbelievably outer barbarian. I was over-awed to discover that you printed your own books and kept your printing press in a back room. It was rather as if an American President arrived and drew a cyclotron from his hip pocket. You had the aura of a magnate for me. In my simplicity I had never thought of just printing one's books oneself. And we sat down at an enormously long refectory table, if I recall, with candles. And then you suddenly quoted Greek to me, and though I had learned my Greek without the strange English pronunciation, to which you added the especial flavour of Australian vowels and elisions, and although I am practically illiterate in Greek, by magic in your declamation I knew it was

Sappho. That is the most memorable moment in the whole meeting, the intensity of that Greekness, and Elza sitting there, sphinx-like. . . .

I had also met my Brisbane friend Rosemary at the large house of the Segals, Australians who lived not far off. She was now married to a bearish bumbling White-Russian, who wrote pastoral poems and had been kept for many years by the wife of one of our leading novelists. (The novelist was a homosexual and his marriage was one of frank convenience, a social cover.) The amiable White-Russian, suddenly discharged, had to find someone else ready to shoulder the pleasant responsibility of looking after him in a rough and rude world; so he married Rosemary, who was delighted at such aristocratic connections. The White-Russian wasn't so delighted at finding her less rich and less easily led than he had thought; but he shrugged and wrote some more pastorals, which were printed in small Russian pamphlets at Rosemary's expense.

One evening at the Segal house I was cornered by a puzzled old Russian lady who talked for hours about Shakespeare. 'Of course you admit that he's hopelessly dull, overrated, positively unreadable and vulgar. And on the stage he's impossible, so crude, so empty. To what do you attribute his reputation? Perhaps you have found music in his sonnets? So have I.' She signalled to the others. 'It is most interesting, most consoling. I find that Mr Lindsay agrees entirely with me. Only the sonnets of that monster Shakespeare are any good.'

Rosemary gave Elza some fashionable clothes, perhaps thinking she wore her long dresses because she possessed only a box of stage-properties. Elza put one skirt on and came to me in my room. 'Look how tight it is across the bottom,' she said. She had brought a mirror with her and twisted round to see herself. 'I feel horrible, I can't bear it.' She pulled the skirt off and tore it up.

About this time occurred an episode which convinced me that I had really changed in my attitudes. One lunch-hour I had a pint with P.R.S. in the Plough. When I left, I was followed out by a young woman, Topsy, whom I had often see there and chatted with. She was surprisingly small, her charming doll-face with its big serious eyes surrounded by a great mop of curly hair. She asked me to have a drink in the side-bar. There she took my hand and said in her childish voice, 'Why don't you ever notice anything? You go about in a dream. I've been trying to make you look at me for months.'

'But I've often looked at you.'

'No, you haven't. Look at me.'

I looked at her and I certainly saw something different.

After some more word-fencing I said I must go. She pouted. 'Meet me in here just before the pub shuts after lunch tomorrow, will you?'

I said yes, and went off. Next day I passed the pub at the trysting-time. I even stood a few moments on the opposite side of the street. But I knew I had no intention of going in. I knew I had broken the spell of the Fanfrolico ethic (the poet must submit to the pull of life, never evade the new experiences offered him, etc.); and I felt remarkably happy, despite a few faint twinges of regret that I'd never kiss the dollish girl with her pleadingly wet eyes and her small pouted mouth. I walked on.

I lost touch with Heseltine after he went to Wales. A while back he had responded with scholarly seriousness, as if to some important questionnaire on Elizabethan madrigals, when I suggested he might aid Douglas who was compiling a book of obscene limericks for his American market. This book, in which Douglas printed the verses with not-so-funny commentaries, was one of his money-making dodges. I contributed a couple of poems, but Heseltine laboriously types out a vast number, some by himself, others anonymous, on a toilet-roll, which he unwound on to a typewriter and then rewound like an ancient book-roll. The only printable one of his own composition I can recall is that with the famous phallus-pun:

> *Young girls who frequent picture-palaces*
> *don't hold with this psychoanalysis,*
> *and though Doctor Freud*
> *is distinctly annoyed*
> *they still cling to their long-standing fallacies.*

Now out of the blue came a letter violently denouncing me for the preface to my versions of Sappho. Heseltine accused me of being a masochist, concerned with what women felt in bed instead of being interested in my own satisfactions. I was surprised, but decided he must have written in one of his irritable hangovers, when he was liable to look round for an enemy to bombard with abuse. However, another matter of dissention came up through the anthology on drunks that he did for the Mandrake, *Merry-go-round*, under the signature of Rab Noolas (Saloon Bar seen on the window from the inside): 'a gallery of gorgeous drunkards through the ages. Collected for the use, interest, illumination and delectation of serious topers' with decorations by Collins. It was a rather lightweight book, P.R.S. mentioned, and though I had no connection with the Mandrake I offered to fill it out, which I did with some more 17th-century poems and a few ballads of Bloomsbury by myself. Heseltine of course should have been consulted, even though he was not putting his name to the book. I suppose P.R.S. expected me to get in touch with him, and I expected P.R.S. Heseltine angrily struck out all the additions from the proofs. I saw him once or twice, but he was prim-lipped and aloof, very much on his dignity. I did not take his angers seriously, feeling that in due time we'd make things up. I didn't realize how the clock was running down.

P.R.S., given a free hand by Goldston after the Lawrence success, was seeking for an active principle on which to build his press. For a while he found it in D.H.L.'s *Pansies* and Burns' *Merry Muses*. But D.H.L. had his own publisher and was soon to die. P.R.S. turned to Joyce, but again there was not much left to build on. He started an excellent small series to which Owens, Edgell, and himself contributed. His effort to draw Liam in was less successful, as Liam did not find it easy to write to order and turned out a potboiler. I wrote four short stories, *Girl*, for him, which however never got into print; one of the tales was that of Betty and the commercial-traveller.

For the Fanfrolico Press, Allardyce Nichol edited the works of Tourneur, which we did with decorations by Carter. And I commissioned versions of *Thus Spake Zarathustra* from Penton, the *Contes Drolatiques* from Phil, and Machiavelli's *Comedies* from Garman. The lease at Bloomsbury Square had come to an end, and as the owners wanted to raise the rent we did not renew. I approached the wholesalers Simpkin-Marshall, sold them £1,000 worth of books, and arranged for them to take over all our distribution and despatch. For a while we had small and dusty offices near the old one, then we retreated wholly to Woodchurch Road. Phil was my sole helper during this period, apart from the machinist.[1]

[1] In *I'd Live*, Phil tells the tale of his lost MS novel, much more kindly than he told it in conversation. Brian and myself placed with Fabers N.L.'s novel *Redheap* (about his hometown near Ballarat). Its excellent picture of the mining township in the '90's was spoiled by the intrusion of a character who talks Einstein and who wasn't in the version I read in Australia. I disliked the book for its abortion theme, sure that N.L. was there drawing on his own emotional resistances to the marriage which had been forced on him by my advent.

Elza was growing more unstable. She had now made it impossible
for any of my friends to come to the house, and soon she was to quarrel
with Phil. He came home drunk one night. She made some sharp comment and he flared up. He was very rude to her, unable to control the
dislike which he had been accumulating and which the hostile comments of the various anti-Elza parties had strengthened. She ordered him
out of the house. I vainly and feebly tried to restrain the pair of them;
and when he stumbled up to his attic, she told me that I must get rid
of him at once. I was in the utmost misery. I could not defend Phil
when he had been so rude, and yet I could not pack him off. Elza insisted
that she would leave the house herself if I did not tell Phil to go. At
last I forced myself up the stairs to where Phil was lying still
dressed on his bed. I told him that he would have to go, gave him
what small money I had on me, and sent him out into the chilly
night.

I watched him go without argument, and felt like one of the damned.
In *I'd live* he tells the story of his wandering night, though he charitably
disguises the reason for his sudden homelessness. After calling on the
Pentons, he went to Victoria station, was ejected after a while from the
waiting-room, drifted off to Kensington where Jeanne Ellis was staying
(he was already in love with her), and ended, via Kilburn, outside the
Segal house, thinking of Muriel, a gay young girl he'd met at our place.
He slumbered on a bench, then tried to break into West Hampstead
station, tearing his trousers, wandered off to a coffee-stall opposite
Baker Street station, tried the tube, and came to rest at last in Blasco's
room.

My surrender to Elza in Phil's ejection revealed what a change had
been going on in me. The weakness I now showed towards her was the
reverse side of the strengths shown in turning down the mop-headed
girl and in trying to reorganize the Press on a less idiosyncratic basis.
It portended dire things for me.

Elza herself was also undergoing some process of change which I
could not fathom. She asked a young architect to tea, saying he had
been a good friend of hers once. I recall his startled face when I arrived
home. He lost no time in finding an excuse to depart. (Later I found he
had been one of her clients in the Pre-Young period.) She told me that
she was with child. No doubt she really believed it, though in fact she
was not pregnant. We had never taken any precautions, and I feel sure
that her various operations had made her sterile. But the fear and the

desire of pregnancy played an important part in her psychic life from now on.

One day, as I was coming home, I met the Owenses, who took me into a pub, and after some embarrassment told me that they had been worried by some of the anti-Elzas talking about the need to get rid of her by pushing her under a bus, or something like that. They did not specify which of her many enemies had been indulging in this loose talk, which I did not take very seriously, knowing how such schemes can be elaborated in the midnight of booze without having any reality in the hangover dawn. However, I made the mistake of telling Elza what had been said. I did so only because I wanted a good alibi for having come home later than usual with a smell of beer; but in her disturbed condition she was strongly affected and her feeling of being ringed by malignant foes was deepened.

Her poems were growing more assured in their style. On the one hand they expressed a direct gratitude to me:

> *Always my mind calls forth this day*
> *when naked in the wood I lay*
> *and you came by and suddenly stood*
> *above my body in the wood*
> *among the deathless flowers where*
> *the crocus budded from my hair.*
> *I spoke; you answered and awake*
> *stretched out your curving hands to take*
> *my beauty, and at last grown brave*
> *all I had sought to give I gave:*
> *older than earth that beauty lay*
> *among fears sleeping till this day.*

She was able to write unselfconsciously about her beauty because for her it was indistinguishable from the life of nature or from poetry itself.

> *O Beauty strike not but unbind this darkness*
> *knotted in my hair that smoulders*
> *to clouds of dust and clotted light*
> *behind my tired eyes.*

> *Music shall hear me now, if I but speak*
> *and at that echo you'll turn*
> *and see me standing there*
> *suddenly naked as a scent.*

F*

But there was also a growing awareness of division in herself.

A woman resentful
in her common pride,
fear holds me down and turns
my happiness to hate;
crooning in her lustful rage
pulls down my hair and rules
my soul's uncrowned estate
while I crouch at her side,
my lot now the fool's.

Apollo, Apollo,
undo this snare again,
release me and let me
be happy in my pain. . . .

And all true lovers take this warning!
be brave and love again.

She continually wrote of herself in the third person and was obsessed by the image of two birds of prey fighting.

She was still active in many ways. As the rent was now too high for us, she suggested dividing the house into two and letting the top half. She found a carpenter who did the necessary work without removing or damaging any part of the existing structure, and let the upper storey to a newly-married Jewish couple. The husband was a furrier, and almost at once he began furious quarrels with his wife. The main point at issue, as far as we could learn from their shouted altercations, was his determination to make the wife accept his two brothers on terms that she didn't like; she insisted she had married him but not his brothers, and wasn't going to be made a mat for the three of them to trample. But, bitterly protesting, she had to give in.

One of the neighbours wrote in complaint to the house-agents, and a representative of the latter turned up one day, a wizened man in a bowler-hat, who did his best to be as sympathetic as possible to such weird clients as Elza and myself. Hatton was working the machine in the basement and I didn't like to go and tell him to stop; I expected the wizened man to ask at any moment to be shown the basement and to discover we were using the premises as a workshop. The thudding of the machine sounded to me hopelessly loud; I felt the house steadily shaking. But the man made no sign and went off, saying that he thought he could square the matter if we accepted an increase in the rent. So our profits from the furrier were almost all diverted to the house-owner.

P.R.S., looking for a hero as his firm's keystone, had come on Aleister Crowley, or Crowley had crept up on him. About 1929, the latter had taken up with Maria Teresa Ferrari de Miramar of Nicaragua, who, though married once or twice before and the mother of a child, fell heavily for him and his magic. She suggested indeed that he should get astride a unicorn and depart in secret for Jericho. He was expelled from France despite her efforts to enlist the help of the Nicaraguan consul; at Tilbury they were both locked in their cabins by the British and returned to France; they then got a visa for Belgium. (Crowley was thought a secret agent for the Germans; he had many German supporters and some dubious connections.) He wanted to marry Maria but found it difficult to get the permission of her very aged father who was somewhere in the Nicaraguan wilds. Expelled from Belgium, he went to Germany and brought the marriage off before a British consul. After that he was allowed to land in England. There he smelt the Mandrake and made for it.

His biographer states:

The directors of the Mandrake Press were Crowley's friends. Brothers Uranus and Volo Intelligere had each contributed a thousand pounds towards this venture, five hundred of which Crowley, as a gesture of independence, diverted to another struggling firm of publishers, a transfusion which helped to ruin one and was insufficient to save the other. However, during its brief run the Mandrake Press managed to bring out two volumes of the *Confessions* (which covered Crowley's life to 1903); his novel upon a theme of magic, *Moonchild*; a booklet of three stories, *The Stratagem*, and an arid apologia of Crowley, *The Legend of Aleister Crowley*, by one P. R. Stephensen, a director of the Mandrake Press. (J. Symonds)

He adds that the Press published D.H.L.'s paintings and 'also showed the originals, but the police closed the exhibition'—hardly a correct statement. I have no means of checking the details about the directors and their financing; I certainly never heard any such story at the time. The account goes on:

The *Confessions* might have paid their way, or even made some money, if the bookshops could have been persuaded to take them. But such was

Crowley's reputation that the salesman employed by the Mandrake
Press always, to their amazement, returned without any orders. Booksellers
weren't having Crowley at any price; especially with his demoniac self-
portrait on the cover and the phallus-like feature of the A for Aleister in
the oversize signature beneath it.

P.R.S.'s own account runs succinctly:

The Mandrake Press did not 'lose money'. It wound up partly because
Goldston could shrewdly anticipate that the effects of the 'Depression' in
1930 would be adverse to Limited Editions, and partly because our star
author, Aleister Crowley, was so difficult to handle that Goldston and I
sold our interests to three of Crowley's nominees, who carried it on for a
while and then wound it up.

These nominees seem the directors to whom Symonds refers.

One amusing episode suited for P.R.S.'s dashing methods occurred
in early 1930, when Crowley was billed to lecture at the Oxford University Society on Gilles de Rais. The Catholic chaplain of the University,
Father Ronald Knox, wrote to the club's secretary and the lecture was
called off. The Mandrake printed the text as a sixpenny pamphlet and
undergraduates with sandwich boards sold it in the High.

To Symonds' and P.R.S.'s accounts of the Press's demise I may add
Phil's. He was more in touch with P.R.S. and the Plough than I was at
this time:

Inky had the misfortune to start just when the limited edition mania was
dying, and his efforts to combine reprints with general publishing and
fiction proved too great a strain for the Mandrake's low finances. Wilfred
[Hanchant] had been called in, after Inky's retirement, to see if he could
salvage anything or open with a new, more lucrative programme, but it
was hopeless. . . .

I had known of Crowley in Australia through Tinny Jerdan, who later
committed suicide in London, as I tell in *The Roaring Twenties*. He had
talked about Crowley with me on Mount Tambourine, and he lent me
several of Crowley's works during my subsequent visit to Sydney. I
thus glanced through the *Equinoxes* and endless yards of verse, including
the obscene booklets. I felt Crowley a fraud at first sight, since no one
with genuine insights could be such a second-rate imitator of Swin-

burne. (The link of the self-intoxicated quality of Swinburne's poems with the Crowleyan self-deification is worth noting.) I also had had pointed out a Sydney disciple, Frank Benett, a Lancashire bricklayer, who dubbed himself Sir. Then in the fifties, he frequented the Roma Café, reputed to perform mystical dances in the nude at the rate of two to three guineas a time. He established a branch of Crowley's Order and was at Cefalu with Mary Butts.

In 1929 Maria, Crowley's wife, was drinking heavily. I met the pair of them a few times, casually, in Goldston's shop. She was a fairly well-blown woman, oozing a helpless sexuality from every seam of her smartly cut suit, with shapely legs crossed and uncrossed, and keeping all the while a sharp glittering gaze on her swarthy and unsavoury husband with his bow-tie, his staring uneasy pop-eyes, his prim lax rosebud mouth, his sallow skin and brown shaven egg-shaped head, which at the time I mistook as naturally bald. There was a mustiness about him that perhaps came from his scent of mingled civet, musk, and ambergris, which was said to have a compelling effect on women and to make horses neigh after him in the street. Maria spoke in various languages, including English, which I could not understand, and he listened attentively like a well-behaved poodle, giving an impression of uxorious dependence. However I gathered that in private she made many scenes, accusing him and his friends of attempting to poison her. After about a year he left her.

Politically, Crowley was ready to offer his system to anyone as 'the alternative to fascism and communism'—democracy being 'the political idea of Christianity in its dying phase'. In 1924 he wrote to Frank Harris, 'To put it very crudely, Industrial-Capitalism is heading for the cataract. The only alternative yet is Bolshevism, which won't do either. Now the Law of Thelema offers a Third Way. These last years I have been training various peoples to act as a Brain for the human race.' He didn't mind who his allies were, as long as they paid dividends. He asked Trotsky to put him in charge of a world-crusade against Christianity, while writing to King George V with proposals for a religious crusade led by himself. His one unchanging panacea was the use of the sex-act for reaching and realizing God.

The only allies he ever actually found were in the Nazi underworld. He had long had German connections through the *Ordo Templi Orientis*, founded in 1902 by K. Kellner and taken over by T. Reuss, who was certainly in the German secret service. Reuss called on

Crowley in 1912 and said, 'Since you know our hidden sex-teachings, you had better come into the Order and be its head for Great Britain.' Crowley accepted. During the 1914 war, in America, he expressed astonishment that the British did not appreciate his subtle tactics of writing German propaganda in such exaggerated terms as to render it ridiculous! Goldring notes:

There were other *gurus* at work during the last (1914) war and no doubt even now active in this (second) one—whose teaching might be described as 'esoteric Nazism' flavoured with the sexual perversions of the Marquis de Sade. It is significant that mages of this type almost invariably pointed to the Germans as the future 'master race'.

Phil, I mentioned, had fallen in love with Jeanne Ellis. He thus describes her at this time:

I loved her at sight when she entered (the room at Woodchurch Road) in her shy, hesitant manner, poised tiptoe as if she half-expected to be insulted and was prepared to run; and then heard her low voice, so quick that it stumbled, and she would hesitate, stuttering a little, mumbling. Her brownish curls, for (like Elza) she wore no hat, fell so far forward that they half obscured her face in an exasperating fashion; yet her blue eyes, I could see, peeped brightly at me from the shadows. Her gown was rather of the Bloomsbury fashion, narrow-hipped and wide-skirted, and of an old-gold colour. She wore no jewellery of any kind, save beads about her throat, naught but the simple gown and shoes, and appeared to me quite exquisite. . . .

Her hair was of a light chestnut colour, and fell in curls to her strong, sloping shoulders, and it took me years of pleading and bullying to entice her to draw it back from the face, for I judged that the Grecian style of hairdressing would be most suitable to her. But she wished always to hide within her hair, letting it swing forward to conceal her cheeks and vizor her eyes. . . .

His imagery is precisely correct. He catches Jeanne's guilty fears which by some subtle alchemy she transmuted into a peculiar charm, her dainty trepidations, her flaunted slink, her challenge masked as a rustling retreat, her use of modest evasions to suggest a body softly opening at the first thrust of penetration, like petals soundlessly falling apart at a bee's snuggling intrusion.

I did my best to deter him by unkindly retailing all the tales I knew of her fornications; but he was besotted. Clearly he meant to force their relations into the open, and clearly Ellis would blame me. I uneasily waited for the blow. About this time a couple of Serbs from the embassy visited Lionel's studio and we drank with them. One of them insisted that war was the ideal state of the human race. For some time I tried to draw him out, to find if he had some complicated philosophical defence of his position; but he merely grinned and kept saying, 'No, no, I just mean it's good. It's what I like.' Next day Lionel came to groan a little and lie on the cool linoleum of my floor to ease his stomach. It's the last memory I have of him.

Phil had been readmitted as press-worker, though Elza didn't want him to have his room again. I was helping him financially as much as I could, and asked Jeanne to make some little drawings for Chesterfield's *Letters*. I was now setting and printing Elza's second book of verse, *Older than Earth*. With most of the books I did the setting and Hatton the machining, though I recall toiling at the machine for long hours over the Catullus and the Herondas.

Phil had brought over some photos of Ray's paintings and I had the idea of doing a book in which the three of us collaborated. As two of the paintings dealt with the buccaneer Morgan and two others could be plausibly linked with him, I suggested Morgan as the theme. Phil wrote an essay, *Morgan in Jamaica*, and I a poem on Panama beginning, 'Thousands of parrots waited on his sleep'. (When Alec Brown read this poem, he startled me by crying out, 'I wrote that!' I thought for a moment I must have plagiarized him in a dream, then he explained, 'I mean it struck me so forcibly I felt that I ought to have'.) We did the whole of this book together, and it seemed that the real reason we had come to England and carried on the Press was to beget the collaboration.

I now went out very seldom, and almost always with Elza. We mainly went to the Kilburn cinemas, and lamented the advent of the Talkies; it seemed that the era of strong pattern and rhythmic sequence on the screen was over. (Through P.R.S. I had seen many of the early Russian films, including *Potemkin*.) We also saw the first film of a young Scandinavian, Greta Garbo, whom Elza much admired. We went to a party given by Bradley where I met Allen Lane. A very popular woman novelist was there, trying to look like a hollyhock or some simple but overgrown cottage-flower, and being coy about her books. 'One can't succeed at any level unless one is sincere,' I said. 'The populace can at least always spot insincerity.'

'O, I'm always sincere,' she said with a meek lisp, taking another cocktail, and turned back to the fair Gerhardi with his blue shirt and bluer eyes.

But in taking Elza to dine at the flat which the Atkinsons now inhabited in St John's Wood, I brought disaster on my head. Rupert, with his hair draped sideways over his head to hide the baldness, was his kindhearted and slightly distracted self, praising the virtues of colon-irrigation and exhorting me to try it. (About this time he gave Phil the £5 enabling him to start off a ménage with Jeanne.) But twice during the excellent dinner and once over the coffee, Marie slyly introduced the name of Betty May and asked me questions about her, looking surprised when I answered curtly. I didn't dare to glance at Elza, but felt sure she was taking everything in. Rupert was quite unaware of any tension; he always studiously ignored what Marie did in her spare time, and this night he was absorbed in colon-irrigation.

I suppose I must have conveyed to Elza the sinking heart with which I listened to Marie's stressed questions. As soon as we reached home, she turned on me and demanded to know why Marie had kept on referring to this Betty. I tried to pass the matter off airily, but she was now convinced that I was hiding something. All that sleepless night we continued the argument, she demanding the truth and I denying that there was anything to tell. I suppose there was a guilty weakness in my speech, which drove her to persist. But she had for some time been developing a persecution-mania, which, as usual in such cases, had a certain basis in fact; for anyone obsessed with suspicious fears inevitably becomes surrounded with ill-wishers and enemies. She had been building up a feeling of my untrustworthiness; for did I not fail to prevent all our acquaintances from turning into hostile witnesses and conspirators? She had made me the sole barrier between herself and the world; and so she felt that unless I were wholly hers, almost indistinguishable from herself, I was liable to turn into the other thing, the threatening world. She was painfully sensitive to the least movement of emotion or action on my part that seemed to break our bond and link me with the known and unknown forces lurking darkly all round her. In a sense, then, it was not my relations with Betty May that now concerned her; it was the need to find if I belonged to her or to the others. And the matter of Betty May merely sparked off the inflammatory material that had been piling up over the last year.

I could not see it like that at the time. I could only feel that I was guilty of the thing she accused me of—though I felt at the same time bitterly oppressed by the unfairness of being charged with an infidelity after having at last overcome the forces that had made me unfaithful. Again and again I told myself that I had the right to deny the charge; for if I did not deny it, I would give the effect of replacing my present self with the self who had been fascinated by the fatal-woman in Betty. I would undo all the change I had brought about in myself through pang and struggle; I would wreck everything; I would merely hurt and weaken Elza herself.

These qualms were only too true. But in the face of another endless day and night of inquisition I could not sustain my resolution. I ended by admitting that I had slept with Betty, though insisting that the whole thing was far in the past and had driven me through unhappiness into the very strengths of single-hearted devotion that Elza wanted. My explanations, pleas, assurances were brushed aside, were not listened to. Elza plunged into one of her black and numb silences, out of which she emerged to pull me down on to the couch in the big room that Phil described. But if I thought that that ended the matter, I was mistaken. At first Elza said that she was going to leave me. Instead of accepting the fact that our relation had reached an impasse, I pleaded with her for a chance to prove my change-of-heart. She insisted on my telling her every detail of my relations with Betty, and seemed both to absorb with an intense excitement, and to suffer at, any facts she could pluck out of me. Finally she said that she would stay, but that henceforth she would go everywhere with me, no matter where I went. I abjectly agreed. And at once knew that I wished her to go.

Yet the least suggestion on her part of going stirred me to a panic. The deepest emotion in me was a need to prove to her that I was now responsible; and this emotion was stronger than all my fears, irresolutions, desires to escape the whole wretched situation, to be alone and at peace with myself. Stronger even than the humiliations, the doubts I felt at the thought of being forever dogged by her, of knowing what all my friends would say: 'We were right, she has finally got him down and destroyed him—what a weakling, what a fool!' Stronger even than the desire to live. I wanted only to make reparation.

17. LAST FANFROLICO DAYS

APART from Hatton at the machine, there was now no one helping me; Lionel Ellis was the only friend I had left—that is, the only friend not excluded by Elza's system. Yet as we both revived from the exhaustion of those scenes before Christmas, I felt a certain serenity: as if the worst had happened, as if I were at last cleansed of some perilous and poisonous stuff in my bosom. All my difficulties and shames seemed unimportant beside the gains. I felt sure that it was now only a matter of time and Elza would realize the changes in me, we would come through to the tranquilly-assured bond which we both wanted. I was happy sitting in the garden on an old wooden seat, setting *Zarathustra* in Walbaum or a selection of Davenant's poems in Poliphilus.

For someone who like myself had accepted the Australian segregation of the sexes in their spheres of action and who scorned the henpecked male as the lowest specimen of his species, it was indeed a personal revolution to have broken with almost all my friends on behalf of a woman whom they disliked. I felt her to be half in the wrong; but when I tried to apportion blame or responsibility for what had happened, I was driven back on myself. All the arithmetics of guilt and innocence broke down, and I was left simply with the conviction that I could not do other than I was doing. As far as I was concerned, I was wholly responsible for the situation; to share out guilts led only to righteousness and resentment; I must work out my salvation by absolutely accepting Elza as she was, a creature of desperate anxieties. I had gone deep enough in her being to become for her the symbol of all fear and hope, and I must accept that fact or be damned for ever.

As we saw practically no one now, it did not matter that she wanted to go everywhere with me. As I was looking up various things at the B.M. and transcribing Chesterfield's letters, I got her a ticket for the Reading Room. She made notes for me and for some reason I cannot now recollect I asked her to read Otto Rank's book on the Birthtrauma. This was a sad mistake. The book much increased her psychic confusion, her sense of a primal wrong; it deepened her fear and convinced her that she had somehow been murdered. I did not at the time realize how far it had affected her, but I saw her anxieties intensified. Another book, which she read at home and which further upset her, was Hemingway's *Farewell to Arms*; the desolate conclusion and the death in childbed completed her recoil from life, her feeling of being trapped and surrounded by murderers. Sex became steadily identified with murder. Again it was to be some time before I understood what was going on in her mind.

In March D.H.L. died. I wrote a *Letter to his Spirit*, which I sent to Charley Lahrs, who said he'd print it; but it never appeared. I feel sure however that I was in too great a state of confusion to have said anything worthwhile. But at least I felt the need to make a summing-up statement, to round off the strange process that had been the dialogue of D.H.L. with all of us throughout the Twenties. Already I dimly felt that a period had come to a full-stop. No doubt much of the emotion derived from my own personal, moral, artistic and economic crisis, but in fact that crisis was at every point bound up with the larger issue, the collapse of the Twenties and all that they implied. It was simply my individual refraction of the larger issue.

Ellis blamed me for the theft of Jeanne by Phil; our friendship dissolved. If things had been normal, I should have sought him out and put my case, and we should probably have patched things up. But in my imprisoned state I accepted this last misfortune as an inevitable part of the pattern of isolation. I was finding it ever harder to run the Press. Our sales were not bad, and the £1,000 from Simpkin-Marshall had got rid of our main debts. But the burden was too much in my lonely position. I was afraid of the Press's demise, because I had no alternative method of earning money. If things had been normal, I should have turned to others—P.R.S., Edgell and Garman, or one or other of my various contacts in the publishing and periodical world. But in the circumstances I could not do that. I was enclosed by Elza's neurosis, which in some unexplained sense was my own—a complex of fears which precipitated all the feared things and made it impossible to find a way out.

However, a god-from-the-machine turned up: B., who had been a director of Simpkin-Marshall and with whom I had had dealings in that firm. He now had a publishing house of his own and asked me to come and see him. Elza and I went. He said that he was interested in having his own fine-press, but did not feel inclined to make an offer for taking over the Fanfrolico. I told him that I was thinking of calling a meeting of creditors, and he asked me to get in touch with him after that.

I called a firm of accountants in to take charge of our insolvency. Things were not in a particularly bad way. Phil records that the accountant said to him, 'This should be a banking, not a bankrupt firm.' But I was at the end of my tether. At last the creditors met and I was asked to attend. I sat on a bench outside the room, expecting to be called in. Till that moment I had not felt much about the proceedings; but there, outside the room with its faint buzz of discussion, I felt an unutterable shame and dismay, as if I had betrayed everyone. I was not called in. After a while the accountant came out and said that everyone was satisfied I had acted honourably, and had no wish to ask me any questions. I think it was above all the fact that I had used practically the whole £1,000 to meet debts and had clearly not hoarded anything whatever, that thus gained the creditors' goodwill. I am not sure how much the firm ultimately paid; but from my last contact with the accountants I think it must have been more or less twenty shillings in the pound.

I handed over all the stock, including the incompleted sheets of *Zarathustra* and Davenant, keeping only our house-furniture, the paintings by Ellis, and a few etchings by Norman. The agents accepted the relinquishment of the lease, though our tenants in the upper storey turned nasty, expecting to have their modest rent raised. We moved to a large room over a shop in Priory Road, in which our paltry things were packed, so that we could just crawl through tables and chairs to the divan. I went to see B. and he offered to finance me in a new press. The agreement was not set down on paper and was rather vague. We proposed to find a house in the country where we could install a press, which we would work for B. Meanwhile he was ready to pay me a few pounds a week against a book I wanted to write on John Donne. I had in hand about £5, and Elza had a few shillings.

Within a few days, with the aid of *Daltons*, we had found just what we wanted. Our first journey, to a site outside Chelmsford, was fruitless; then we came on a disused forge a few miles south of Dunmow, with cottage attached. By concreting the forge floor a good workroom could be created. The price was about £300. B. agreed to buy the place and to let us live in it free while our agreement operated.

We had only about three pounds a week and I could not pay the bill of the removalist who brought our things down. He held on to the paintings by Ellis—my portrait, a large nude in a sort of Venetian pastoral setting, and a sketch of Jeanne combing her hair. I wrote to Ellis asking him if possible to reclaim the pieces as I did not see how I was going to do it in any measurable future. There was no reply and I do not know if he got the letter.

18. A BACKWARD GLANCE

WHAT had we achieved in the Fanfrolico Press? Nothing, if one is to judge by the total absence of any comment in the literary records. True, we played our part in the raising of book-production standards in general, which resulted from the expansion of fine-presses in the Twenties; and we did some useful books, such as the edition of Tourneur, as well as stimulating interest in Beddoes.[1] It was in *The London Aphrodite* that we made our wider impact, and this was too unconventional a product to meet any recognition from the critics, then or later. In the U.S.A. where critics are less strangled by the public-school tie, there have been some attempts to see the magazine in a serious perspective. Thus F. J. Hoffman remarks:

. . . its exaltation of Life and its disregard of both past and future structure, has been one of the characteristics of the twentieth-century explosion. So, for example, the opening editorial of the *London Aphrodite*, edited by Jack Lindsay and P. R. Stephensen: 'We affirm Life, and for definition quote Nietzsche: Spirit is that life which cuts itself into life. We affirm Beauty, and by that term understand a sensual harmony, a homogeneous ecstasy, which, constructing intellectually, yet hates nothing so much as the dry cogs of the objectified and objectifying intellect.' (*Freudianism and the Literary Mind*, 1945)

And, pointing to *The Modern Consciousness*, he adds that 'the *Aphrodite* was perhaps the best modern exponent of Nietzsche's position'.

Still, in our Dadaism and our Integrations alike, in our neoplatonist individualism and our revolutionary glance at the proletariat, we were too violent, too intense, too out-of-step, behind the times and ahead of them, for any direct effects of our propaganda to be identifiable. We remained at root an Australian explosion in the English scene, which

---

[1] When in 1959-60 a widely-travelled exhibition of fine-press work as a tribute to William Morris was got together, our *Guenevere* was the only direct work of homage to Morris. In point of sales we were the most substantial Press by far after the Nonesuch.

politely ignored the noise, held its nose, and went on with its own business.

But the question of direct influence in the immediately succeeding years does not help us much in assessing an expression of the Twenties. Soon, with the Great Slump, there was an almost clean break in the intellectual scene. A different political and a different cultural situation arrived. Even D.H.L. went wholly out of fashion for many years; the only point raised about him during the Thirties was whether or not one should call him an outright Fascist. Huxley became an outmoded petty-liberal with an atomized view of life. Rickword dropped out of poetry. Even where there were genuine anticipations of the new phase, the work of the Twenties was ignored, e.g. no one pointed out that P.R.S. had founded Marxist literary criticism in 1928-9. True, the achievement of the Twenties, in all its diversity of positive and negative elements, necessarily underlay the struggles of the Thirties; but for the most part the participants of the new phase were too interested in getting on with their jobs to bother about their debts to the previous decade.

We may drop then the question of obvious effects, and ask instead how typical we were of the period. Looking back, one sees that for all our idiosyncracies, which provided a stumbling-block and a source of mockery for the profane, we had many points of close contact with the contemporary situation. Our aesthetic at many points was allied to Yeats'; our ethic was in some respects near to D.H.L.'s (as witness his letter to me about the rightness of my rages), though it contained some of the things he most denounced; our satiric angle often coincided with that of Douglas and Huxley, both of whom were friendly to us. Our critical dialectic had its roots in Romanticism, in Morris and in Nietzsche, but also looked to Marxism, the direct point of contact being established by P.R.S.

The main significance of the Twenties lay in the blasting force of its critical attitudes. All conventional and traditional values were questioned and put in doubt. The emphasis shifted from the meandering intellectual criticism of Shaw and Wells, with a leap into vague utopias, and from the art-for-art's-sake dissidence, with its opposition of philistinism to a rather rootless or decadent art. What emerged instead was a conviction that the whole development of society and art was wrong, and that the burden of defence had shifted from the artist to the upholder of the existing world. The new criticism varied from the passionate quest of

D.H.L. for the human essence in its uncorrupted state to the nihilistic cavillings of Douglas and Huxley; but, whether passionate or nihilistic, it regarded with scorn the entire smug set-up.

Our positions then, despite oddities, were highly typical of the period and contributed elements which were lacking in the other expressions. We can therefore claim our due place in the historical picture.

In one sense we were all phoney or confused revolutionaries; and P.R.S. initiated the awareness of this crucial point by applying words of Lenin to D.H.L. and Huxley:

Lenin's criticism applies, for example, to the raving 'transition' mob in Paris, who assume, amid a thousand other vagaries, that word-chopping and the use of lowercase for caps, is revolution. It applies also, splendidly home, to Wyndham Lewis, that fantastical 'enemy' of everything and nothing, who garbles and espouses in turn Communism, East-versus-West pictorial sociology, Shakespearean heterodoxy, and aesthetic Fascism—with photo of author and all his Press-cuttings.

Lenin's criticism applies also to a 'modern' of great literary genius, D. H. Lawrence, who in *Lady Chatterley's Lover* sets out a quasi-revolutionary thesis of attack upon the Gentry by means of sexual-social humiliation —first making the mistake of selecting the wrong opponents, for the unfortunate and dispersed English Gentry hardly matter at all now, having long been displaced from their feudal hegemony by capitalists à la Monde; and secondly, using a purely abstract weapon of attack upon the ruling class, viz. lumbar mysticism; and thirdly, not even relating his chosen characters and conflicts to actuality: making the gamekeeper an almost-gentleman with a foot in both class-camps, so that the Lady was not even properly humiliated 'from below', because she knew her lover could talk and behave like a Gentleman whenever he chose.

With various changes, the same general charges could have been made against ourselves. They could also have been made against Graves, who in *Goodbye to All That* had written: 'I had sworn on the very day of my demobilization never to be under anyone's orders for the rest of my life.' But to reject Authority in the abstract is to come back to individualism in its most egocentric form, back to the very thing that started off the chain-reaction leading into the Authority one rejects. Graves traced the experiences that brought him to rejection, but omitted the revelatory crisis and the resolving consciousness. 'No more anecdotes, and, of course, no more falsities, religion, conversations, literature, arguments, dances, drinks, time, fun, unhappiness. I no longer repeat to myself: "He who shall endure to the end shall be saved." It is enough that I have endured.' That is stoic *apatheia*, but reduced to the point of low intensity in which not only the world of struggle, but the whole world of ideas is renounced; and Graves has remained remarkably true to his oath, his creative work showing intellectual activity without the intrusion of a single idea (in any comprehensive, dynamic, or organizing sense). A strange rigour. The revolutionary emotion is maintained in a vacuum; a conviction of integrity is preserved by a ceaseless hysterical *noli me tangere* masquerading as uncommitted judgment. (From a different angle the *noli* cry was deep in D.H.L.) Lenin had summed up these attitudes as specially characteristic of the 'the petty-bourgeois "gone mad" from the horrors of capitalism' with all 'the weakness of such revolutionism, its futility, its liability to transform itself into obedience, apathy, fantasy, and even into a "mad" infatuation with some bourgeois "craze"'.

I have already discussed the way in which Heseltine fled from his deepgoing sense of a wholly corrupted world into a sort of deliberate schizophrene condition. Here we must look at his end, in which awareness of his betrayal of life caught up with him. The way in which this awareness struck him was closely parallel to the way in which I had broken down under Elza's attack; he too felt his error, not in its wider social bearings, but in the attitudes to women which it had brought about.

He had been depressed at Collie's death by galloping consumption; and he found his sources of income drying up. The song market had been spoiled by radio, and he had largely used up the sort of music he wanted to transcribe. (For his last work of transcription, the brilliant version of Giles Earles MS book, which was published after his death, I can claim some credit, since I had introduced him to the MS by asking him to copy out and edit the music for *Tom o'Bedlam*.) His many schemes, for a magazine and for opera, broke down; he asked Victor Carne to help him to a job in Columbia Gramophones; he wanted to write notes for classic recordings, and act as adviser, and offered as a start to conduct gratis his own *Capriol Suite*. The wage he asked was £5 a week; he was turned down. He applied to various official seats of musical learning; and again was turned down. He burst out in fantasy-schemes such as letting caves in Kent and Sussex to flagellants. And his spirits hovered between the hope of a new start and the conviction of doom. From a farm in Hampshire he wrote:

I have a hopeful premonition of something extremely fortunate making its way towards me. In any case I shall live no more in London unless I have some definite work to keep me there. . . . I shall sell practically everything I have except a few books, and then set out afresh, without impedimenta to tie me long in one place—and hope for the necessary god to descend from his machine.

He had returned to the mood of 1919-20, but without its social consciousness. He wanted a wholly new start, but was afraid of what the effort implied. He turned back to a girl he had loved some eleven years before, and turned back to Delius. In a letter of June 1930 to the girl W.B. we find him still yearning to get away from the London of evil and trying to realize what flaw had made him fail love:

On that miraculous day, now more than two months past, when I was with you in those lovely places, I was so oppressed by the beauty of it all— and you were the key to it and all the downs and rivers and birds were you —that I was quite inarticulate, and even a little afraid of you and all the loveliness around me. . . . I know now—and you have known always, I believe—that in failing you I have deliberately betrayed my own soul and all the faculties of mind and spirit. I do not pretend to understand the source of the appalling perversity in my nature that has caused me now for years, with deliberate and callous cruelty, to torment and persecute that only precious part of myself, which is you, until I know not now whether the semblance of its death is death its very self and no semblance at all.

He says that he cannot understand why he betrayed, reviled, mocked, and ill-used her 'with a barbarity that must surely have been implanted in me by the fiends of Hell'. He keeps on examining himself and is tormented.

And though you who know my heart have known that I was so encompassing my own destruction, I am writing this because I want to make full confession to you myself, kneeling at your feet, not for forgiveness but that you may know that all my cruelties have come back to revenge themselves on me, and because my one remaining joy is in the awareness of the horrors of my past actions as revealed by the anguish I am suffering at this memory of them—and I like to hope that awareness is itself a sign that I am in some measure expiating them.

I cite this letter because it brings out so poignantly the inner conflict which Heseltine had been striving to hold down all those years, and because it shows him in an emotional fix extraordinary like mine at the same moment. Both of us were forced by the logic of events to pull ourselves suddenly up and recognize that the dynamic on which we had been relying enclosed an unrealized or evaded cruelty. Heseltine, unable to bear the strain, put out the cat, and gassed himself. The door was broken in on the morning of December 17th; he had feared to face the Christmas which he loathed and for which he set so many carols. He had failed to link his remorse over personal cruelties with the sense of a murderous world which had obsessed him in the years leading up to 1920. I also was failing to make the same sort of correlation for myself; but by enduring to the end I was to make it, not telling myself it was enough to have endured.

There is an odd similarity in the way the various persons with a displaced revolutionary emotion whom I have discussed all used a woman in order to objectify their needs and define their positions. Heseltine used W.B. to turn back the whips upon himself; D.H.L. used Frieda to dramatize his inner conflicts; Graves used Laura to bring to a head his desire to say farewell to all that; and I in the same sense used Elza to ensure that I should accept no half-measures, no egoisms disguised in highfalutin terms.

D.H.L. fought out his conflicts to the bitter end. Heseltine devised his schizophrenic mode of life to sever art and struggle; his deepest experience had been his revolt against the forces making for war and the city of corruption; but his art expressed nothing of this. The deepest experience of Graves was the discovery of the human hell revealed by war and the rejection of the authority that permitted and needed such a hell. But after his first recoil from the inhumanities of the war in France, his art expressed nothing of this. His novels do not raise even in abstracted forms the problems of his discovery and rejection. By a creed of *apatheia* he was able to seal down the crevasse, now and then opening small cracks in his poems and hastily closing them up again.[1]

---

[1] Though the method flattens his novels and makes him a bizarre critic flying off at any tangential point, it has worked well for the kind of verse he wanted. I

Heseltine, living more dangerously, found the mask of Warlockism break up in his hands; but by then the split had gone too far. He could only dream of regeneration and die.

I think what I have said above touches the innermost conflicts of the Twenties, its creative liberations and its limitations. A necessary part of the spiritual scene was the scepticism, the withering ironies, of Norman Douglas[1] and of Huxley; but whereas Douglas stuck out stubbornly for a hedonist egoism as providing a stable basis for the exposure of the irrationality and falsity of the social situation (atomized into its idiotic details), Huxley was aware of the insufficiencies of this position and tried to use the ironic method to state the inner conflicts developing underneath. In *Antic Hay* he found the finest balance between the witty exposure and the disconcerted yearning for some kind of integration; and

notice, as I write, a review of *More Poems*: 'He is thus a great rhetorician. The thoughts in his poems are always sprung on us in their purest possible shape and at their moment of maximum impact. It is a technical mastery which goes with a complete openness to experience, a resolve to find, not impose, form . . . [He] does not write poetry so much as find poems, a succession of separate victories for spontaneity, propitiations of the White Goddess of changeable love and unpremeditated experience. . . . As an artist he never repeats himself and never develops.' (P. N. Furbank, *Listener*, May 18, 1961). I agree with the proviso that the 'maximum impact' is that of a momentary concentration and dispersion of personality, not that of the whole man in consistent struggle with life. (When I knew him he was still haunted by terror-dreams; many of the poems of the Twenties record nightmares of a strangling kind.)

[1] Though N.D. would have snorted angrily at the idea that he had a social conscience, such a conscience underlay much of his indignation. In Florence, the conversation having turned on excessive legal penalties, I mentioned a Sydney dentist who around 1900 had been hanged; it had been found that, when he gave women gas, he cut off a small bit of their pubic hair and gummed it in a book with their names added. There was no evidence that he did more than that. N.D. was strongly affected by the story, kept on repeating it, asked me to tell it to Mrs Compton-Mackenzie, and so on. (I did not meet him again till 1944 when I was stationed in London and Nancy Cunard asked me to lunch with him. I found him shrunken and cantankerous, but saw him a few times to listen to his rages against wartime conditions and Britain in general. A few years later he wrote me some words of liking for an essay on Fairies in *Life and Letters*, on a card of Nancy's from Capri.)

Even Nina who seemed always as impervious to a general idea as anyone can well be, had her brief revolt under the influence of Gaudier-Brzeska. 'Henry knew five languages and translated for me' at an anarchist meeting in Soho before the 1914 war. 'I did not know much about anarchy but I thought that any kind of revolt against anything was good. I decided that it was dreadful not to have been born in Whitechapel and that the proletariat were the only people who were capable of anything.'

it is significant that the material of this work owed so much to Heseltine-Warlock. After that his work weakened; for he was losing his ironic bases without effectively building up any lyrical integrations. (At root this is what P.R.S., analyses about him in the *Aphrodite* and what I wrote to him of *Point Counter Point*.) Hence the way in which he turned to D.H.L., and then, unable to use his formulas without becoming a mere echo, to pacifist yogi-ism, in a revulsion from the sterile intellectualism he had landed in.

Huxley thus faded out along a side cul-de-sac. D.H.L., with all his limitations, held the centre of the picture, seeking in the last resort for what remained truly human in a dehumanized capitalist world, despite the cash nexus and all its deadening routines and mechanizations. And I think that although we made our attack on him, partly stupid and partly attempting to sift away the maddened and confusing element in his work, we were on his side and in many ways close to him. P.R.S. made one of the possible logical steps when he moved in the Mandrake to the championship of Lawrence; his misfortune was that Lawrence was near his death and could not provide much further ammunition in the fight.

It seems to me, then, that we did have a valid place in the decade and that if we are left out of the picture the intelligibility of that world is lessened.

One important writer has been omitted from the above generalizations: Edith Sitwell. Her early brilliant developments of what I called the colour-image, the new concentrations on the basis of the Rimbaudian derangement-of-the-senses, developed by 1928 into *Gold Coast Customs*, in which she brought out all the social relations inherent in the aesthetic struggle she was waging. This process of hers was an expression of what I was talking so much about, the deepening of the Image of Beauty; but I somehow missed *Gold-Coast Customs* at the time. In this I merely reflected the *zeitgeist*; for that poem did not affect the movements of the Thirties, to their great impoverishment. However the development from *Façade* to *Gold-Coast Customs* (with its seminal image, its author has told me, in a blackened death-dance figure in a Hunger March) was of the highest significance, and revealed precisely and deeply the creative pattern which underlay the Twenties, though almost all the writers failed to find it in its fullness in their work. Edgell Rickword, who had initiated the poetic exploration of the city of alienation, stopped writing poetry after he arrived at Marxism. A great misfortune: for if he had persisted, he might well have kept intact the links with what was

vital in the Twenties, and thus have deepened the whole poetic movement of the Thirties.[1]

[1] Of the other persons who come in the narrative, Moeran and Lambert
drank heavily and thus destroyed themselves; Lambert was strong enough to
survive into the post-war world but had dissipated his lively talent. Philip
Owens, whose *Marlowe* never got past the proof-stage in our Press, wrote
Portrait of a Nobody during the Thirties and was killed in the war in a jeep on
Mytilene, serving in Intelligence. Brian Penton returned to Australia and became
editor of *The Sydney Morning Herald*, dying of cancer. P.R.S., after various
literary exploits, founded a nationalist party, and spent the war-years in a
concentration camp. In a sense he was trying to live through D.H.L.'s *Kangaroo*,
bring it true. Nina survived into the 1950's, still resolutely and toughly living
as in the Twenties. I last saw her about a year before her death, a sadly shabby
sight, in a Soho winebar. I am told that 'hauntings' by Crowley played a main
part in driving her to her death through a window.

AFTER

_19._ FORGE COTTAGE

We were happy settling in. The cottage had two rooms below and a small kitchen, two rooms above. There was a large open fireplace into part of which a range had been put. Next door was the family of a farm-labourer, with whom we became friendly. A few more cottages, a pub, and a farm with outbuildings made up the hamlet of Onslow (or Hounslow) Green. Once B. came down to inspect. He approved of the place and I had a few beers with him at the pub: the only time I went in. He paid for the forge to have a concrete flooring, but went on delaying about the despatch of a press. I had told him that I would start work as soon as the press arrived. He was in fact drinking hard and was not, I think, doing well as a publisher; he had started in the midst of the slump and did not have any knowledge of books apart from a certain trade-gumption acquired in the wholesalers.

We came to know most of the people around. The old parson looked apologetically in and we had a chat about the Cappadocian Fathers and about Donne. There was also a retired civil-servant who lived in a large house about a mile off and who tried to act the role of Lord of the Manor, scoffed at by the villagers. One of the neighbouring women told us that he used to get into the cottages by asking for a glass of water, then he'd make a grab at the woman of the place. She added that when he tried to put his hand up her skirt, she said, 'Lemme alone, you dirty old sod. I'm one man's whore and that's enough.' She was a handsome merry woman who might have come out of a medieval _fabliau_, broad in the beam, brown as a nut, honest as the day, and quite shameless. Elza liked her and her bawdy sayings. 'The parson's given up asking me to church,' she said. 'Last time I farted in the middle of his sermon. I didn't mean to be rude, you know, he's a dear old boy, but I got to dozing, and when I doze I don't know what I'm doing. Lucky it wasn't worse.' She gave her gusty rusty laugh.

There were tales of the last proper Lord of the Manor, a great cussing character, who once rode his horse into church and who had a score of bastards. In a tumbledown cottage a few miles to the west there lived a widowed man with his three daughters. They all slept together and one of the girls had a child which everyone said was her father's. The youngest of the three frowsy tattered girls used to hang about the back door of the pub on a Saturday night, offering herself to the men who came out to visit the Gents. Her price was sixpence. 'She makes up to five bob on a good night,' said our bawdy friend. 'Not to be sneezed at these hard times. I'd consider it myself, only that old Bob of mine is that particular, he'd say I was getting myself talked about.' She and Bob were a happy loving couple, without a care in the world, it seemed to us, except when the slugs got at their cabbages.

There was also an idiot girl who roamed about and stood staring at nothing. One day I found her staring in at the window while I sat typing. She didn't answer when I spoke; she had a cleft palate. But Elza gave her some biscuits and she went away, chewing one and putting the others in her torn blouse. 'She's handy for them that are too mean to pay sixpence,' said our bawdy friend. 'There's a lot of mean sods round here, you'd be surprised. Sometimes I think it's awful being a woman, only Bob wouldn't like it if I wasn't, so I shut my trap and put up with things.' With a broad wink and a great laugh that swung the loose breasts in her loose blouse.

There was also an old witch who drove over from the Rodings in a decrepit cart with a bony horse on its last legs. She went slowly past, with many creakings and clatterings, talking to herself and now and then shaking the reins. The kids watched her in subdued awe, from a safe distance. She sold herb medicines. 'Relieves you of your rheumatiz and gets young hussies out of trouble, sometimes anyway. I never tried her. I'm one of those that like trouble, I can't get enough of it.'

The old rustic life was still thriving in the hamlet; and Elza felt at home in it. We had quickly taken roots here as we hadn't at Alphamstone or Takeley, perhaps because I wasn't spending part of the time in London and because the hamlet had its own close-meshed communal life. Elza was stimulated to start a novel on Saturday Night at a pub; but she could not sustain a long work in prose and after a while she took to dictating it to me. I revised the completed thing—one can hardly call it a novel; it was more an extended documentary account, with a very slight story—but nine-tenths of the result was Elza's. I wondered where she had gained her knowledge of what a country pub was like;

for neither here nor at the other Essex places had we drunk in the local.[1]

About this time on a visit to London to give some information which the accountants dealing with the Press wanted, I called in with Elza at the exporters, W. Jackson, off Chancery Lane—I forget why! they must have written with some queries about their stock. Elza mentioned her book; they asked to see it; they liked and published it.

I was myself working at my book on Donne, which kept running away with me. From a biography it wandered into an extensive commentary on the poems; from a commentary on the literary aspects it meandered into a psycho-analytical study and then into a long prose-poem which attempted to show the stages by which the reckless witty *libertin* became the devoted lover of Anne More. The thing grew huge and unwieldly, and in my disturbed and bewildered state of mind I could not devise a clear scheme on which to cut and rewrite. I was trying to find where I was myself going, by the exploration and elaboration of Donne's stages; and without knowing my own destination I was creating a wilderness of analysis on the pretence of mapping out Donne's spiritual progress. When at last I sent the MS in desperation to B., he didn't know what to make of it.

But very soon afterwards he died. Whisky and anxiety had proved too much. My two or three pounds a week abruptly ended, and it was only a question of time before the house was sold up over our heads. I managed to place one article, in a weekly, *Everyman,* but had no other luck. I was determined not to appeal to those who had been my friends but whom I had allowed Elza to exclude, Edgell, Brian, P.R.S., or Phil. I felt that I had no right. Having accepted Elza's control of the circumstances of my life, I had to find my way forward within the terms of that control or perish. The matter was so simple that I do not recall debating it at all in my mind; I merely accepted it without question as the premise on which any action must proceed.

On top of these disasters Elza suddenly, without any discussion, decided that at all costs she must have Robinetta. This was the first time she had mentioned the girl since she called on Edith Craig. There had been nothing to stop her having the child with us at Woodchurch Road

[1] She had written a short tale for the *Aphrodite,* obviously a piece of direct autobiography, about a starving girl who wanders in the streets, at last is driven to make a pick up, yet, when the man leaves in the morning, cannot bring herself to ask him for money.

as far as I was concerned; there was a large house and garden. But with
my many problems pressing in on me, I had not suggested it; I felt
that any decision must come from Elza. I did not ask myself if it was
fear of me that prevented her from proposing the child's return;
besides, she had become so self-assertive after driving the Pentons out
that there seemed no reason to doubt that if she had wanted the child
she would have raised the matter.

Despite my difficulties I rather welcomed Elza's demand. I told myself
that the child would produce an easing of the situation. She would
stand between Elza and me; and Elza's affection for her would surely
have the effect of breaking down her own intransigence, of ending her
'imprisonment' of me, and of letting me out 'on parole' in quest of the
necessary money for the household. I wrote in Elza's name to Edith
Craig.

No reply came. I was surprised, as I had understood that Robinetta
was to be returned whenever Elza asked for her. Though we could ill
afford it, we made a trip to London and called at Miss Craig's address;
but were told that she was away. We realized that she had no intention
of returning Robinetta, whether that had been her intention from the
start or she had come to it in the process of looking after the child (who
was attending a semi-dance school at Hampstead). We wrote to Robert
and he offered Elza his support; other persons whom Elza made an
effort to involve did not reply.

Elza told me that I must get the child. I think she expected me to
kidnap her, but I said that we would go to a solicitor at Braintree. We
walked across, through Felstead, where I lingered a few moments to
look at the old buildings, and went into the first solicitors' office we
saw. We could not have made a better choice in all England; for the
elderly man who listened to us was won over by Elza and threw himself
heart and soul into our cause. Except for some fees to Counsel we never
paid anything; we never received any bill. The solicitor knew that we
could not have met it. He advised us that our only recourse was a
Chancery suit.

The suit went on a couple of years. Many of the countless affidavits
and statements were drawn up by myself, and merely re-typed at the
office. Elza had worked herself up into a state of deep angry tension,
which she vented on me. She clearly now looked on me as a weakling, a
useless person unable to reclaim her child from an unjust world, unable
to make a living. I felt a certain bitter satisfaction in knowing that my

futility derived in large part from the impotence she imposed on me; she wanted to have me her slave and at the same time a strong man. I knew how she resolved the opposition: if I loved her truly, I would be both entirely hers and strong. I agreed with that thesis, but felt that she was inhibiting me from being 'entirely hers' in any free and vital sense by trimming our relationship into rigid rules and expressing her insistence that I should be a complete lover by a flat distrust of me. The least attempt on my part to argue this point of view produced in her a blind rage and convinced her that I wanted to escape once more into irresponsibility.

I tried to understand why I had given in to her pressure and 'confessed'. There is always, I thought, an element of revenge in a confession: the classic Dostoevskian position. One confesses in a hope of purging one's guilt, of spreading the guilt out, of proving that in the last resort society itself, the family and all that conditions the family, are the guilty things, having made one what one is. One hopes to gain a new start. But the element of resentment, making the confession an accusation as well as a plea, at once cripples one. One pre-supposes that the listener (the wronged lover, the police inspector, the whole damned world) is going to feel exactly the same mixture of emotions as oneself, will reach out to embrace one and bring about an identity of aspiration: the same rejection of the past, the same intense desire for a new life, a new heaven and a new earth. But this embracing union of confessor and listener is about the last thing likely to come about. The listener wants a different set of pledges, while the confessor feels the act of confessing itself to be the proof of his deep need for a regenerated self.

Re-reading *Hereward*, I saw how I had there forecast just what I was going to do. I felt all the more confused, as if throughout I had schemed for the exposure of myself, as a strange test of us both, a test I still could not understand. At the play's climax Torfrida discovers Hereward's entanglement with Alftruda, and he protests:

> Hereward: *I feared to break because I feared to bring*
> *this pain upon you that I've brought at last—*
> *but it's your fault. Why was your heart so hard?*
> *I would have come then and confessed to you.*
> Torfrida: *No man confesses.*
> Hereward: *But I would, I would.*
> *It has been beating fists in every pulse,*

thumping upon my life like terrible messengers—
ah, can you understand what it is like
to have your life a room with many doors
and terror knocking madly on every door?
That's what it's been. If but I could have told you—
why was your heart so hard?
Torfrida: *You never tried....*

They upbraid one another, with Alftruda mocking them. Torfrida goes and Hereward turns gladly to meet his death of betrayal.

Yet when the time came, I had not wanted to die, as my Bussy and Hereward had. The *liebestod* had lost its glamour; the romantic basis of my poetry had fallen away at the crucial point, and I was left with an unsolved problem. I was alive, and enduring. What I carried over from the previous phase was the belief that I must never impose a solution on my conflicts. Desire was good; all will was self-will and evil. For it worked by seeking to impose a solution, a goal, a system, on others, and so must work out as self-righteousness and dogmatism, as parasitism and powerlust. My only hope was that by desiring harmony and union I would break down self-will in Elza, in whom since Takeley it had burst ever more strongly out.

I had to keep working in the hope of writing something that would sell, though I could not plan anything on the basis of making it marketable. As I had no belief in my own prose, I took the drawings Norman had made for Abercrombie's *Phoenix* and which had never been used. I shut my eyes and shuffled them up, then I set myself to work out a story to correspond to the new sequence. I hoped that I would be able to sell the result on the strength of the illustrations. For a character sufficiently like the girl in *Phoenix*, and yet different, I chose Cressida, Phil's great love; he had written a short verse play in Australia, *Cressida's First Lover*, and I decided to steal this title, as he had done nothing with his play.

I was about half-way through when Elza suddenly deepened her attack. I had noticed that she was growing more hostile and difficult, suffering a revulsion from sex altogether and yet caught in a half-dream that some simple earth-love, a peasant-force, might awaken her body and fulfil it as none of her lovers had done, as I had failed to do. Something like the unexpurgated version of D.H.L.'s tale *Sun* as a day-dream (which in fact it was anyhow on D.H.L.'s part: though he saw himself as the peasant and Elza saw herself as the woman-to-be-earthily-awakened). Now the revulsion-aspect triumphed, and henceforth there were never any physical relations between us. But the rejection of sex was the least furious of the attitudes she now turned on me. I had failed to get her back her child, I was a failure in all repects. I was a liar who had not succeeded in cleansing and freeing myself from all the hellish aftermath of the birth-trauma. I must now proceed to become fully sane.

'You are hiding behind your beard,' she said. The remark was true enough, but she had forgotten that she made me grow it. She borrowed a razor from the farm-labourer next door and I shaved. She tore up several of my books which had drawings by N.L. in them. She wanted to get rid of anything of the past. She gave my one warm coat—that which Gruner had given me—to the farm-labourer.

With my shaven face I did indeed feel strangely naked. I agreed with her in general that I still had far to go before I had fully sloughed my old self; but I could not see what more I could do at the moment. The mere fact of being the person who had the responsibility of making money, so that we could survive, had a tightening-up effect; it prevented me from entire surrender, from letting go and dying and becoming a new man. Her answer was that I had no business to take on myself the responsibility of money when I shelved the responsibility of becoming a whole-man, a man freed from the curse of the past. Let money go to hell.

We had long arguments. I clung to the general scheme of my Australian notion of life: the man for action (in its pure form, creation), the woman for love and children, the home. The man begets the creative image, the woman the child. Elza's retort was that woman's capacity to bear children did not affect the essential fact that her personality was humanly no different than the man's; she too could be creative. There was no simple line of sex-division; sexual characteristics were secondary.

I wanted to accept her viewpoint, but couldn't. Every idea I had of life and art broke down if I did. I had given up my thesis of the poet at the mercy of his instincts and impulses. Using John Donne as my admired examplar, I now accepted the true progress as from the Libertine who loves the Centrique Part in any woman, in a kaleidoscopic world of variable Venus, to the Truelove of a single woman, who, as a living centre, illuminates the rest of the universe, including all other women. But I could not go further and say it was male vanity and sexual fear which differentiated between the sexes at all and allotted them different functions. I was now nearing the D.H.L. idea of sex as my final defence.

But all the while something in me was breaking up. My ideas grew more and more entangled and uncertain. I could neither revise my Donne book nor finish my *Cressida*. I no longer had any stable basis on which to evalue event or construct character. All personality seemed built on false premises, an unsafe structure flimsily set up on quicksands; consciousness as I had known it, a total false-face, an illusion pasted over an illusion. Nothing was real but the need to crawl as far back as possible down the tunnel of memory, to the very mouth of the womb. If one could only somehow repeat the birth-experience inside the focus of one's consciousness of failure, of warped patterns, then one could perhaps correct what had gone wrong, get a really fresh start from the very first moment of the blast of light, of joy-pain, of hope-fear, of life-death. Every other way allowed the primal flaw to reassert itself in unrealized forms, however earnest the wish for a new start might be.

I decided to fast in the belief that privation, by permitting no alleviations of the anxiety, the backward-quest, was the only sure guide to the depths, to the light-in-darkness. I retired to bed upstairs, taking with me some bread and lemon-water, and fasted. Exactly how long I stayed there, I am not sure; for after the first few days I lost count of time; but it must have been at least a fortnight, perhaps three weeks or more. Now and then Elza brought me some water in which lemon-slices had been dropped; otherwise I had nothing. After the first few days I did not feel any hunger. But in my dreamy lost state I found it hard to concentrate. Just as I would seem to be nearing some significant trauma or twisted wound in my remote past, my mind slid away and I drifted from one vague dissolving image to another. When I regained control of my thought-processes, I felt hopeless. The traumatic spot (assuming that it existed and I did manage to come near it) was impregnable. Without concentration I could not break through the intense resistances; with it I would not drop slowly down to the hidden levels where the wound festered.

After I had been about a week abed, Elza came hastily up one morning and said, 'Alec Brown is here.' I dressed myself as quickly as possible: that is, pulled on shirt, trousers and shoes, and went down. I felt rather shaky and light-headed, but did my best to disguise my condition. Alec was driving through to his home-area in Norfolk, Diss, and was full of cheerful talk about his work. All I can remember is saying that I meant to write a book about local characters and ways of life, calling it *Roundabouts Dunmow*; for later, seeing that I did not use the title, he published a book *Chadwick Roundabouts*. I could not avoid eating a little while he was with us; but as soon as he had gone, I stripped and retired to bed again, resuming my fast.

Now, however, some images did persist and seem to be really drawn up from my submerged self. I saw myself walking in a small public garden just after Ray was born; he was being wheeled down the path in his pram by my mother, a lacy Victorian figure, and I fell down some stone steps on to my face. Further back, when I was about one, a curtain caught fire above my cot and blazed whirling red and black into the window. . . . Gradually I seemed to be nearing the birth-moment. At last, after hours of wrestling with obscurely violent sensations, my body caught in rhythmic pangs, I leaped from bed and ran to a mirror. Frantically I searched my face and found thin white scar-lines, almost indecipherable but brought out by the seething of the blood around them. I was convinced that I had found where instruments had torn my throat and lower face in dragging me from the womb, and that I had had a very difficult birth. (I did not get out of bed with any idea of looking for the lines; I was simply driven to the mirror; and only when I saw the lines did the idea of birth-scars come to my mind.)

Now, I have no conviction as to whether I had indeed forced myself, in my fasting condition, back to the earliest level of memory in the completed organism, or whether I had desperately fabricated the images in order to prove to myself and Elza that I was regenerated. (If the latter case were true, I must have noticed the scars unconsciously and now used them as definite evidence of my return. I later wrote a little of these experiences of mine to Jack Elkington, whom someone, my mother I think, had mentioned as being present at my birth. But instead of answering any of my questions, he riposted with one of his own: Had I been taking drugs? I presume that he had in mind the fact that some drugs can produce a series of birth-images such as we find in Coleridge's *Kubla Khan*.)

I called Elza and tried to persuade her that I had now come to the end of my quest. She turned a stony face on me. I went back to my fast. Now I no longer made any effort to direct my thoughts and a strange series

G*

of images rose and drifted before me, changing from the microscopically exact to the incoherently vast: great deserts and cosmic wastes. (No doubt a prolonged fast, under conditions of extreme anxiety, can act in much the same way as drugs. My theory later was that it released the accumulated toxins in organs like the heart and the liver, which had an intoxicating effect in the literal sense of that term. The toxins were brought out and cleared away; the visions were of the vanishing evils of the body.) I saw enormous skies of cataclysm, Turnerian in colour at the outset, and slowly hardening into a lurid coppery glow. A skurry of countless forms, cosmic tadpoles and starry viruses, a mad descent of the damned. The small spikes and blobs expanded hugely, then contracted to points again and fell to a level somewhere below my sight, where I could yet see them in a painfully oblique angle. My broken body flapped like slow wings over the infinitesimally tiny forms in their ant-trail of busy fury across the abyss. Great coppery suns set in ragged crevasses. Apocalyptic imagery: sudden storm and flight of flashing angelic figures in battle with dark cloud-veering shapes. Then nothing but geometric forms breaking and revolving round a lost centre, perpetually on the edge of attaining a perfect balance, which I feared. Once the symmetry interlocks, all things will end. Then back to the cosmic spaces, myself crushed between mating earth and sky.

Some of the images may have been drawn from art, others constructed out of mythology; but the experience was none the less disturbing and engrossing. In my weakened condition there were long periods of dull lassitude. I floated with outstretched wings over the void and was not interested; then came moments of extreme urgency when life-and-death (of myself, of all things) depended on the outcome. My son, in whom I am well pleased. And dark mocking laughter. Day and night as one, a slow alternation of shaken patterns, howevering on the point of chaos or of interlocked immobility. All the while Elza said nothing, though she came up at moments to look at me with an inscrutable challenge and contempt. I longed for one word of encouragement.

Finally, one afternoon, in a sudden long wave of coppery light, I saw the over-life-size figure of an Egyptian goddess with lion-head, Tefnut or Mehi-t, at the other end of the room. At the same time the form seemed Betty May lion-headed, standing in majestic unconcerned power, a strange animal-power, not malign, yet terrible in its predatory innocence. I saw the form in a preternatural sharp light which revealed every detail in a flat microscopically-near precision. I saw every hair of the lion-face, every pore of the large coarse milky breasts. At the moment of vision I had no fear, no belief or disbelief; I merely saw. All my being was absorbed in the act of seeing. Then I leaped out of bed. The image vanished. I was afraid. I ran for the window and stared at the roadway of common traffic with tremendous love and relief. No one was in sight. Then a dog passed across at the end near the farm. I loved the dog. I loved the world and wanted to escape from the pointless hell of my own mind with its vicious circle of remorse. If I had reached the stage of projecting my images as apparently real things I had better stop before I went mad. I went slowly downstairs, found some milk and drank it.

I told Elza that I was cleansed of my illusions; I had realized my relation to my father and my mother; it had been the failure to achieve this realization that had driven me along a compulsive path of romantic self-dedication, with a dream of *liebestod*. All the while I had been running away from my responsibility to my mother; I had feared to face my failure to take charge of her in the helpless state into which she had fallen when I was about fourteen; I had put myself at the service of the father who had thrown her into her lost misery; by accepting his ethereal art-message I had felt redeemed from the earth-fate of my mother. Woman, what have I to do with you? I am doing my father's business. I had been relieved of my sense of guilt by a deepening of guilt, by making the guilty act seem the affirmation of a higher need, an overriding justice. What I had thought my creativeness was a false intoxication proceeding from my passion, my mysterious crucifixion under the father's will. But at the very heart of my acceptance of that will there had been a slowly growing revolt, an effort to understand the truth. I had turned to her, Elza, because I recognized in her my lost mother; I had wanted to redeem her from her trampled desolation. But I had been unable to grasp this impulse in its fullness except by the dramatization of my inner struggle through the conflicting claims of Elza and Betty—Janet now being obliterated as the image of the father-submission I rejected. It was therefore wrong to penalize me for my 'betrayal', which had been my only way forward to a complete devotion. Without it I could never have shocked myself into facing the truth of my relation to my parents. Now I was free from the repetition-compulsion uttered in my art-theories, my romantic concept of the relation of art and life.

As an expression of my belated defence of my mother, I wrote an angry letter to Norman. I think it must have been Phil who told me that

N.L. contemplated reducing my mother's not-large allowance (£5 a week was all she ever had to bring up us three boys and keep herself) on the grounds that her sons now made their own living. I am now not at all sure how definite the rumours of reduction were; but it suited me in my present mood to accept them. I wrote to N.L. accusing him of various meannesses towards my mother and demanding that he should not reduce the allowance. I assume that he got the letter and tossed it aside. He did not reply.

Though I was making the mistake of seeing my whole life as a mere projection of unrealized relations to my parents and of thus omitting the society in which the family operated, I had learned important truths about myself, without which I should never have made any decisive steps forward. And I owed these truths wholly to the relentless pressure that Elza had put on me. Previously, in discussing Freud, I had said: There seems a great deal of truth in his work—in his dynamic concepts of the unity of the psyche and in his subtle web of associations, in his understanding of the nature and action of symbols; but for the life of me I can't see how the Oedipus Complex applies to myself; I have no feeling one way or another about my mother—though I can see how the Complex has a wide application.

Now I felt that whatever was the case with other people I certainly was a perfect example of the Complex. I had been left by the disappearing (dying) father with my mother as the head of the family; and a peculiarly strong tension had been brought about as she lay increasingly helpless (at my mercy) from my puberty onwards. I was the family-head (father) with my two young brothers and my mother looking to me; and I had been driven into ever-deepened revulsion from the position by my mother's collapse, which I did not know how to deal with. Inevitably then I was psychically in the classic role of Oedipus.

I expected Elza to turn to me now with happiness and say that the basis for a stably harmonious relation had been reached. But she merely listened with an aloof critical interest, as though I had had the first glimmerings of sanity but was not at all yet to be trusted. In an effort to find external verifications of my change-of-heart I burned all my MSS I could lay hands on: the many plays and poems written in both Australia and England, which had not yet been published, and surrealist novel, the translations of Essenin, and so on. I also burnt all the letters I had been keeping, of which the most important were those of N.L., Norman Douglas, and Gordon Bottomley. But no holocaust had the least effect in moving Elza. And I began to doubt my own sincerity. Was I acting like this because I really wanted to cut all past connections? or was I only trying to placate Elza? Her disbelief in me had the effect of creating afresh a division inside myself. I did not yet suspect how deep were her fears, how hopeless was the task I had set myself.

Once she said, 'Your eyes are sane while you're working.' I should have understood how all her energies were taken up in watching me. All her fears and revulsions had become concentrated in me; and I was therefore the last person in the world who could help her to throw them out and to become stable. I was in the position of a psycho-analyst who has seduced, cheated, and betrayed his patient, and who then cannot understand why the processes of transference fail to work. The more he tries to detach the patient from himself and return her in a balanced state to the world, the more he awakens her distrust. And in my case the situation was made yet more involved by the fact that I was simultaneously attempting the decisive analysis of myself and that the world to which the patient had to return was my own bed and bosom.

I had some vague understanding of the impasse already, and as things went on I saw it all clearly enough. But always it seemed too soon or too late to insist on a break. The uttered or unuttered threat of suicide always stayed my hand. Besides, it was not so easy to affect my own transference. The more difficult things became, the more I felt that I was facing a test, an ordeal, which I must accept if my humanity were not to perish. For a few years the mirage of a final reconciliation as a reward for suffering and submission also operated; then I ceased to believe in it. I simply endured.

She liked to be in control, even while resenting her position. My submission fed the tyrannical side of her fear, and it was illusion for me to believe that only flaws in my submission prevented her from turning afresh to me with love. Not that now I loved her in any normal sense of the term. One cannot love what one fears. Since fear had now come ineradicably between us, our love had become a form of hate, an uneasy alliance of enemies, so that my mirage of an ultimate reunion could only mean a reversal of the roles, myself supplanting her in control. She felt this well enough and was determined to keep the whip-hand. She was determined never again to be hoodwinked by 'love', by trust in anyone else's goodwill. I was the last person in the world she could ever trust, because of the complicated process that had gathered in me all the oppressors and betrayers of her defiled life. She hated me now with a

steady calm hatred, which was tempered to a kind of tranquil benevolence as long as she felt sure that I obeyed her in all things and thus
reflected her will without the least contradiction. So she too was tormented by her mirage. She wanted me to become an automaton of her
needs, which she interpreted as my becoming my pure-self; only if all
selfwill dropped away from me would she be able to give up her sleepless task of watching, which kept her hard and unbending, and took away
all possibility of relaxation, let alone pleasure, from her life.

For the moment however there was a truce of exhaustion. I tried to
complete *Cressida*, and finally managed to do so, keeping up as well as I
could a manner in which I no longer could put my heart. Elza read the
MS and insisted that Cressida and the lad she has carried along with
her should be married at the end; I thought this out of key but did as she
said. Then I sent the MS to the agents Curtis Brown. About the same
time I thought of the Limited Editions Club of New York as probably
one of the few fine-book producers able to weather the economic storm.
I wrote and proposed a version of the *Golden Ass*. They promptly
commissioned the work for £100. However, £50 of this was used up
before I got it, for at our solicitor's advice I agreed to put that sum into
a trust-fund for Robinetta; they advanced the money as a loan.

Suddenly Elza announced that she was going to see her mother. She
had previously always spoken of her mother as long dead, the distracted
Mme de Locre of the aristocratic Paris Garden; but now, without any
explanation, she told me that her mother was married to a market-
gardener in Combe Martin and that she herself was an illegitimate child.
Her father had been an elderly doctor who holidayed yearly with his
family in north Devon; he fell in love with the young girl who worked
for them, and got her with child; he arranged to go off with her to New
York, but his wife proved too much for him; he gave in and allowed his
child, Elza, to be looked after by an uncle of hers in Bristol. After a while
Elza's mother married the market-gardener, and now had several
children by him.

I had heard so many stories from Elza that I didn't believe this one;
but it turned out to be completely true. I sent my few N.L. etchings to the
Leicester Galleries and my books to Foyles, and got a very poor price.
We also offered our few sticks of furniture to a Dunmow dealer. We now
had enough cash in hand to buy our tickets for north Devon and live
there a few weeks. Elza, concerned at the effect I'd have on her family,
insisted on buying me two ready-made suits from the local Co-op. One,

which we took on the spot, fitted me to a certain extent; the other, sent after us, proved about five sizes too large, but we made no effort to send it back and have it changed.[1]

[1] I recently revisited Onslow Green to take a photo of the house, and found it gone. At first I thought I must have mistaken the place, then I saw the concrete flooring I had had put in the smithy. At the pub close by I learned that shortly after we left an old man fell down the stairs with an oil-lamp and the house and smithy were burned down.

THIS is the part of my life when I am vaguest as to chronology; I was living so completely inside myself. However, my fasting experience must have occurred in mid-winter, helped on its way by the news of Heseltine's suicide; and it was sometime in early spring that we arrived in Combe Martin, that long sprawling valley-town, with market-gardens on the slopes and the tall tapering shapes of ruined mine-towers on the skyline. Elza had taken a thin corridor of a bungalow, about half-way along the village and half-way up the northern slope. We went to see her mother, who proved a cheerful stocky countrywoman with a broad Devon accent. The only thing at all akin to Elza were her eyes, of a pale bright blue. But one could see, on a second glance, that she must have been a pretty thing at the age of seventeen before her waistline thickened and her face was burned by the suns and the ovens of a hard working-life. Her husband was a bluff self-contained man, somewhat older, who received Elza with a friendly nonchalance, despite the fact that her arrival must have stirred up all the village gossips with the tales of his wife's young days. The children, boys and girls in their late teens, were clearly curious. One of the girls, bringing some vegetables and finding me at the washing-up, reported that we were 'chicken': that is, tenderly devoted to one another.

It was necessary for Elza to make an impressive return, but we had none of the paraphernalia for it. I must have looked gauntly distracted, obviously no rich husband; and Elza's distinguished eccentricities of dress were not the sort of thing to evoke a village's respect. From this period she began to wear ordinary clothes. Her mother was certainly very relieved to see her. She had heard nothing since Elza left Ilfracombe, did not even know of her marriage; she had given her up for lost, imagining a fate which in many aspects was all-too-exactly what had happened, but hardly guessing that her girl could have climbed so far out of the ruck and the muck as in some ways she had. Yet the relief was chequered by confused fears; she didn't enjoy her past coming up again after so many years of respectability; she sensed something was wrong and that our visit had an unstated motive.

Elza found her tongue loosed by the familiar setting of so much of her childhood. At about six she had left Bristol and had lived with her grandfather and grandmother here. Then she had run away to a job in a hotel at Ilfracombe, where the manager seduced her. Not that he was the first. She took me to meet a woman who as a girl had been her closest friend; they used to go out with this latter's two brothers and make love in a scrambled way among the bushes and nooks of the valley, changing round and laughing at one another. The friend, now a married woman with a couple of children, received us with a prim mouth and scared eyes.

There were endless tales of the troubles she had got into. She must have been a wild child, rebelling against the least show of authority and resentful at being relegated to her grandparents while her mother, now married, was near at hand. She had a conviction that the Bristol uncle, a commercial traveller, had embezzled the funds that the doctor had settled on her, and then tossed her back to the village. From a few remarks of her mother I think there was probably much truth in this belief, though she may have exaggerated the sums of which she was cheated. She also had a very circumstantial account of the various ways her uncle abused her in a small carpentry workshop he had at the rear of his suburban house. At the time I credited all she told me; but now I am not sure. She had suffered so much outrage and she had brooded so long on her uncle's theft of her 'birthright' that she may well have built up a fantasy of complete depravity on his part.[1]

Various outlying relatives, hearing of her return, called in to see us, friendly and suspicious, and invited us to tea amid their best china-ornaments. I found the whole thing wearying and felt in a false position, but did my best to help Elza keep her end up. In my spare time I was working at the *Golden Ass*, using a rickety writing-desk, and feeling an ever-greater fellowship with Lucius transformed into a beast of burden and seeking the rose of regeneration. We were near the end of our cash. When I went to post the MS to the Limited Editions Club, I didn't have

[1] Among other things I now learned that she was a real connection with De Hérédia; before meeting Robert, Elza had had an affair with a youth of that name, whom she described as the poet's son. Presumably he was some descendant of the family, how directly from the poet I do not know. But he certainly existed; Elza had much to say of him; he seemed to have moved her a great deal.

enough to pay the postage. I took the parcel back, removed most of the packing material and any unnecessary sheets, tied up what remained in a tubular form, and just managed to buy the stamps. As soon as I handed the parcel over, I felt scared that it would come to pieces before it reached New York. However, it arrived safely, and in a few weeks the cheque turned up.

Before that I had had some more luck. The Bodley Head accepted *Cressida*, with the proviso that the marriage was an unconvincing finale. I rewrote the passage and received a cheque for £25. To my surprise the firm said that they did not want the drawings with the tale. To keep going with our daily expenses Elza had meanwhile had a heart-to-heart talk with her mother and borrowed a few pounds, which we repaid as soon as the first cheque arrived. At the same time she told her mother about the Chancery suit. I had the feeling that the various revelations both worried and relieved her mother, who now felt that she understood better the strange daughter come back in a strange guise. Our solicitors had advised us that it would help us if we had an affidavit from Elza's mother supporting our case. We went with her to a firm they had named at Ilfracombe, and complied with the formalities.

A mistake was made in the document which our opponents tried to make much of, though I don't think the judge took it seriously. Elza's mother was described as Widow. Edith Craig's solicitors sent a detective down to Combe Martin to check up and found that the mother did exist but was not a widow. I hadn't noticed the error in the flurry of the moment and couldn't see that it mattered so much; but our solicitors said a Widow had a much more free legal personality than a Wife. (This was not the only mistake we made; but the other was an error of judgment, possible through the almost free hand I had in the affidavits. In a moment of wrath I put into a plea against Miss Craig some matters of libellous hearsay, purveyed to me by Elza, and was properly rebuked by the judge-in-chambers, who also, however, rebuked our opponents for trying to describe my writings as immoral.)

Shortly after the acceptance of *Cressida*, but before the cheque came in, I received a card from Allen Lane to say that he would be motoring in Devon and would like to call on us. (He was still in the family-firm, the last of the name.) Though I would have liked to see him, I felt it would be impossible and wrote putting him off. For the next ten years no guest put his foot in our doors (except once a student at Truro, and once Randall Swingler at Dartmouth). I did not know that my uneasy card of late spring 1931 was putting off not only Allen Lane, but the world.

We now felt that we must retreat somehow from Combe Martin, but didn't know how to make a graceful exit. Elza found out that several miles to the east, at Blackmore Gate, a fine house was to let at 30/- a week. The person who had main control of the leasing was a rich woman living on our village's outskirts; and we called on her. She clearly did did not quite know how to treat us. In the hopes of getting the house I laid what stress I could on my appearance in *Who's Who*, but on the other hand the woman clearly knew about Elza's parentage. She tried to ward us off, but without much decision. I managed to go over her head to the Barnstaple solicitors in charge of the estate, and they drew up a lease.

But the lease had still not arrived on the Saturday when we had arranged to leave Combe Martin. I felt desperate. We had to go some-where; Elza's relations knew that we were negotiating the lease of the imposing house; a decrepit taxi was calling for us. I decided to assume that the lease was held up by some accident and to enter the house by hook or by crook. When we arrived, we piled up our things on the door-step and said goodbye to the car-driver, who would report to the village that we had duly taken possession. Then I prowled round the house and found a side-window open. So we entered without breaking anything. I then rang up the solicitors and told them that we were in. Some hours later a bewildered clerk came by train from Barnstaple with the lease. I had succeeded in forcing the hand of the uncertain owners. I presume that the solicitors had rung up the lady of Combe Martin, who hesitated about calling in the police to have us evicted.

Well, there we were, with our solitude established, in a sort of magnifi-cent manor-house built of local grey stone, with about twenty rooms and large grounds. In the gentlemanly way of pre-war leases (which was to save me from ruin many times in the coming years) the first payment was due at the end of three months. Three months: time to write a couple of masterpieces and perhaps make some money. In a large cellar under the huge kitchen there was the complete apparatus for generating electricity; meanwhile we had some candles. But the days were lengthening and we could rise at dawn. We each chose one of the rooms upstairs with a splendid view, and put a suitcase and a small portmanteau in for furniture. That was all we had for the moment. We slept on the floor.

That night, after darkness came, I was disturbed by a loud scrabbling and banging at the back door, and went with some trepidation to see who was there. When I opened, I had a fleeting glimpse of a large white object that shot up, knocked me over, trampled on me, and rushed into the house. My candle had gone out, but there was another in the passage. I rushed to get it and found my assailant had been a sheep. With some difficulty, its hooves clatter-clattering on the wooden floors, I managed to push it out. It baa-ed disconsolately for some time, scrabbled, and went off. Some days later I found that the house had previously been tenanted by a caretaker with a couple of children who made a pet of a small lamb; the lamb grew into a sheep, but the children wept and clung to it; they saved it as their own till their departure about a week before. On the night of our arrival the sheep had broken loose and come in search of its playmates.

In a cupboard next day I found a gadget for impressing the address of the house on note-paper. I selected my best bits of paper and impressed the address; then I wrote to some shops in Barnstaple, the names of which I gained from a copy of the local newspaper. I ordered enough blinds to cover the windows of the ground-floor; also some of the more durable groceries. At the last moment I also ordered a quantity of dried fish, with a few fresh ones, from a large fishery-store. (I developed a feud with the latter shop, for they delivered the fish to a blacksmith at the cross-roads below in the valley: the place where they had left goods for the last inhabitants of the house. They didn't inform me, and the fish were unclaimed so long that they went bad. I refused to pay and was threatened with prosecution for debt.)

Luckily the caretaker had not taken away a fair amount of vegetables he had been growing; and in the barns and sheds at the back I found packing-cases and lengths of wood out of which I constructed tables and wardrobes. I started on a pair of beds; but as I had no tools except a defective hammer found in the pantry, I gave up and used my impressed note-paper to order the cheapest pair of camp-stretchers I could get. Now we were fully equipped.

What was I to write? I couldn't follow *Cressida* up with a similar kind of work; and my ideas about people and life were still in too chaotic a condition for me to attempt an ordinary novel. I decided to try a fable about Satyrs and Centaurs—about the war that wiped out those odd creatures, so that only a memory of them remained in Greek art and poetry. Thus I felt I could continue my anatomizing of what was wrong with mankind and why they were heading for disaster. Once I had begun,

I wrote with considerable speed and hopefully sent the work to The Bodley Head, from whom it soon came back. Depressed, I sent it to the agents, who failed to place it.

I thought the work had gone to join the limbo of so much of my writing; but after Phil's death in 1958 I found a copy of it in his big box, among other MSS of mine and a large number of his summonses and debt-writs. To my surprise the work was much more amusing than I had remembered; its weakness lay in the fact that there was no central idea to explain the stupidities, irrationalities, and highly-involved confusions that led to the exterminating war. A ridiculous chain-series of events was shown accumulating disorders and antagonisms; but the only general idea to be inferred was that the inner disorganization of men prevented them from dealing in time with trivial alarms and conflicts, which gathered steadily their destructive momentum. The culmination came when the physicist of the Satyrs projected on to the Centaurland a terrific force which too late he realized would set up a chain-reaction and recoil on its begetters.

Once again I expressed my conviction that modern science was set on a road of disintegration which would threaten the earth's very existence. The physicist stays on at his mechanism, trying to find the flaw in his system in the few minutes of life left to him. ('I may find the necessary formula before I am exploded.' 'What use is that?' wailed Paniscos. 'What use is anything?' replied Assaon tartly. 'It will be a most important discovery.')

But what most surprised me in re-reading the MS was that the novel held in abstracted form the method I was later to apply in my historical fiction. It showed an obsession with points of social explosion, with the causes of mass-movements, the relation of individual aims to the larger whole which is seen only in refracted or distorted ways; and it strove to find a technique for gathering a multiple set of divergent lines into a single pattern. My fasting vigil under Freud's aegis had brought me half-way to the clear earth. It had rid me of other worldly fantasies and lodged me nakedly in the reality of the family; what remained was for me to place the family solidly in the reality of social process. But that was no easy task. Meanwhile I could see only individual acts and emotions in infinite interaction, with the aggregate of separate impacts making up a complex mass of turmoiling strains and stresses; I could not distinguish any organic unity or purpose in that mass. The birth-trauma alone unified.

At the same time as I worked on *Satyrs* I began an attempt to general-ize my experiences on a theoretical level, *Birth and Will*. My aim was to show the way in which the birth-trauma produced various repetition-compulsions, based on an unconscious attitude to the parents—an attitude which turned the parents into myths or god-figures, images of authority or license, fear or desire. As a result, an accumulative set of tensions and strains were created in the individual, who drove himself along the lines determined by his unconscious fantasy of the parents. Will was thus a destructive force, an effort to compel oneself along the fantasy-lines, to impose a pattern of living on oneself; it always created more problems than it solved; it tied one up in knots of worsening frustration and bodily rigidity; it distorted the sexual flow into power-lust; it turned the self into a thing, a means-to-an-end, and thus pro-duced property-lust—all the possessed things being reduplications of the dead thing-self. The alternative was to relax, to stop fighting and driving oneself forward, to fall back into oneself and slowly break the tight grip of fear. Then one could begin to realize the truth of oneself, one's place in the family, one's place on the earth. By finding one's own true centre one entered into the fullness of life, realized oneself as a living part of all things. By straightening out the traumatic knots, twists, and cankers in one's being, one enabled the life-flow to pervade all aspects and levels of oneself. One released one's sex from its clotting in certain zones and points of irritation, and made it an harmonious part of the life-process in one's body-spirit, merging oneself with the universal process.

These ideas were worked out in long and precise detail; especially I used the evidence of language, in which the unconscious hope and fear are often fused. (At this stage I saw all social institutions and forms of expression as projections of the struggle in the individual psyche.) The general method was Freudian; but I did not know any psycho-analytic work with the same points of departure or arrival. I did not assume that the work of analysis had as its aim the smoothing out of inner conflicts so that the purged individual might fit into our given society. On the contrary, I assumed that our society was all wrong, the result of a mass-projection of all the evils I grouped under the heading of Will—power-lust, property-lust and so on. I wanted the individual to resist our society, to reject it, but had no scheme for changing it, beyond the assumption that if enough persons resisted and rejected along the lines I advocated, a different sort of social system would result, one that reflected the pure life-flow in the individual.[1]

I had a letter from Sherard Vines, asking for a contribution to a collection of satiric poems, *Whips and Scorpions*, and wrote *Philocyon*, aimed against my past self. I copied out my Blake book, added some variants, and sold it for a couple of pounds to Foyles' MSS department. I had only a shaky packing-case table and a typewriter in its last stages of collapse, continually jamming. I kept on racking my brains for fresh translation-outlets; but the Limited Editions Club turned down my suggestion of *Daphnis and Chloe*, saying that they meant to do George Moore's version. Later in the year their fine edition of my *Golden Ass*, bound in soft ass-skin, turned up.

I loved the house we'd taken and dreamed of spending the rest of my days there. We went for a few walks over to Exmoor, but mostly stayed within our own bounds. Even there I sometimes encountered wild cats behind the sheds. The house itself, though built in the last century, seemed in its silvery-brown stone to have been hewn out of the earth, not something imposed on the landscape and rejected by it. The farmer below, with whom we became friendly, gave us a hare he had snared; but neither of us, despite our food-straits, could bear to clean it, so that in the end I buried it. Once I used up a lot of our meagre supplies in making, very successfully, an elaborate cake, just to prove that I too could be handy in the kitchen. Elza, with her sudden phobias that could be most inconvenient in the midst of other difficulties, decided that she could not bear the creeper covering one side of the house, and I called in a local builder to remove it and wash the walls with some preservative. He must have reported the matter to the Combe Martin lady, for a few days after the job was finished she turned up. I couldn't ask her in to have some tea, as there was no furniture—nothing on the ground-floor

---

[1] Apart from the books by Freud then available in English, I had read fairly widely in psycho-analysis: the books of Jones (the essay on Salt much influenced me, and both Phil and I had recognized N.L. in his essay on the god-fantasy), Stekel, Rank, Ferenczi, etc. (Ferenczi's 'shock-tactics' had impressed me.) I had studied a large number of case-reports and thus had a good idea of the practical side, especially impressed by finding that the process of psycho-analytic self-knowledge was identical in structure with the poetic process of Greek and Shakespearean tragedy. Works like Freud's on dreams and the psychopathology of everyday life deepened what one had already surmised and thought out about the associative principle at work in the creative process. While admiring some of Jung's work on symbols, I disliked what I felt his vague and messy mysticism.

at all, apart from the neat blinds, but a packing case in the middle of the vast kitchen. So I had to talk as fast as I could, wandering round the outside of the house and discussing the improvement we had made by removing the creeper, and jumping on to any other theme that came into my mind, to distract her. Finally after about an hour, during which I kept an anxious eye on the blinds, afraid that some had not been well-drawn, I said, 'I'm sorry to keep you so long. Sorry there isn't time to ask you in for tea,' and shook hands. Being well-mannered, she mumbled something about not wanting to bother us and went off, probably deciding we were mad and best left to our own devices.

Though with no market in mind, I began on *Daphnis*, and I got an idea for another novel. A group of people week-ending in a remote country-house (exactly like ours) dress up in the costumes of the 1640's; without realizing the transition, they find themselves transported back into the midst of the Cromwellian Civil War, the house is besieged, and various conflicts develop among them.

21. WANDERINGS

THE end of the first quarter was nearing and I had no means of meeting the bill of £20/10/-. Left to myself, I would have stayed on, hoping somehow to raise the money. But Elza decided that we must return to London. The hearing of the suit was soon to come on, and we should have to pay a visit anyhow. With our depleted finances, the only sensible choice was to evacuate. I wrote a letter to the Barnstaple solicitors and posted it as we left. I asked them to cancel the lease, wait for what was owing, and arrange to sell the blinds, sending what they fetched to the firm that had sold them, and letting me know the deficit. I was melancholy as we took the local train, but Elza was always cheerful during a move.

In London we found a flat in Portobello Road, a top-storey that was being given up by two old maids. The latter had decided that city air did not agree with their large number of pets, and they were moving on to the north outskirts of London. We had to listen to long accounts of the ailments to which canaries, cats, dogs (if pekes may be dignified with that name), and angora-goats were liable. Not that they had goats in the flat, but they meant to acquire them in their new place. By these means we gained their confidence and their flat, escaping after four days from our Paddington room.

The episode of the uneaten hare and the general bias of my book on Birth and Will had inclined us against meat-eating. The more I thought about it, the more I felt that the roots of religion and the whole evil power-complex I was trying to understand were to be found entwined with meat-eating and all it involved—not the only roots, but an important set of them. The magical ideas of the hunting-groups, and even more the religious ideas of the settled groups who raised animals for slaughter, seemed to me to have created a series of irrational fears and lusts which has later been rationalized in men's consciousness, but which still operated in their aboriginal form from deep down. Only by discarding a diet based on rotting corpses could men become sane. The fantasy of needing a blood-diet, a corpse-diet, was inseparable from the distorted relation to the parents I had been trying to clarify in myself and which one way or another existed in everyone. The corpse-eater was still in fantasy feeding on the parents.

We discussed these ideas and decided to eat no more meat, no more animal products of any kind (such as milk, cheese, eggs) and to discard mineral salt. Apart from a few extreme applications of our position, when I tried to eat such nauseous things as raw potatoes, we found that we felt very much better in health. Until I was called up into the Army in 1941 I kept strictly to a vegetarian diet, with enormous benefit to my health, getting rid even of the colds that used to bother me a lot and had convinced me of a weak chest. I never had the least illness during the decade to come, despite the many hardships and anxieties, and despite the periods of lack of exercise.

Robert Craig turned up in reply to a letter from Elza, and on learning our views took us to a vegetarian restaurant. I now read some health-reform periodicals, and during the next few years contributed articles and poems to them. The Chancery suit did not come up as we expected. Some preliminary rounds were completed, and the game of affidavits resumed. I was trying to finish the new novel, *Masquers*, and wrote a long-short story, *Come Home at Last*, set in the ancient Greek world, which Elza read and tore up. (Later I wrote it down as close to the first version as I could recall it, and it appeared in a book of short stories with that title. The wife and the girl whose deaths she brings about stood for the opposed aspects of Elza, her cruelty and her tenderness.) I also re-wrote for her a play on which she had got stuck—a typical romantic incest-fantasy, in which a father almost seduces his unrecognized daughter.[1]

Then we moved again. I cannot remember why. Elza's restlessness must have been the main cause; for, throughout the following years, I always wanted to burrow in, wherever we chanced to be, if only to avoid more moving-costs—but also because I urgently wanted to grow roots. Within a week at any new place I had ransacked the public library

---

[1] I was trying to write an introduction to *Daphnis*, citing examples of the Rejected Babe Suckled by Beasts. As I was walking home from Notting Hill I was thinking of Cyros, stopped at a tray of secondhand books and picked up a copy of Herodotos that opened at the tale of Cyros. I bought the book for a penny (my limit for books), and felt an omen in the event as I translated the passage. But no one wanted the *Daphnis*. Elza had been convinced that Seymour Hicks would take her play; she had known him in her Craig-days. We sent the play (as later the one I rewrote for her in Cornwall), with no luck.

for histories, records, and so on, and had begun to feel a local patriotism. Now, using our trusty *Daltons* we decided to settle in some seaside huts below Maldon. At the moment Elza had fantasies of our finding an island somewhere and of herself turning into a great matriarchal figure with hundreds of grandchildren and great-grandchildren.

Autumn was advanced. The Essex coast was bleak, an endless stretch of misty mudflats broken only by mournful seagulls. The damaged decaying huts, with shreds of summer gaiety, were all empty. Elza hated it at the first glance and sulked. I wanted to get at least our week's worth of money. But she wouldn't stay. We took a bus eastward, and by making inquiries put up at a farmstead where part of the main building was to let. We stayed there some weeks. My typewriter ceased to work, and I copied out the last parts of *Masquers* by hand as neatly as I could, afflicted by the stench of pigs and fowl-droppings. I felt the novel was weak. The idea was good, but I could not develop personal conflicts among my masqueraders which really had any deep connection with the historical scene into which they were dropped. As in *Satyrs* there was an effective mechanism, but no organic idea to draw the parts together. I looked out on the yard and said to myself: There is the earth, describe it in all its manifold details; bring it to life in its underlying unity. But I seemed to have no talent at all. I compiled a list of the things I saw; I could not reconstruct the scene or define what I felt when I looked at it. Either a dead enumeration of oddments or a retreat into a personal cavern of despair. I gave up and brooded through the long slow changes of the dusk. Then suddenly I found phrases coming from my pen: 'The knots and snarls of light in the tree are drawn too tight, they crack and explode in momentary spikes of silver. Nothing has happened. Time exists. . . .' I felt Time as my enemy, tearing the world to shreds before I could grasp its pattern, taking me, too, to pieces, like a child with a clock, and unable to put half the cogwheels back. Time that went backwards as well as forwards, but was not reversible. I re-read what I had written. Words, words, words. Nothing to the point. But I did not know what the point was.

I had another problem to worry me. Just before we left the shore-hut a letter from my literary agents had arrived, addressed to me, which held inside a letter to Norman. From the letter it was clear that Norman was now in England; and I inclined to believe, no doubt incorrectly, that the misdirection to me had been deliberate—an oblique way on Norman's part of letting me know that he was in London, and of providing me with his address, without risking the snub that might come from any straightforward note or message. I was convinced that he had indeed come to England to see me; that he had been upset by my attacking letter and had finally decided to come over and see what had happened to me. In all these conclusions I doubtless over-estimated greatly my importance in his mind. From Rose's notes I learn that he had been much embittered by a renewal of abuse in Australia and that as they walked through the Sydney streets on their way to the liner they read the Smiths-Weekly posters: Will Norman Lindsay Be Arrested? The Faber edition of *Redheap* had been banned and an *Art-in-Australia* edition dedicated to his work had been seized by the police. They felt the need to get away from Australia for a while, and visited the U.S.A. as well as England. In London, as Will Dyson was ill, the *Daily Herald* offered Norman his place as a guest-cartoonist at a high fee. 'But Norman was only interested in getting on with his scheme for publishing books,' says Rose. I should guesss however that he shrank from doing cartoons for any periodical with the least left tinge; he thus threw aside a ready-made opportunity for a strong impact on English opinion. He and Rose stayed at a hotel in Russell Square, complaining that the central-heating pipes gave no heat (while Elza and I shivered in Essex with no fires at all). He used to walk to the Pentons' flat in Corman Street for its piled-up grate: Brian at the time working on his novel *Landtakers*. When the Pentons moved to a larger place, Norman and Rose took over the Corman Street flat for six weeks, then left for Australia again. Rose mentions visits from Phil and Jeanne, the latter in her tight-bodiced velvet frocks and flowing skirts.

My father does not seem to have made any inquiries about me at all. The only persons who had my changing addresses were the agents; but since he shared them, he could easily have written me a note. Despite my angers, I still felt the strong pull of his personality. Deep in myself, I longed to go and see him. But I knew that if I did, I should succumb to his charm, I should begin to whittle down and modify my new convictions, I should end by returning, even if in a less intense form, to my discipleship. And deeper than the longing for reconciliation there was the need to hold myself apart and nurture the new life which was still a young and fragile thing. Here, as in all matters, for the next few years, Elza was my objectified conscience, sternly watching me for any backsliding. That was why, in the last resort, despite the many inconveniences and hardships it entailed, despite what may seem from the outside an intolerable narrowing of existence, I accepted her domination. The over-rigid elements in her attitudes may have been unfortunate; but I felt them as the price paid for keeping on a straight and perilous path from which it was all too easy to stray—especially for someone of my character, who, ready to set up Absolutes in solitude, was given to caving-in and compromising when faced with an opponent in the flesh. In part the reason for such compromises lay in my inability to avoid seeing a certain element of truth in the adversary's position and being driven to imagine myself under his skin in order to understand why he had arrived at it. I was ready to fail myself, but I could not bear to fail Elza.

We took buses and reached Colchester. I visited the Castle with its Roman remains and long meditated there. We bought *Daltons* and sat in a flyblown café. After Devon we felt the pull of the West. Why not go further on, further into the wilds? I longed for a landscape where I did not feel the shaping hand of man. The comfortable vistas all round London had ended by horrifying me as revealing only a toy world, a land ploughed and trampled into easy curves. I wanted the sterile stone and the waste that men had not dunged into prosperity. And looking out through the café window I watched the girls, the young men, hurrying or idling through a world they never questioned, a world that was now a madness to me. And I was sorry for them, and envied them, like a dead man looking through a crack in his gravestone. How happy if they only knew. But if they knew their happiness, they would know also its insufficiencies, they would reject it and seek wholeness, they would be lost, haunted with an irremediable ache and yet strangely proud. I have been chosen for this impossible task, the quest of the life-source; I chose myself for it. I am living in a folk-tale, I am Gilgamesh as well as Hamlet, and the end is the same for all of us. Only I have this secret pride. Perhaps it is nothing but a sense of wonder at the infinite riches of the least moment of living. I have discarded all the normal props and protections in order that I may have nothing whatever but life; that I may live in the perpetual wonder. But why then this distracting fear, which breaks the wonder?

'We shall take two cottages,' Elza is saying. 'There are two advertised at Portreath on the North Cornish coast.'

I nod. I too would like to live on my own. But all I can think of is the double rent. Such details never bother Elza; she decides what she wants, what she needs, what is right; and then she simply leaves me to find the means.

We took the next train to London and went to Paddington. From there we wrote for the cottages in Elza's name. By return post our tenancy was accepted. With our luggage and a bagful of apples we took the train; and with every westward mile my heart was lighter. I liked even the ugly town of Redruth and my heart leaped at the sight of Carn Brea before I knew anything of its history. The bus rattled with us down the green valley to Portreath, where the quay was still used for coal-deliveries though the old tackle for hauling the coal up the hillside was broken. The houses stood in tiers on the valley-sides; our address was on the eastern slope. Once again we met one of the worried old maids who let houses distrustfully to us. 'I thought it was two ladies,' she moaned, wondering what to do with the tea she had brewed ready for us. Her lips puckered and quivered. I talked so fast that she gave up trying to make out what our relationship was, offered us tea, and surrendered the keys. With difficulty I held myself back from saying that if we had come to Portreath to live-in-sin in her houses, we should not have needed two of them.

It was now early 1932. A second £25 for *Cressida* had been keeping us going. Soon I was to get £50 for an American edition. For over a year no other money came in. And even then it was very little. I cannot now make out how we managed to exist at all, let alone move about, from now on till late in 1933. True, apart from rents, our expenses were extremely small. I did all my own washing and mending, as well as cooking (as indeed I did till 1941). I lived almost wholly on oats, cabbages, spinach and potatoes, which for the most part I bought from local farmers—if one can use the word farmers for men penuriously growing a few vegetables on small patches of dry and stony soil. I liked these men, and talked with them, as with the fishermen who had lost their boats, or with the miners encountered in some hollow of the hills—sharp, embittered, calm men. I liked the rough barren moorlands with their ruined mine-towers; even the crenellated small cottages and the miserable gardens of fuchsias. I spent a whole morning with men I struck washing and crushing with ancient apparatus in a lonely glen. 'What do they care for us?' they asked. 'Can't they make more money out of sweating the Malayans?' I felt an entire unity with these men, though I did not know how to express it, to them or to myself. The reference to Malaya reminded me of my sage remarks to P.R.S. in

Paris; but what had been a bit of random economic information had here become human reality, knotted in the hands of these miners. And it seemed that I had had to come a long way round to understand my own words.

A few doors above Elza was a fisherman's family. The man was small and wiry, his wife large and snub-nosed, and they had an indeterminate number of children. They joked at one another rather in the vein of our bawdy friend at Onslow Green: she about the lovers she took while he was at sea, and he about his wives in every port. His mother lived on the opposite side of the valley, keeping a stern eye on the daughter-in-law whom she detested for her loose tongue and for her refusal to listen to advice about the rearing of children. The two women rejoiced the village by shouting abuse at one another across the valley; and the wife forced her husband to take out an insurance policy on his mother's life. Then, when she could think of nothing else to annoy, she flourished the paper and commented on the good time they were going to have after the old lady's death. The latter set her teeth. 'I won't die, to spite you. I'll make you pay out a mint of money and then I'll laugh in your face.'

I liked the suspicious Cornish, living in their stony caves of separateness, with a hunger for comradeship which seemed to find expression only in their Methodism. I liked their speech with its dying hint of a Celtic lilt. One day I heard a woman say to a friend, 'Yes, my dear, I haven't washed my feet for a year, and they're lily-white.' I got all the books I could from Redruth library about the locality and about Cornish mining and fishing, climbed Carn Brea, and dreamed of the ancient tinners. There had been food-riots in the Twenties in Redruth; the Cornish were capable of sudden violence, but found a continued union of resistance too hard to sustain. The co-operative fishing-groups had just gone down before the steam-trawlers of commercialized fishing; always someone betrayed the group. And yet there was a strange smouldering desire for righteousness and unity. (I later put what I felt of Portreath and the region in the novel *End of Cornwall*, which Cape published, under the name of Richard Preston. It perhaps showed some knowledge of what was going on that I mentioned then a growth of solidarity among the miners in the very area where shortly afterwards the first trade-union organization emerged.)

But for the time I was having no luck with my writing. I tried a short novel, set in Portreath, in which I used an Australian episode. In Sydney, once visiting a well-known poet-friend, I was told by his wife, when he was out of the room, that she had taken revenge on him by pouring boiling-water on the roots of his favourite flower-bush; during the evening he kept on lamenting the sad looks of this bush and wondering what pest was afflicting it. I transplanted this incident to Portreath, making the flower-lover a retired Cornish seaman. The short novel was rejected when the agents sent it round, though later I included it as half of *End of Cornwall*.

For the rest I worked at *Birth and Will*, and collected a large amount of notes illustrative of its thesis, mainly using language and folklore for my material. I re-wrote a play of Elza's and worked up her early life into a novel under her name, taking down her tale and then expanding it. Neither of these works had any success; the Elza-narrative was too strictly tied to the facts (as she remembered them) and the play was an odd mixture of the plays which Elza had acted in or been connected with, third-rate musical comedy and third-rate drawing-room comedy. I wrote a poem on the deepsea-blue eyes of the girl serving in the grocery-shop; the *Western Mail* printed it, but paid nothing; I gave up hoping for any cash-return from verse. However, I got some healthfood-goods in barter-return for poems in nature-cure monthlies.

At this moment I could easily have given up writing, as there seemed no way to connect my pre-fasting techniques with my post-fasting attitudes. Human personality had broken down into the vast network of complexes born from the birth-trauma and reducible to a limited range of repetition-compulsions. What the world took for personality was only the fabricated mask of difference set over the shared flux of compulsions; as soon as one had seen behind it, one could not feel excited about defining or elaborating it. (D.H.L. had felt something like this when he early rejected 'character-drawing' as against the quest for the nuclear core.) I felt the need for anonymity, for completing my rejection of Will by losing myself in the faceless mass, in any form of productive work where I was simply exploited and had no share whatever in the profits, in the advantages of the situation. For this reason I felt a wish to become a navvy, a farm-labourer, a craftsman; I should have preferred to die than to serve as any kind of office-clerk or to take any kind of fragmented factory-work, which seemed to me the antithesis of everything human: the degradation of labour by its reflection of the disintegrative nature of the cash nexus. I did not seek out a job, partly because I was automatically grinding away at the literary tasks before me, partly because there would have been a strenuous struggle with

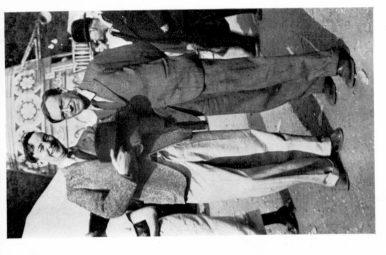

Philip Lindsay (right) at the Kursaal,
Ostend, in the mid-thirties

Philip and Molly Owens with their son

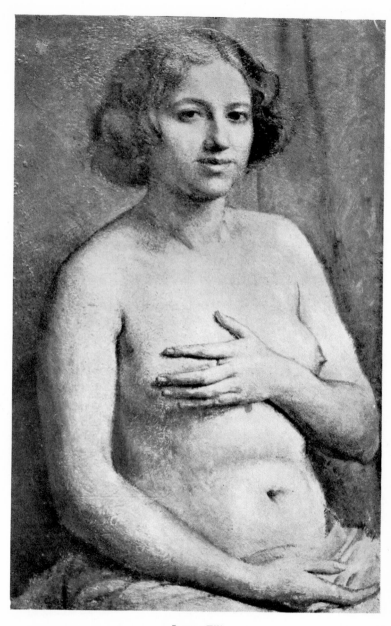

Jeanne Ellis
'The London Aphrodite'

Elza, which I did not feel capable of carrying through to the bitter end. At moments, however, she talked about schemes of hers for a dress-making shop or the like, in which I tried to encourage her without giving away my eagerness; once she had shown any power to stand on her own feet, I should have taken a job on a farm, written poetry again for myself, and published nothing. Beyond that, there was the dream of earning enough to buy a small island where I could build, grow things, and live entirely without the use of money, severing the last ties with iniquity.

That I might have some claim on parish or national powers in the event of complete indigence was something that never came to my mind; and if it had, I should have thrown it out.

The Chancery action now at last came on. We went up to London and stayed in a Paddington room. At the hearing the judge was polite about me and my relations with Elza, despite the efforts of the other side to present the Fanfrolico Press as something disreputable. He, however, inevitably came to the conclusion that the child was best left in the control of Miss Craig for her education, though he gave Elza full free-dom of access to her. I forget the exact wording, but his decision amounted to allowing Elza to see Robinetta as often as was reasonable and to have her for part of any holidays. Elza was enraged, but at first she seemed ready to make the most of the chances offered her. We changed our rooms to a better neighbourhood, Bayswater, and she fetched Robinetta for the day. She decided that we must stay in London so that she could be near the child; she meant to keep continually in touch and offset Edith Craig's influence. I suggested that I should go back alone to Portreath and fetch our luggage. Travelling by night-train, I hastily crammed our things into various cases, lugged them down to the bus-stop, and caught a London train that got me back sometime the following night.

But when I arrived in exhaustion, I found that Elza had abruptly changed her mind. She could not bear to share the child and compete with Edith Craig. She had decided to return to Portreath. Luckily in my rush I had spoken to no one; I had meant to write from London. So, without unpacking, we left London the next day and took up afresh our residences in Portreath, with no other effects than a waste of money we could ill spare, and the creation of some astonishment among Portreath-eans who had seen the going and coming of the luggage. Though the loss of her child played a profound and pervasive part in Elza's psychic life, she never again referred to it in any way.

H

Our landlady now wanted one of her houses and asked me to change over into a small house in the grounds of the hotel nearer the sea. I did so. Farmers used the bit of roadway in front of the house for selling horses, and I much enjoyed the arguments, the sales-jargon, the humorous comments. The shore was shingly, without sand, and rapidly shelving. Without Elza knowing it, I used to get up early and swim. I was afraid of the harsh undertow where the shingle banged against my legs and knocked me over, the choppy waves, in which I once bumped against a solid body, rose spluttering in dismay, and found myself staring into the questioning eyes of a seal. And once, expecting to find nobody about—for I never saw any of the Cornish bathing and visitors were rare, I had thrown off my clothes and walked round a rock to find a girl standing naked, stretching herself with her hands above her head; another girl was bent with her back turned, bare but for her stockings. I retreated, pulled on my blue trunks, and plunged into the sea. Later in the day I passed the two girls on the quay. The one who had been standing with her arms above her head smiled at me, but I gave no sign and went on. To ignore the smile was not easy. It wasn't that I wanted to make love to the girl. What I longed for was companionship without veils. Nakedness was a symbol of the ending of fear, of lies; the tenderness of undemanding touch; the lotus-peace of union with the elemental flow. I felt more fully one with the girl than with anyone I had ever known. But to speak with her would have dissolved the conviction of oneness. And yet in passing her I seemed to renounce all human warmth and contact.[1]

It was easier to ignore the smiles of the hotel manageress, her amber eyes and cat-smile. She asked me now and then to help her with her arithmetic and suggested a drink of gin, which I refused. Every morning I called on Elza for a short while, then returned to my work. Occasionally we went for a long walk together, up the coast to St Agnes and beyond, or down, across the cliff-tops and the dunes, to St Ives. What she did with her time I was careful not to ask. There was an assumption that both of us would emerge from the trammels of the past at the same moment, with the same powers of self-expression. But in fact she had given up any attempts at writing since the days of Forge Cottage, where she wrote her last poem when we returned one misty morning from an

---

[1] Something of the emotion of this moment went later into *Shadow and Flame*: myself drowned and Elza finding the moment of tender touch as a release from fear.

encounter with the redcoats and the hounds of a hunt among the ghostly trees.

The manageress now asked me to change into a round tower with a single large chamber above a store-room, at a few shillings less a week. Which I gladly did. Soon afterwards I received a letter from some Sydney solicitors acting for Janet, who asked for money to meet the expenses of a divorce. Instead of welcoming this letter, writing frankly about my financial situation, and promising to foot the bill as soon as I could, I sent a panicked reply that I could not pay a ha'penny. Perhaps because of this letter, perhaps because of the growing economic strain, Elza turned up in my tower one day and announced that she was staying with me, that her nerves made it impossible to go on alone. In a furious temper, she accused me of having messed everything up. I saw no reason to defend myself. But we could not live together long in my tower-room, however chastely, in a village that had known us as mere, if peculiar, acquaintances.

If only a divorce could then have been carried through, things might have worked out differently. I am thinking of the greater security Elza would have felt, but even more of the change I should have felt in our relation. Married, she would have had the law on her side, to enforce her rights; unmarried, she was dependent on my honour, and that was a court without appeal.

So we read *Daltons*, found a bungalow at Feock, at the top of Falmouth Harbour, and removed there by devious buses. Elza at once disliked the dilapidated place, though the situation was excellent. We walked all over the area and bathed on the beach below. Then we tried Truro, where Elza decided to settle. The only possible house was at the end of a terrace, tenanted by an accountant who wanted to move to a newly-built suburban residence he was buying through a society. He was a snobby pretentious type we abhorred; and after some discussion he referred us to the owner, a canny old Cornish dealer with a villainous twinkling eye, who, I think, guessed our unreliability but dangled a lease before us. In the end the accountant moved out and we moved in without any proper agreement, though the person to blame was the amused pig-eyed owner, who still had the accountant in his clutches. We were now extremely hard-up, and on our negotiating visits we walked all the way to Truro and back to save bus-fares. The time was late August or early September, for I recall how we ate the ripe blackberries from the hedges as we wandered endlessly on. It needs a very large amount of blackberries to give even the temporary illusion of a full stomach.

Just before we moved, Robert came down to see us; he was arranging to divorce Elza. She was moved at the sight of him, reluctant to accept the divorce, and clearly contemplating a return to him at the last moment. And strangely I felt jealous. I wanted her to stay: as though, despite the burden she was, I had no trust in my continuing to strive for the new way of life unless she were there driving me along.

With blackberries, cankered apples plucked across a fence, and sixpenn'orth of turnips, we survived and reached Truro. We had no furniture at all; but a bit of luck saved us. *John O'London* accepted three articles of mine on the ancient novel, and paid on the spot. We ordered a table, chairs, and beds on hire-purchase. About this time I got a letter from P.R.S. saying that he was on his way to Australia, wishing me all the best, and hoping he could be of service to me. I used a penny on a stamp to tell him to go to hell. It was highly ungrateful of me to respond so rudely, but I could not let pass any chance to throw a stone at my past.[1]

As soon as the *J.O'L.* cheque was cashed, we went to a healthfood-store and bought several shillings worth of things, unheard-of delicacies for us. But we had eaten so little for so long that we felt sick as soon as we started on the plenteous meal. However, I enjoyed having the town library nearby and began reading anything there on Roman history, my mind harking back to Catullus and his world. I got the idea of writing a biography of M. Caelius Rufus, Catullus' supplanter with Clodia. Not a great deal was known of him apart from the speech on his behalf, against Clodia, by Cicero; his handful of letters to Cicero and the latter's replies; and the fragment of a speech he gave—together, one assumes, with the abusive poems by Catullus to his rival Rufus. But I thought that I could eke the book out by extensively sketching the background.

Somehow or other an Oxford undergraduate, who knew and admired the work of the Fanfrolico Press, got in touch with me. I have forgotten how he did it; perhaps the librarian told him I was in Truro. Anyway he called and we let him in, gave him a brief meal, and became friendly. On his return to Oxford he borrowed many books from his college library on the period of Caesar and sent them to me. Among them was E. S. Beasley's *Catalina, Clodius and Tiberius* (1878), a book which had a decisive effect on my thinking. It somewhat idealized Catalina and Clodius, but it brought out strongly the nature of the popular discontent in their period and the way that Cicero and the other ancient writers had blackguarded it. Slight as the work was, it was just what I needed to fertilize my mind at this moment, to release me into a radically critical attitude to the ancient sources I knew so well. For the first time (apart

---

[1] I give without comment his own statement about his development in Australia, made in August 1961: 'It began with my book, *The Foundations of Culture in Australia*, 1936. I was then associate editor with W. J. Miles (an old Tory Australian Nationalist, founder of the Rationalist Association in Sydney—and father of "Bea" Miles) and conducted a monthly paper, *The Publicist*, in Sydney for 5¾ years from July, 1936 until March, 1942, writing at least 5,000 words a month for it, covering a very wide field of literary and political criticism. Our stand would nowadays be declared as Australian Neutralism—no participation in England's obviously coming second war against Germany. This the Communists and Jews interpreted as pro-Nazism and anti-Semitism. Under their pressure, after Japan entered the war, I was interned without trial for 3½ years by order of H. V. Evatt, and was in an Australian Concentration Camp from March 1942 until September 1945. Of this incident I am inordinately proud, even though, as Nietzsche remarked, "Martyrdom *proves* nothing" '.

from vague adolescent intuitions) I felt, however crudely, the role of the people in history; my idealist preconceptions, sapped from one angle by my Freudian ordeals, now began breaking down in all directions. History was no longer moved by the Idea, but the Idea was born from History, from the masses, from the production and renewal of life in and by the masses. My long criticism of religion had prepared the way to this position: and now that I had reached the position I saw the nature of religion from a new angle. I grasped in sudden, sweeping intuitions how the abstractions had arisen from the fertility-rituals in groups rent by inner divisions; I felt the desperate fears and hopes as forces rending my own flesh. Memories of my readings in Jane Harrison returned, consolidating my new convictions and opening up fresh vistas.

I did not however at a blow rid myself of the limitations of my Freudian period. A wild confused fight went on between my belief that all social forms were projections of psychic conflicts and compromises, and my new positions that the spirit could only be understood historically and that history itself arose in the last resort from the struggle to know and merge with the earth (in work, in sex, in art). I blundered along, re-reading Catullus, Lucretius, Cicero, Propertius and the rest. At the same time I started on a novel, *Flatdwellers*, which tried to use a block of flats as a social group—refraction of the larger whole. But I was bewildered in my ideas as to what part personality played in a world of psychic projections and mass-creations of history. There was no coherence in my group of flat-dwellers, and I tried to find a guiding idea in the dim struggles of the main heroine to develop and stand on her own feet—Elza in her early years.

Elza was tired of Truro and the usual rent-problems were looming up. The accountant, asked to wait, turned nasty and got a court-order against me. Two bailiffs tried to break into the house, but we baffled them, bolted all doors and windows, and announced from the upper storey that we had no intention of surrendering. After their threats and cajoleries had failed, they swore that they'd besiege us. But they were negligent, and it was easy for one or other of us to dodge out now and then. Still, the periodical banging on the front door became irritating. Elza found a recently-built bungalow at Portloe, not far to the east, which we took, and we arranged to move on a Sunday when we knew our bailiffs would be at home enjoying a well-earned rest.

We moved successfully. But about a week later the bailiffs tracked us down and this time we didn't have time to bar them out. 'Everything we have is personal belongings, tools of trade, or things on hire-purchase with only the deposit so far paid,' I told them. They said they believed me, but must report that they'd seen over the house. So, all good friends now, we showed them over and they made jocular remarks about our poverty. 'You see you couldn't escape us,' they said with pride, 'but there's nothing here we can seize. We'll do the best we can for you. We always do that for those that treat us decent.' They shook hands and departed. No more was heard from Truro.

I decided against trying to revise *Birth and Will*, but couldn't bear to burn it. I dug a deep hole and buried it in the hard earth. Elza felt ill in a listless sort of way, but refused to let me fetch a doctor. The house was situated on the upper ground, with the road winding down to the small fishing village. Once more I would have been ready to settle, but Elza wanted to move. I had no money at all and wrote to Will Dyson asking if he could help me; I mentioned that I was doing so because I recalled the letter of his my mother had always carried in her bag. He at once sent me a friendly note and a cheque for £15.

From some local paper we found rooms to let at Porthleven in a ropemill and took them by post. We got someone to carry us and our belongings across in a lorry. Our premises consisted of one room on the ground floor beside the firm's office, and two above. Elza took the room below as it had an oil-stove, and I took those above, where I had a small oil-burner of my own for the oats or vegetables which I cooked.

Once more I tried to drive roots in, talking to the old fishermen on the grey granite quay and walking along Looe Sands or towards St Michaels Mount. Also, I liked living in the middle of a workshop. From my windows I watched the rope twined or stretched. I finished *Flatdwellers*, which had become a large kaleidoscopic work, with much use of interior dialogue that owed more to surrealism than to Joyce; but there was still no central idea. I had regained high-spirits in writing and used extended lyrical metaphors, trying to define Jenny (young Elza) so as to give myself faith in her purposes of self-renewal.

I sent the MS to the agents. Phil had written to me, care of The Bodley Head, and I replied that I was extremely hard-up. I told him of the Caelius book. He wrote back: Why not drop straight history and try a novel on the period? I pondered over his words and suddenly felt the need to write a story about Catalina. I began *Rome for Sale*.

Oddly, about this time I developed the only strongly-felt antagonism to socialism I ever had. As N.L.'s disciple I had paid lip-service to his anti-popular positions, but had not really felt them in my bones. Now, however, in my intense regard for individual responsibility, for my own special responsibility towards Elza, I felt fiercely hostile to any system which would make things easier for me, which would take Elza off my hands and in any way mitigate the rigours of my self-dedication. I wrote poems on the absolute rejection of property, of all possessive emotions, as the only way into a true humanity: *There is a State and Act called S. Francis*. For a while I turned my ascetic demand against socialism, feeling it to offer plenty without first purging the individual of his lusts for property and power. I did not yet see socialism as the form of society in which at last the struggle I wanted became generally possible.

I also completed a series of poems dramatizing my divided state of being in terms of a character James Allague. 'Drunken Christ, crucified Bacchus, we live and grow despite our shames.' But I made no attempt to place any verses, except a satirical *Cradle Song* and a lyric which I sent to Roger Roughton's *Contemporary Verse*, where they were printed. (An issue of this magazine had been sent me by my undergraduate friend: the only such periodical I saw during these years.)

I now received a note from Colin Still, a publishers' reader of much power at the time. Still said that he had read *Flatdwellers* and was impressed, but felt there was no public for experimental novels. He encouraged me to keep writing and suggested it might be possible to cut the more unusual parts of the novel and trim it to a more conventional shape. I asked for the return of the MS, but soon found that to remove its extravagances was to kill it stone-dead. So I wrote to Still with an account of *Rome for Sale*, which I had not yet carried far. He expressed much interest.

I was then held up from the novel by a lucky chance. Noticing an advertisement for a school-series which included a book on the Greeks. I wrote to the editor Gerald Bullett, proposing one on the Romans. He asked for a specimen chapter, liked it, and commissioned the book. I thus earned £30. But meanwhile Elza's outbursts were growing worse. At any moment she was liable to come upstairs and start abusing me. After one of her ourbursts I wrote in the blank pages at the back of my edition of Catullus by L. Mueller:

Let me recall this always, written after a scene with Elza. There is no question of self-pity or of fantasies that a life together is possible. Any such weakening in my part reacts most miserably upon her. She wants freedom underneath, the same as myself, but her form of father-fascination makes me tethered to me while I am tethered by a single point of weakness. The whole thing is not a question of sex or of anything beyond the fact that the psycho-analytic relationship must be broken, and it can only be broken by the most ruthless standing on my own feet. As soon as there is money to stabilize her position I must go. First, however, to break things we must get separate houses under different names. The merest expression of fear or uncertainty on my part breaks down her efforts to escape me. Things must ultimately turn out the same for both of us, but that does not mean we should not part. The responsibility of the psycho, is that we should share revenues—nothing else. Let me put this down in case I forget it, the utter horror of contact with her, the poor tormented way in which everything I do or say is turned by her into hatred and murder. May I go mad myself if anything ever blinds me to this.

Well might I add that last sentence; for the least softening on her part, the least appeal to my pity, and all my resolutions crumbled away. However, at last I was goaded to say to her that it would surely be best for us to part since she had such a low opinion of me. She agreed. I left all the money I had, apart from the fare to London, with a note saying that I would send her more in the near future and see that she did not starve. Then I knocked at her door and announced my departure. She merely stared at me with hate.

I had Phil's address in London and went straight there. But there had been no time to warn him of my coming, and I had to wait outside for about three hours. I had only a few pennies left and didn't know what to do. Then he and Jeanne turned up, welcomed me joyously, and took me in. As soon as we were inside their small flat, I broke down and wept for some hours, in a mixture of relief, remorse, and inability to believe that I had come through into a life with my fellows again. Philip did his best to strengthen me, and Jeanne fluttered round me with her bird-hands and her small mellifluous voice. They were still hard-up and had little furniture. The only article they could offer me to sleep in was a sort of big cradle, bought for their baby Cressida Anne, who had been sent to the country. My legs stuck out at the end, but it was more comfortable than the floor. In the morning, as we were break-fasting on toast and porridge, a wire arrived for me. I had left Phil's address in a note to Elza, so there could be no question who had sent the wire. I fumbled at the envelope, afraid that Elza might have done

H*

something violent to herself. But it was only a demand that I should
return. Phil told me not to be a bloody fool, but I replied that I had no
choice. With sinking heart I took the train back. (Phil and Jeanne had
been married since April.) Phil gave me the fare.

To my surprise Elza did not show any particular emotion at my
return. I realized that she had dared me to go because she was convinced I couldn't do it; she always tended to assume that I was in the
same impasse as she was. That was the only way she could keep her sense
of superiority. My return apparently had the effect of enabling her to
reassert her conviction that after all I couldn't really go and stand on my
own feet.

Soon we were back at the old tensions. I worked hard at *Rome for
Sale*. I wanted to express the tragic role of Catalina, caught into accepting
leadership of a doomed movement, and to show the change of all his
hopes into their opposites as the expression of the contradictions in the
movement itself. I still felt that the tragic pattern was the deepest
revelation of the human condition, that consciousness was developed
by a process which ensured that it arrived too late to affect things, that
the flaw in life was discovered at the point where consciousness had
decisively broken through, and that the peculiar struggle in tragedy was
this tension between the doomed action and the liberated consciousness
—one line going down, the other line going up at the same time, and the
two meeting with full concentration and contradiction at the climax.
Against Catalina I set Cicero the professional compromiser and falsifier,
the rising middle-class-character wanting to be accepted by the land-
owners, and Caesar, the supple schemer who bided his time, waiting
for the moment when a maximum amount of change would be possible,
but making the possible always his limit. To bring out the lost tribal
unity to which the angry hopes of the dispossessed looked back and
from which the more complex aims of renewal in Catalina and Caesar
drew sustenance, I sketched in a background of the recurrent rituals in
which the life of the earth and men's fertility-needs were expressed. The
action thus had to cover a single year, a single twirl of the earth-cycle: to
bring out, as strongly as my powers allowed, the way in which men's
relations to nature pervaded all their economic and cultural activities.
Further, as I struggled with the form, I realized that I must attempt to
define the situation from a number of levels—personal, economic, legal,
religious, and so on—all of which had to be grasped in the last resort in a
single focus. And that for my colour-key I must draw on my total

impression of the art, literature, and religion of the period. Thus the particular intonation of an age, its unique coloration and resonance, might be reproduced. And through all the individual movements and impacts there must run an organic connection with the deepest conflicts of the age—the conflicts between all that was most human and integrative, and all that was most inhuman, corrupted and divisive. Though I was by no means fully clear, I already had the intuition that the human aspects were linked with the unions of men for productive, creative and joyous purposes, and the inhuman with everything that divided up the human process, money, privilege, social and economic differentiation of any kind, the systems of power and parasitism begetting class-societies. I felt more and more that the creative key lay in the free and harmonious relations to nature, which were strengthened and deepened by the uncorrupted unions, and destroyed or perverted by the divisive forms.

Slowly and doggedly I was coming to see history as the pattern of this struggle. With moments of painful confusion and loss of the trail, and with moments of enormous delight, as I felt I had picked the trail up again. The year-pattern I saw in terms of Attic tragedy. In drawing away from the limiting aspects of psycho-analysis, I was re-discovering the cultural anthropology I had read, the work of Jane Harrison, Cook, Cornforth, Gilbert Murray, and others.

At the same time the feverish quest for an irreducible element in experience, in history, which I could accept and bless as good, as truly human, was given its force by my personal situation, my almost total isolation from normal everyday life and its consoling contacts. The imprisoning pressure of Elza's neurosis (reflected in my own anxieties and instabilities) helped to hold me back from accepting anything save that which satisfied the whole man. In a sense, while I thought I was sacrificing myself to help her, I was doing in fact the exact opposite—using her to knit my own resistances and drive myself along the lines which my deepest self wanted to follow.

Slowly and steadily, for the first time since the undermining of our Fanfrolico synthesis, I felt a growing zest, a simply sustained happiness, a sense of continual discovery which stayed with me even in my sleep—or so I was convinced. For I awoke fresh and filled with a sense of urgent tasks. (Ever since my Freudian fast I had had no dreams. I told myself that my unconscious was too afraid to provide me with symbols to analyse for its undoing, or that I had cleansed myself of the need to throw up the masked ghosts of fear and desire. I had absorbed my mythopoeic or symbolizing powers, such as they were, into my working faculties.) I had, as I had never had before, a pervasive and secure sense of union with sea, sky, earth—and despite, or because of, my isolation, a sense of equal union with people. I felt that my relation to nature was becoming serene and pure, and that therefore my feeling for people was being purified. The pity I had felt and still felt for Elza had become a pity for all living, a sense of my unity with all the torn and suffering lives. For all were crucified: that was the truth of Christianity. I felt anew an intense sympathy for, and antagonism against, that creed. In some of its aspects it seemed to me to have reached the deepest truths yet stated about the human condition; in others it turned away from its profundities and did everything possible to distort them, to hand mankind over to the murderers.

My departure for London had upset Elza more than had appeared. She grew restless and less harsh. Finally she said that she wanted to go to London. I would have preferred to wait till I had finished *Rome*; but I at once agreed. I sent the MS as far as it was completed, to Still. We left our few bits of furniture to be sold, and as soon as I had any cash in hand I paid off the debt on it. The ropemaker, I am sure, was glad to see the end of us. A kindly man, he could not but have been aware of the discords between Elza and myself, and the separate way we lived. But he was too mild and easy-going to throw us out.[1]

---

[1] Edith Young in *Liza* strangely makes Michael and Liza (myself and Elza) go near Porthleven at the point of tragic breakdown. Also, I was interested later to find that Christopher Caudwell went to Porthleven not long after our stay, to think out his new world-outlook of Marxism.

23. LONDON AND A NEW START

WE found a top flat in a house in the Paddington area, and I set to work on *Rome for Sale*. I visited Phil, who now had a large ground-floor flat only partly furnished; his fortunes had started going uphill. I also went a couple of times to see Still and discussed among other things his thesis that *The Tempest* incorporated the structure of the mystery-rite as carried out at Eleusis. I felt he was correct enough—but not because of any esoteric lore on Shakespeare's part. In *The Tempest*, the first great work in which we may say that the creative process is made the object of the poetic consciousness, we inevitably find the tragic structure glossed and illuminated in a new way, though in the work itself tragedy dissolves in dream and symbol. Still told me to take my time; he was going to instruct Nicholson and Watson that they must do *Rome*, and he could get me an advance if necessary. Elza refused to call on Jeanne and as a result Jeanne shrank from calling on her.

I completed the novel. Still asked me to prune it a bit if I could, but not to worry if I couldn't. I cut out two episodes. Nicholson, whom I met, was an intelligent publisher, and I felt that I had at got last somewhere and found a basis of existence as well as a form of work that interested me and allowed me to make a maximum use of my past preoccupations while revaluing method and material in terms of my new attitudes. Elza was much affected by my success in having a work thus accepted. She assumed that she too would very soon find her way forward along similar lines. I discussed things with her, and she said that she wanted to study the 18th century; she even decided that it would be best to live on her own. She had made a brief effort to contemplate a resumption of normal relations between us; but the idea terrified her and brought her to the decision of a break.

I agreed with her. We once more consulted *Daltons*. I had a look at a place advertised in the apple-area of Kent, but found it too small. Then I decided to take a cottage advertised in a lonely part near Speen in Buckinghamshire, while Elza thought she would like to go somewhere

along the south coast in Dorset or Devon. She found a place near Lyme
Regis.

I bought her several books on the social history of the 18th century;
and we parted with something like goodwill. She was firm and calm;
it was rather I who tended to feel and show some regret. After seeing her
off at Victoria, I went to Paddington and took a ticket for High Wycombe.
By bus I reached Speen and then walked out to the cottage, which was
on the top of a hill. There was another house not far off, and a farm
screened by some trees. Otherwise the site was lonely and deep in
greenery. Away to the back were large woods. The countrywoman who
owned the cottage I found was living in some rooms built by the well at
the side, but I hardly ever saw her. To my delight the old timbered
cottage itself, sparsely furnished, with a huge fireplace, was thickly
stocked with books, mainly dealing with the history of religion and with
anthropology. From my landlady I learned that they belonged to the
previous tenant, who had committed suicide; his relations had not yet
collected the books. The man had written for the Rationalist Press
under a pen-name; a melancholy recluse, he had ended by being crushed
under the weight of an irrational world.

I stayed in this cottage for some three or four months, over the worst
of the cold weather of 1933-4. I had no thought of the dead man except
gratitude for his library, which was just what I wanted after *Rome for
Sale*. I read through the whole of Frazer's works, those of Hartland and
many other anthropologists whose work I had known only slightly, as
well as a large number of works in various languages on Biblical
criticism and the origins of Christianity. Nicholson had agreed to do
two anthologies of translated poetry and prose: *I am a Roman* and
Medieval Latin Poems. First I concentrated on the latter, and often went
up to the British Museum to copy out medieval texts. I also wrote to
Stephen Gaselee, with whom I had corresponded earlier about Petronius,
and was invited several times to his house near Gloucester Road. Here
I ate a conventional meal and drank some wine—my only lapses before
1941. He had a young, handsome and silent wife; and to my shame I
once spilled a whole glass of wine on the table linen. But we soon retired
to his book-lined study. Though his lines of interest were very different
from mine, he was always ready to spend any amount of time to help
me in difficulties or to advise me what editions or commentaries to
read. After I left Speen, I kept in touch with him by letters; and
generally I got a reply dealing with any knotty point in medieval Latin

by return post. Once, however, he was gravelled and consulted A. E. Housman, sending me on that scholar's authoritative answer.

I enjoyed the journeys into London. Often I walked all the way from Speen to High Wycombe, and once I was jostled by the portly Chesterton on his way back to Beaconsfield. I did not call on Ramsay Macdonald's daughter, whom I had met at Oxford and who had taken the Speen pub which I passed on my way out to my lonely hill. Arriving home in the dark, I lighted an oil-lamp, put a match to the pile of wood I had prepared in the brick fireplace before leaving in the morning, warmed up some of my perennial vegetable stew and opened a tin of soya beans, and settled down to read Frazer or the verses of Hugo of Orléans and the Archpoet. When I did not go to London, I walked in the woods or went westward to where the hills fell away into open vistas. I felt intensely happy, but always over my happiness there hovered a slight cold shadow of fear that Elza would not keep to our bargain.

I wrote to her a few words every day, and sent her money weekly, cutting my own expenses to the bone so that I could give her twice as much as myself—though the agreement had been equal shares. I spoke to no one. At moments in London I was tempted to ferret out Phil or Edgell. But I never did. I had a feeling that I best warded off the danger of a new attack from Elza, a collapse on her part, by living with an ever more sharp discipline. My ideas were rapidly expanding, on the basis cleared by *Rome for Sale*, and I enjoyed working on medieval Latin.

Elza asked for more money. I drew further on the publishers and sent what she asked. Then came the expected and dreaded telegram, to say that she was ill. At once I went, arriving about ten p.m. In the morning I got her on to the train and brought her back to my cottage. She was not suffering from any specific illness; she was merely worn-out and miserable. For about six weeks I nursed her, doing all the cooking and housework. She gradually regained her spirits and found a house in Brixham in South Devon. Again I gave her all the money I had in hand, and promised a weekly sum; but I had the feeling that this time I should be called to her even sooner.

I was right. Within a couple of weeks she wrote saying that she would go mad; I must come to her. I went, leaving my cottage with deep regret. Furniture had been sent from one of the large hire-purchase firms, selected by Elza from a catalogue. I now ordered exactly the same ugly things for myself. Already she was on bad terms with our neighbours; and a day or so after the second lot of furniture arrived, the

police called, saying that these people had complained of someone
stealing their firewood; obviously they had hinted that we were the
culprits. I told the police to look in the house if they wanted; and rather
apologetically they glanced vaguely around and went off. The house was
new and jerrybuilt, on the high ground east of the harbour, overlooking
the sea. I liked the fishing-port and did my best to settle down.

Rome for Sale was now published and went quickly into a second
edition; it also appeared in the U.S.A. Still had added an introduction,
which I did not see till I got the book. In it he made a rough comparison
of the Catalinarian revolt with Fascism. I was a bit staggered at this, but
did not protest—though I was sufficiently uneasy to ask Harper's to
omit the preface from the American edition. Mussolini's régime I had
disliked and despised, but had not taken it very seriously except as one
among many symptoms of social decay; I had used the term 'Fascist
skull-and-crossbones' in the *Aphrodite*. Of Hitler and Nazism I as yet
knew practically nothing, since I read no newspapers, partly through
poverty and partly through obsession with my own problems. All I
knew of the Nazis came from a translation of their basic points in a
John-O'London picked up at Porthleven: a programme that read as a
demagogically radical creed. I had no means of telling how truly or
untruly it reflected the party policy; and indeed had only glanced at it,
assuming the Nazis to be some ephemeral gang of noisy cranks. Though
I now began a desultory scanning of newspapers, it was not till the end
of 1935 I realized anything of the significance of the international events
going on. For one thing, I had a profound Australian distrust of anything
whatever in newsprint.

I was working on *I am a Roman*, prose and verse extracts translated
from Latin to exemplify the Roman way-of-life; and had sketched out
the idea for a second novel, *Caesar is Dead*. I had realized now that the
only way for me to compose was from the mass-effect to the particular,
from the large-scale rhythm to the individual involvement; I had to
begin with a feeling of vast forces at work, clashing, fusing, breaking
apart, and by holding fast to the epical pattern, to make out, inside the
stormy whole, the faces of people at the key-points of death and
renewal. Then gradually the individuals grew in size, taking into themselves the original tumult of clashing masses and big involving rhythms,
so that they became significant of the main lines of force. Here I decided
that I must open with a long many-angled account of the day of
Caesar's murder, without Caesar himself being directly shown, and

then, after the explosive moment seemed to blast the multiple individual purposes into unrelated shreds, to express the mounting tide of popular and legionary wrath, which deified Caesar and swung Antony into power as the Avenging Mars. In *Rome for Sale* the religious rituals had been deliberately kept apart from the narrative of events, to bring out the gap between the past group united in the fertility-cult and the present conflicting classes. But now I needed to show the fresh liberation of the religious emotions slumbering in the masses, who had been caught up in a revolutionary situation—though a situation which halted far short of actualizing freedom and equality. I needed to show how the masses deeply affected the direction of events and yet in the end appeared only to have intensified oppression and State-power. The form of the book thus emerged as a sharp broken pattern of rapidly changing events, with the mass-pressure reflected by the development of a growing coherence of narrative movement. The uprush from below steadily shatters all the ambitious plots, cabals, and temporary compromises of the politicians. Antony, the leader least driven by personal schemes (except in so far as he seeks to evade the push of his wife and to enjoy himself), is the one who becomes the vehicle of the mass-emotion. The book was to end in his effort to find a point of arrest in conjunction with the young man, Octavius, who comes up in rivalry with him as the actual heir. I felt the need to convey the way in which the baffled aspirations of the populace, which led to Caesar's deification and disrupted the balances of the schemers, were in essence begetting both the Empire and the Christian protest against the State.

The books I had read in the Speen suicide's library thus turned out to be the best possible aid to my tackling the second volume of the trilogy I had decided to write.

I had arranged for the publishers to pay me £5 a week against royalties; and as I was able to keep this system going till I was called up into the Army I henceforth had a stable basis for my existence, even if the sum at times was hardly adequate.

I was working hard. The noise of my typewriter must have grated on Elza's nerves as a proof that I had mysteriously managed to come through into earning a livelihood while she was further off than ever from such a thing. She had long given up any pretence of studying the 18th century; and from now on, as far as I know, she never read another book of any kind. She was becoming violent and could not bear even to see me. At the back of my *Catullus*, under what I had written at Porthleven, I find I scrawled about this time: '. . . all truces are lies. That is why they afflict us both with dependence, an effort to bring out the truth. She wants the same as me—to escape. Look out for self-pity—which is *the lie*.' And then in pencil: 'If I am such a stinking lunatic as to forget all this, may I be boiled in oil. Remember how she smashed my window merely because I opened the door at the same time as she was going into the hall.' My extreme weakness in the face of the slightest appeal from her was the reason for the vehemence of the last sentence, as with the similar exhortation at the end of the Porthleven entry. But no matter how strongly I called on myself to remember in all its anguish and horror the moment of contact with her suffering resentments, I could not sustain the oath of cold objectivity. The next moment I saw only her misery, her vicious circle of frustrations, for which in their final stages of precipitation I had been responsible.

Often at this time she came into my bedroom and switched on the light, holding the hot and glaring bulb close against my face, my eyes, and stared at me. Painful as the sensation was, I felt only pity for her maddened effort to recognize the unknown murderer. Once she came into my work-room and flung my typewriter on the floor, so that I had to send it away to be mended. Once, as I opened my door, she threw a carving-knife and missed my eye by an inch or so. Knives at this time fascinated her and I knew she wanted to attack me with one. I did not however at any moment feel fear; only disgust and pity. Perhaps she knew this. During these months when I often thought she might come in and attack me in my bed, I never slept more soundly. An extreme fatalism mingled with my spiritual weariness. If it works out like that, I thought, it's too bad; but felt no impulse to protect myself. I do not know if this calm of mine saved me or made her worse.

Strangely, she now had no physical resemblance to the delicate pre-Raphaelitish dreamer I had first met. Ever since her return home she had been growing more like her mother, and now she had turned into a plumpish, heavily-built person, her face rounding out and losing the translucent pallor which had struck everyone in her earlier days. Her complexion had coarsened and had a rough redness about it. She often reverted roughly to the tones and idiom of North Devon, which had been quite absent from her speech. No doubt a mixture of psychological and glandular disturbances worked to produce these effects.

My efforts to psycho-analyse her had all recoiled on me. She had gained only a deepening of certain fears and obsessions, had turned the tables and forced me to psycho-analyse myself. So while I had been liberated, she had been more closely bound down. Our isolation had the effect of cutting her off blankly in a dead space, paralysing her whole emotional being. On me it had the effect of intensifying my social consciousness and making me feel with a terrible poignancy the need of union with my fellows in a worthy cause. The quest for this cause had become one with my search for a creative method, for themes in which I could embody all that I had experienced of deep-going change and renewal. I had turned from the groping journey down the dark tunnel of my own buried past, into the effort to enter into the conflicts and aspirations of history; but into the latter I brought the agonized dynamic of my need to cleanse myself, to find bedrock.

About this time Graves published his first Claudius book, which the *Bookfellow* sent me to review. It happened that I had just read Tacitus through in the Latin, and Graves' novel struck me as almost a straight paraphrase, with a minimal amount of invention and without any central idea or any effort to build the social picture. But, feeling that perhaps I was jealous of its success, I leaned over backwards to praise it, though pointing out a few errors such as the misdating of Catullus' death (through an antiquated mis-reading of the squib on Vatinius). Apparently these quite minor cavillings annoyed Graves; for when the *Bookfellow* sent him my *Caesar is Dead* he made no comment on the work as a whole in his review, but contented himself with trying to find factual errors. I disagreed with all his points and dropped him a note, saying why and mentioning some real mistakes I had myself spotted after publication, *e.g.* the mention of stirrups. Graves had said my passage purporting to be from an elegy by Gallus was too coloured, and in that he was correct, though I could formally defend each phrase: which I did by looking up examples under the key-words in the dictionary. Replying, Graves remarked that he had a dictionary as well as I: which was smart on his part but did not dispose of the examples. However, his contention in general was right, and I re-wrote the passage. (Later, during the war, I heard that Graves had gone to Brixham: no doubt a pure accident, but giving me an odd feeling of his following in my track.)

One day Elza opened my door suddenly and threw a note in. The note demanded a move, but the wording was vague and I assumed that she wanted once more to be on her own. Gladly I found a house in Lincombe Drive, Torquay—a rambling complicated three-storey structure of wood, built on the slope overlooking the eastern coastline, almost directly above Kent's Cavern. I arranged for the furniture to be taken there and sent on my typewriter to Phil in London. Then at the last moment I found that Elza expected me to go with her. For a brief moment I felt inclined to walk out; but as usual I accepted her wish without question.

For a short while she was happier, as she always was in a new place. She settled in on the ground-floor, then decided to move upstairs. The house was easily divisible: both the ground-floor and the upper section had their own entries, kitchens, baths. I reclaimed my typewriter by railway from Phil and set to work on the third novel about the Caesarian revolution. I had now realized that the connecting character in the trilogy was Mark Antony and the last volume must deal with the break-down of Cleopatra's schemes. Her vision of a theocratic empire on the system of Ptolemaic Egypt in many ways anticipated what was to happen in the 4th century A.D., with herself as Isis suckling the Divine Babe (Caesar's Son) providing the iconography of the Virgin Mary; but history would have been incomparably poorer if the leap had been made at once to the conclusion, without the slow working out of the inner struggle between the remnants of republican *libertas* and the new centralizing power. I tried to express the full contradictions of the situation, taking Antony in his final phases of collapse; to catch the difference of the historical level from that of *Caesar is Dead* I used a straightforward narrative dealing with two persons, a boy and a girl, who were in themselves unimportant and through whose problems we saw the last convulsions of the slowed-down revolution and the enhancement of personality which was to appear both in the extensions of Roman law and in the protests of Christianity. In the last pages, where the lad in his flight with the girl up the Nile had to deal single-handed with the pangs of childbirth, I hoped to convey the feeling of the new epoch that was being born.

In choosing the Caesarian revolution as my theme I had in a sense been exploring the poems of Catullus, which had always meant a great deal to me: finding myself through the discovery of all their social and political implications, or rather of the dialectical relation between their intense personal definition and the larger aspects. While from one angle I had begun by trying to grasp the historical events as projections or facets of the poet's passionate personality, in the process of realization I was forced to invert this effort and to explore the roots of personality in the social process. A set of tensions was thus set up between outer and inner reality, through which I sought to define the full structure of movement. While in one way the story was an allegory of my own struggles, in another and more important way it was a vehicle through which those struggles were enlarged and I transformed my isolation, my sterile reductions of experience to the early pangs and traumata of growth, into a sympathy with human life in its entangled richness of good and evil, its distorting compulsions and its liberating leaps into new dimensions, new wholes.

There is much more I should like to say of my struggle with the trilogy and the ideas I sought to embody. But I have said enough to show the general lines of approach. Perhaps I may, however, once more stress what I felt about the enclosing relationship to nature as providing both the moral and artistic clue. The dialectics of social struggle remained barren unless realized within this larger whole; and by the touchstone of the pervasive relation of individual men and of society to natural process one gained a true understanding of what was at stake in all the conflicts, in the conscious and the unconscious aims. One saw what alienation was, and what human unity and freedom were. In all my work I have continued the effort to apply this moral criterion, which is also an artistic method.

24. BREAKTHROUGH

My main interest at the moment, apart from my continuing preoccupation with the meaning and pattern of history, was biology. I had read Darwin's *Origin of Species* and was powerfully affected. The effect came, not from the book's conclusions which I already accepted in a general way, but from the tremendous force and weight of the exposition, the method. The slow remorseless way in which all interpretations but the materialist are excluded, the masterly insistence on the simple and the concrete, had a decisive influence on my thinking. I then read all Darwin's other books, and followed up with many contemporary ones on biological themes. I was also reading D.H.L. for the first time with a strong sympathy. I still rejected much of his ideas and tendencies, but I had found out the quick of the man, all that he meant when he declared that our civilization 'has almost destroyed the natural flow of common sympathy between men and men, and men and women. And it is this that I want to restore into life.' I realized the deepmost nature of his criticism of our cash nexus society, and what he had meant when he told me to stick to my hates, since they were the best and truest part of me; and I felt bitterly sorry that I had neglected my chances of meeting him when he was alive. I was also re-reading Dostoevsky, Tolstoy, Dickens, and reading Proust for the first time—previously I had been put off by the kind of person who admired him. Also, after Darwin, I read Spinoza, and came through him to Bruno. (I wrote a long poem on Spinoza, which was printed in the *Irish Quarterly*.)

I had also begun writing a considerable amount for the *Freethinker*, with a few contributions to the *Literary Guide*. I should like to mention an article in the latter, dealing with an attack on Darwin by Belloc, since it brought out clearly the philosophic position I had now reached, synthesizing Freud, Jane Harrison, ancient Stoicism, Spinoza, Darwin.

Defending the latter from the charge of mechanism, I argued that one gained from his work the conviction that there was no teleological universe, no 'purpose-behind'. There was only the vital totality of forces at any given moment, from which the future organically evolved. My argument implied that the living moment, the existential present, included freedom as well as determination, it was spontaneous as well as fated by the previous moment. Though I did not go any further, I should have claimed that the totality could not be seized by analytic thought—though such thought played a necessary part in one's comprehension of it. Intuition and analysis merged in the whole-man; and by one's existential wholeness one could know, even if one could not ever finally encompass by analysis, the living moment.

I was now at a half-way point between my Fanfrolico positions and those of Marxism. In *Dionysos* I had rejected all abstractions in the name of the ceaseless experience of existence.

Do we strive to make life approximate to an abstract idea? That is to hate all that breaks the abstract law, to hate all that is vitally alive and moves by the laws of its unique and dynamic identity. That is to hate life.

For life eternally outruns all statements that can be made of life, its complexities for ever go one step further than the ground covered by the widest of generalities. We must continually formulate our experience in image and thought; but once we conceive that the thought exists in itself and not as part of a continuous and deepening process, it becomes completely false. Once we try to substitute re-experience of the thought for the developing experience of the energies loosed by the thought, we are growing abstract.

I had now lost the bias to the irrational present in that passage; I accepted history and evolution as fully real, as the wider processes in terms of which any individual existence alone could develop; I saw that any biological, social or individual purpose must be inherent in the material situation and could not represent a transcendent or abstract intrusion of mind or spirit; I believed that the processes of knowledge, in so far as they proceeded from the whole-man, were knowledge of a real and material world. But I had not yet properly separated out the social from the biological, and as a result I still was confused as to the dialectical relation of the individual and society. My concept of a totality of given forces at any moment, with an inner dynamic of organic purpose, still had an element of *mystique* about it. This came, not from stressing the element of the unknown and unknowable, but from the lack of any guiding principles for the analytic attack. I was aware emotionally of the importance of love and work for individual and social development; I felt their link with the brotherhood of struggle. But I was still far from any clear idea as to the precise effect of productive forces and relations in determining the general structure of history. Still, though Darwin had temporarily made me think of society in biological terms, he also prepared me for a materialist explanation of its movement and changes; and as a novelist I had already begun investigating and concretely defining relations which I could not yet formulate as a thinker.

I kept on writing poems, wholly for myself, in which the unslackening pang of loss was fused with my deepened sense of unity with nature. In some the pang spoke harshly:

> *I have nothing left and nothing remains to be done.*
> *In me is enacted the ancient sacrifice*
> *and it means nothing. Nothing. That is my hope.*
> *Put it aside now, put it aside at last,*
> *let nakedness be gaunt with the thistle, and dumb.*
> *Say nothing. Lean and turn with the thinning shadow.*
> *Put it aside and wait till the Agony's past*
> *here on the winter's slope. . . .*

But for the most part a sense of intolerable sweetness had the last word, which I tried to put into a poem on Van Gogh, my hero of this phase.

I was indeed intensely happy, with a daily sense of vast discovery and a crystalline conviction of harmony with nature. I lay naked in the sun outside my bedroom window where there was a sort of cavern guarded by flowers and bushes; and to listen through the night to the faint clear sounds of Mozart or Wagner from a house higher up the hill, gave me a purer sense of what music was, than any concerts or records I had ever heard. My gratitude was infinite. There were a few moments of friendliness with Elza, when we visited Kent's Cavern or watched the butterflies with long curved beaks which they inserted, hovering delicately, into the flowers on our terraces. But soon she grew hostile and retreated into herself. She was continually harassed by smells. First she insisted on having all her floors lined with cork-lino, then she said the smell drove her out of her senses, and so on. I had so much that I needed to read and think about, to write, that I did not want to disturb her and provoke her rages. For weeks I did not go out. Such groceries or vegetables as we needed could be delivered—a note being left out for the man from the delivery-van. I kept myself fit by sunbathing and exercises;

I had never felt better. But my happiness did not lie only in perfect health and satisfying work; it derived in the last resort from the secure feeling I had of a total renunciation, above all my sense of owning nothing and wanting nothing. During these years I was a better person than I had ever been before or have ever been since, because of my complete elimination of any property-sense from my being; and for this reason I was also deeply and stably happy.

Mary Butts, who had published a novel on Alexander the Great, *The Macedonian*, wrote to me. She was working on another about Cleopatra, and sent me the MS when she completed it. I ran through it for factual errors and found about fifty. She thanked me and said she'd incorporate my corrections, but a while later she wrote to say that she was feeling very depressed and ill, having fallen down a cliff. She had lost my list of errors and asked if I could remember what I had written. I compiled a fresh list as best I could, and sent it to her. I did not hear from her again. (She died in March 1937, a few weeks before her Gabriel.)

After my trilogy I felt winded for a short while. Then I wrote *Despoiling Venus*: the story of Caelius Rufus, done in the first person. I had wanted to compose something which would define his strong, lost, embittered personality. This novel was a pendant to the trilogy, making the direct link with Catullus and Clodia. Next I decided to go further back in time and used the Egyptian record of an envoy who went to Lebanon after timber near the end of the 2nd millenium B.C. Egypt at that time was on the downgrade, and Wenamen's difficulties and mishaps amusingly brought out this situation. I followed the record closely, though introducing a Greek, a tough rough character, to represent the up-and-coming culture, which seems very crude next to the highly sophisticated though tired culture of Egypt. Through Phil I had got in touch with an Australian working at Saggara under Emery. I sent him the MS, which both he and Emery read. Neither of them could find any mistakes or slips in fact or in tone, though Emery queried one botanical detail. I had soaked myself in ancient Egyptian art, literature, and religion before I began the work.

I also wrote a boys' book, a tale set at the time of Spartacus, *Runaway*, for the O.U.P., and a long short-story, *Storm at Sea*, for the Golden Cockerel Press, which was illustrated with woodcuts by John Farleigh. Further, I found that the daily papers had started competing with short stories. I wrote large numbers of these, all of which were printed. The best I collected in a book *Come Home at Last*. One longer story about the heroic end of Cleomenes in Alexandria was published in the *London Mercury* (now not Squire's). I was working about fourteen hours a day. Having no interruptions, I was able to stick to any job day after day without a break, using pen or typewriter ten to twelve hours at a time. My simple meals took little time to prepare.

A letter arrived from Jeanne, saying that Phil had accused her of being unfaithful, and asking me to convince him of her innocence. I was moved by the letter, and besides I was ready to champion any woman in the name of the united family. So I wrote to Phil in her defence. He replied, with testy correctness, that I was butting into a matter about which I knew nothing, that Jeanne had been playing hell with him, and that he was going off to the West Indies. He had obtained a librarian's job at Government House, Jamaica, through the offices, I think, of Compton Mackenzie. The work was easy and the Indies were congenial, but he could not bear the way the Whites treated the West Indians, with whom he hobnobbed on friendly terms.

The English, I gathered, sat on the stage or somewhere near it during shows, while the locals were kept to the pit, where Phil sat among them. He soon found himself choked out of his job and decided to return to England. For some time he had been doing much work, or, to be more precise, earning a lot of money by wasting time, in connection with films. He had been artistic director for Korda's film on Henry VIII, on the strength of the novel, *Here Comes the King*, which had been very successful; and after that he became friendly with Wallace Beary and the Fairbanks. At the time I had written to him sarcastically suggesting that he choose definitely between films and books; and indeed my advice was good. But he could not resist the easy money and the excitement of pottering about in the film-world, going on trips to Spain or somewhere else to get local colour for never-made films. And this just at the time when he should have been concentrating on his novels if he were to develop them with full effect.

Once again Elza suddenly decided that she must move. We found a house at the back of Preston further west along the bay. This was a fine house with a large garden and many fruit-trees. Elza was always friendly during moves, perhaps because then she had something to interest her. I was aware that her total lack of any form of activity stood heavily in the way of her recovery, and in our friendly periods I did my best to develop the least show of attention on her part into some more enduring line of thought or action. I had to be careful, as the slightest effect of pushing her aroused instant antagonism. But though she momently took up this or that subject, she was incapable of any sustained action on her own. I never knew how she spent her time in her long withdrawn phases.

I had myself now reached a point where I needed to deepen and extend my understandings of history and individual existence. I had found that I could enter effectively into the latter only if I was at the same time exploring in some new way the relations of individual and social movement, historical change. The timeless element only came alive when I was deeply involved in the colours and patterns of a particular time. In the hopes of extending my method I wrote a slight contemporary novel *Shadow and Flame*. The main character was a gentler sort of Elza, the person she had seemed at our first meetings. She has married a young bookish chap who knows nothing of her past, and they are holidaying at Portreath; as strain develops, he is drowned in the shingly undertow and she is thrown back on her old ways. But now she manages to escape the spiritual undertow which has always brought her down; she finds, with an artist's aid, what I may call her Lawrencian body; she achieves calm, relaxation from the rigours of fear, acceptance of herself in the tenderness of undemanding touch—unpossessive contact with another. The tale was thus once more an allegory of Elza standing on her own feet, with myself eliminated and with the solution using something of D.H.L.'s terms reinterpreted in terms of my own experience.

The book was promptly accepted by Chapman and Hall, the reader being L. A. G. Strong. (He did not know at the time I had written it, as it was signed Richard Preston, under which name it appeared.) I got an amusing letter from a reader, who described herself as highly musical and married to an unappreciative husband; she added that she would like to spend a week-end with a witty young writer, giving herself 'without reserve'. I replied that Richard was neither so witty nor so young, but out of curiosity asked for a photo. She answered at length, but without the photo; and though I did not write again, she went on pouring out her soul, even sending small presents. What had convinced her that I was the witty young writer she needed was a passage where the heroine walks along the clifftop from St Ives with her bladder near bursting, too shy to withdraw behind one of the scanty bushes.

However my uncertainties as to what next to do were settled by Warburg, then in Routledge's, asking me to write a biography of Mark Antony. I was thus plunged afresh into the Caesarian world. And shortly afterwards I found what I needed for a fresh stimulus. I saw an advertisement for works by Marx, Engels, Lenin, and decided I ought to look at them. My knowledge so far had been almost all derived from P.R.S.'s writings in the *Aphrodite*, his copy of Marx's *18th Brumaire* which I had read and which had in fact merged with Beasley's book in providing much of the political outlook in *Rome for Sale*, together with a few scattered remarks in conversation. I had a woefully inadequate idea of Marx's positions: which had not prevented me in the past from laying down the law about them. Now, however, I obtained and read the main works of Marx and Engels in English, with *State and Revolution* and some other writings of Lenin. From almost the first moment I felt that at long last I had come home; I had found the missing links in my dialectical system. I had brought that system from its idealist basis in Plato-Blake-Nietzsche down to earth and had at moments intuited something of the nature of productive activity; but only now did I see that activity in the fullness of its nature. The conflict of liberty and brotherhood which I had tried to discuss in *Last Days with Cleopatra* was now seen as securely resolved by the return of the means of production to the producers.

My ripeness for Marxism was shown by the fact that in a few weeks I had read and absorbed all the main works by Marx and Engels, with a sprinkling of Lenin's theses. Needless to say, I had not understood them as fully as I thought I had, nor were the answers to all the problems so unanswerably present as I thought they were. All the same, I had really reached bedrock; and though in the twenty-five years since January 1936 I have found the problem of developing Marxism adequately to be incomparably more difficult than I had imagined, I have never wavered in my conviction that Marxism does lay the basis for a world of unity (of equality, brotherhood, justice) and for a unitary consciousness in which the old contradictions and limitations of thought and feeling are overcome. What I have had to learn, often very painfully, is the depth of those contradictions and limitations, and the complexity of the struggle that has to be waged in order to overcome them—a struggle which is simultaneously social, political, intellectual (scientific and artistic), and which is going to take a long time.

I thus inevitably oversimplified things in my delighted discovery of

Marxism. Where I have differed perhaps from the many other intellectuals of the period, who in their own ways then came to Marxism,
has been that when I bumped in due time up against the brick walls, I
blamed myself for the oversimplifications, not Marxism. From the outset I took seriously the proposition that the dialectical method must
expand and deepen to admit every new truth, every new exploration of
reality; I did not believe that the way forward lay in trimming the truths
and editing the explorations so that they did not jar against the already-
built system. In consequence my progress as a Marxist has led to many
conflicts with my comrades, in some of which, though not all, I have
been wrong.

But that experience lay ahead. For the moment I was enjoying all the
excitement of the secrets of heaven and earth laid bare. I subscribed to
the *Daily Worker* and plunged into immediate politics as zealously as I
had once avoided them. It was with much satisfaction I realized that
Edgell, Garman, Alec Brown and others had reached the same conclusions as myself, though by less devious byroads; and that in *Left
Review* there was a rallying-point of the movement. With a shock I
grasped something of what the rise of Fascism in the Thirties had
meant: the breaking-out, through the thin crust, of the evil forces I
had often talked about in the Twenties as sure to reassert themselves. I
got hold of any books I could about the Soviet Union, and in particular
searched eagerly for translations of Soviet novels or plays. I soon had
read a couple of score or more, most impressed by Sholohkov, Gladkov
(*Cement*), and Leonov (*Skutaresky*, done by Alec Brown). With enormous
love and gratitude I looked towards the new world into which my
aloneness had suddenly turned: the Soviet Union and the Communist
Parties.

I wanted to join the C.P. at once, but was deterred by the unsolved
problem of Elza. There was no branch close by, but I could have found
one at Exeter or somewhere nearer. I had learned that the only thing
with any strong effect on Elza was an accomplished fact. If I had joined
up and then told her, she might have accepted my action and have made
some effort to go out into the world again. Probably things would not
have worked out that way; but they might have. I should have tried. My
failure to act at this moment haunts me as the one real error of those
years.

But in positing the issue so simply I know that I do not do justice
to the complexity of each changing moment at the time. After more than

five years' daily crushing of my own self-will, I did not find it easy to assert myself, even when now I had discovered an authority in the world which I could respect. When I had diverted my immature revolutionary emotions in 1919 into the championship of Norman's ideas of art, I had found life infinitely exciting; in effect I had accepted him as authority. My unstable and conflicting emotions of admiration and anger towards him and his work were supplanted by a single-hearted allegiance, and there was a powerful identity between the actual father and the father-image of authority, built up in my spirit out of complex family and social elements. The authority I now accepted was set flatly against all the existent forms of authority that I knew in the social scene. In my Fanfrolico years in London I began to break up the N.L.-image and ended by losing any faith in it; I turned instead to Elza as the martyred mother (in whom I slowly recognized an identity with all the suffering and downtrodden elements of life). Elza then, in her suffering self and in her remorseless need to keep insisting on moral purification, became my sole image of authority. However, as I dramatized my experience and situation in my work, I gradually got an objective basis, which had ended by splitting the authority-image in Elza. Now I saw her pitiful self on one side and the claims of the suffering and downtrodden on the other side. The Soviet Union and the C.P.s of the world became the new form of authority to which I could yield a pure allegiance, for they were pledged to the ending of the class-system and all the sufferings and contradictions that that system implied—all that Marx had gathered under the term which I still did not know, Alienation.

This was the moment then when I should have been able to break from Elza in the sense of standing up against her, obeying my need to express the new allegiance openly and *then* seeing what I could do to help her.

All that sounds simple. But in fact I was caught in a set of contradictions that were not at all easy to resolve. My new position, which brought to a head the striving of many years, involved as its essence the need to achieve a unity of theory and practice. As long as Elza could contain the authority-image I had expressed that unity by my submission to her; now I could express it only by joining the C.P. Deep in myself I felt sure that I would drive her to suicide if I did. How could I express my solidarity with the oppressed and exploited of the world by stepping over Elza's dead body to give them a cheer? The more I felt sure that I would kill her or drive her out of what remained of her wits by the step it was necessary for me to take, the less I could take that step. I felt more cornered than ever. The whole mechanism of fear and self-pity which had put me at the mercy of Elza took control once more.

Clearly throughout my post-1930 relations with Elza I was revealing the masochism of which Heseltine had scornfully accused me. Without that masochistic strain I could not have carried out the steady sacrifice of my self-will; I must have gained a certain satisfaction from being Elza's victim. And yet I do not feel that the whole thing can be reduced to such simple terms. There was indeed the weak side to which they apply; but the need for moral self-renewal which expressed itself through my weakness seems to me the dynamic of the process, the ultimate touchstone. I renounced my freedom in order to gain a place in the universe; and though for long it seemed that I had lost any basis for reachieving human solidarity, in fact the drive throughout was the need to reachieve it. Step by step I moved towards a fuller sense of what constituted humanity; and that progress was the proof, the only possible proof that my submissions were not as irrationally masochistic as they might well appear. I had come through to the point which has been well defined thus:

. . . submission is not the only way of avoiding aloneness and anxiety. The other way, the only one which is productive and does not end in an insoluble conflict, is that of *spontaneous relationship to man and nature*, a relationship that connects the individual with the world without eliminating his individuality. This kind of relationship—the foremost expressions of which are love and productive work—are rooted in the integration and strength of the total personality and are therefore subject to the very limits that exist for the growth of the self. (E. Fromm, *The Fear of Freedom*)

In the sense that this passage gives to the words, I had used submission to break through into a spontaneous relationship to man and nature, realizing that the key-expressions of this relationship were love and productive work; and I had struggled to define this attitude in my writing. Through Marx I saw that history was more than a cyclic conflict between freedom and brotherhood, individual self-expression and social unity, and that the logical step after the creation of an industrial proletariat was the socialist ownership of the means of production and distribution. But this new idea was not merely the addition of a cornerstone to an edifice in process of construction, it involved a radical reorganization of my whole dialectic. I had been tending in this direction

ever since I wrote *The Modern Consciousness* in 1928; but the moment o₄
arrival was none the less shattering.

After my fast at Forge Cottage I had had a long period when I
struggled against the reduction of society, history, people, to a set of
psychological projections and traumatic compulsions. Now I had to
struggle against the reduction to economic forces and relationships.
Once again personality seemed unreal, a rationalization imposed on an
unrealized complex of compulsions. I decided to write a novel on the
last days of Bruno, his return to Venice which led to his being handed
over to the Inquisition. He had known the danger he was putting himself into; in a sense he had sought destruction. But more deeply, he
had tired of his rootless wandering life, his intellectual activity without
a basis in any apparent group or people; he wanted to find again his
place in the Catholic body, with a desperate hope that by the sheer
force of truth he could convert that body or at least find in it a minimal
basis for the propagation of his ideas—so that out of the resulting
conflict a union of his lonely truths and of Catholic solidarity might
result. (In historical fact, some 250 years were to be needed before the
line of thought Bruno-Spinoza-Kant-Hegel-Marx could find its catholic
body with which to unite, and then this body turned out to be the
international proletariat. Bruno was trying to short-circuit history by
turning to the one world-body of his epoch; he was also perhaps showing
a nostalgia for his own childhood and an intuitional revolt against the
new individualism which he was helping to found and which was to
play its part in making capitalism possible.) There could only be a
tragic end to his quest; and in his possessed distracted days in Venice I
strove to show the hopeless contradictions that drove him on. In his
agony before the inquisition I was drawing on my own memory of the
demoralizing dilemma of facing with rational arguments a force which is
simply asking a total submission—a submission which one may want to
give but which one cannot fabricate. As I had put it in one of my Elza-
poems:

> *The walls of the world have fallen, yet I'm enclosed.*
> *No man, imprisoned in a foul jail,*
> *may know this suffering; for while he rots,*
> *he writhes with renewed worms of rancour and plots*
> *to escape, and when his efforts fail*
> *he still can blame and hate*
> *the men who thrust him there.*

††††††††††††
† GUENEVERE †
††††††††††††

TWO POEMS BY WILLIAM MORRIS
THE DEFENCE OF GUENEVERE
AND KING ARTHUR'S TOMB

with eight decorations by
DANTE GABRIEL ROSSETTI

and a foreword by
GORDON BOTTOMLEY

printed and published by
THE FANFROLICO PRESS LONDON

The title-page of *Guenevere*

Jack Lindsay on the sea-front at Douglas, 1942

Jack Lindsay at Bournemouth, 1939

For me all such evasions come too late.
I cannot even claim the right
to be sad because I am lonely.
I am ravaged by the ceaseless Face of light.

I cannot blame, because I know
that I am alone in the world, mated only
with the untouched Accuser. Nothing avails
to repay where what is demanded is not part
of self or the world, not coins or the heart's idols,
but the whole of a life. This is the clutch
in ancient days called Christ, *the insatiable voice*
of pain insisting upon absolute choice.
In vain I cry: You ask too much, too much.
It is not mine to give.

But I was also thinking of the victims of Fascism being tortured as I wrote. And though I did not know it, I was exploring also the pangs of a Communist brought up cruelly against the dogmatisms developed in his own creed as part of such aberrations as occurred under the later Stalin. I was dealing with the conflict of freedom and unity which carries on into socialism, however much it is being steadily resolved by the forward movement of the socialist society towards communism.

I am speaking here of the completed work; but nothing I have written caused me greater pangs and confusions. I had to write and re-write, I had to fight every inch of the way—as if I were reliving all my past years with Elza as well as sharing a cell with some anti-fascist fighter in Hitler's Germany; I had to rediscover in Bruno the complex origins of my Marxism and regain through my reconstruction of his personality, his thought, his desperation, a belief afresh in the individual as well as in the forces of history.

When the book appeared, nothing of what I had attempted was visible to my fellow anti-fascist intellectuals. This was the first shock, giving me a slight inkling that I had a somewhat romantic and over-simplified idea of what our anti-fascist unity was, and of the way in which Marxism acted as a liberating force.

I inevitably carried an existentialist stress into Marxism, but I did not, and do not, see that this was necessarily wrong. Existentialism in its modern form is a one-sided dialectic which seeks to correct certain

I

abstractions and distortions in the Hegelian system. It goes too far in its swing and achieves an aberration far greater than anything in Hegel; yet its protest remains of significance as an attempt to vindicate concrete experience and the whole-man. In so far as Marxism has carried over abstractions from Hegel, the existential protest has a certain validity, which however diminishes with each step of Marxism towards a fuller concrete grasp of life in all its aspects. That is, existentialism in its protest has an absolute value against Hegelianism, but not against Marxism. It keeps its value only insofar as Marxism holds mechanist, idealist, and over-rationalized elements—as Marxism will continue to do in some degree until the realization of world-communism and the total withering-away of the State.

Here is a crucial point in my outlook, and I feel that I must clarify it further in order to bring out as richly as possible the inner struggle of my advance into Marxism, a struggle which, at a different level, is still with me now. Kierkegaard put ethics in the forefront as the key to the release of the whole-man; Nietzsche stressed an aesthetic view of the world for the same reason. Both were reacting against the views of the rationalist 18th and 19th centuries which in effect identified Being and Thinking. I think, therefore I am. This abstract elevation of thought and reason is linked with the expansion of mechanist science, and reveals a key-aspect of the alienating process, which above all drives a wedge between reason and emotion, logic and imagination. Kierkegaard saw that the purely intellectual or rational (scientific) mode of life was insufficient, and he used all his sharp irony against the idea that an intellectual system could set things to rights by merely offering the rejected elements a place in its rational ordering. Nietzsche in the same vein attacked the notion of scientific objectivity, not in the name of relativism, but in that of the whole-man; scientific values must not be cut away from the values and purposes of the whole-man; he saw the science of his day as hopelessly compromised with the deadening forces of dehumanization.

I believed, and still believe, that such contentions were correct, however much I dissent from the ways they were worked out. Kierkegaard split his 'existentialist simultaniety' with an abstract concept of choice between belief and unbelief, between finite and infinite, and so on. Nietzsche lost his concept of the whole-man in a medley of biological and subjective fantasies, and never faced what he meant by Eternal Recurrence (a blind repetition or the acceptance of necessity which becomes freedom). Jaspers was thus able to formalize the split at the heart of the existentialist notion of wholeness, a split which inverted the struggle against alienation into an acceptance of alienation as the precondition of choice. He divided Being into three forms: being-there (the world of scientific 'objectivity'), being-oneself (the transcending of being-there), and being-in-itself (the world of transcendence itself). The weaknesses and errors of the unsystematic dialectics of Kierkegaard and Nietzsche are thus systematized, upheld, and brought within the general framework of philosophy. The vital intuitions of those thinkers are carefully undermined. Though in Jaspers' system the thinker is said to participate in all three realms of being and thus to approach the unity to which his reason aspires, in fact the interrelations are metaphysical and we are back at rationalist domination, against which existentialism made its protest. A gap has been driven between being-there (the given self, the given world) and being-oneself (the dynamic self of living experience, with all its potentialities and complex changes); the task of achieving a true dialectical unity has been evaded once more in the name of abstract choice. (The dilemma made manifest in Jaspers is in fact present in Kierkegaard and Nietzsche; but because they do not systematize, it is disguised under a brilliant handling of momentary aspects of experience, with their contradictions and their impulses towards resolution brought out.)

Something of the Jaspers' system had still clung to me in my defence of Darwin, though I was already rejecting the gap between being-there and being-oneself. At the same time I was also beginning to comprehend that scientific method and fact were not given, unalterable things. Now that comprehension became explicit and drew me forever away from the existentialist gap of passivity. I saw that it was necessary to distinguish between scientific methods and views as developed in a world of alienation and those that would develop in a classless society moving towards communism. The deadly gap between science and feeling, reason and imagination, which was the clearest mark of the alienating process, would have to be closed if the whole-man was to be more than a ghostly figment used as a merely logical link between the two spheres; and this implied a struggle to develop both science-reason and imagination-feeling along new lines so that they could fuse in a higher synthesis. Existentialism, I saw, used its genuine insights into alienation to obscure the real solutions, to return to the metaphysical sleight-of-hand it had set out by rejecting. The problem was to end the gap between being-there and being-onself, not to rivet it by a scheme of transcendences which were in fact only a sanctification of the divisions of alienation. The gap must be closed by a steadily-deepening unity of thought and act, theory and practice—whereby both thought and act themselves would be changed.

Where I differed from most of my fellow-Marxists, though it took me some time to grasp the meaning of this difference, was that I refused to assume that the taking-over of the given mechanism of Marxist dialectics automatically solved the problem of alienation and closed the gap. I saw it, indeed, as the first and necessary step towards the solution. But the insufficiencies of the existing scientific outlook and method remained even when science was set socialist tasks instead of capitalist ones. The social aims were bettered, but the actual modes of thought and being were still tethered to the insufficiencies and distortions of a discipline developed under the full blast of alienation.

At the same time, I realized, one could not hope to step overnight into a science from which all the old mechanisms and idealisms had been purged; those limitations went deep into the premises on which all scientific thinking had been built up, under the Greeks or in the epoch starting with the 16th century. In carrying on from those given bases, a fierce struggle was needed to work out new fundamental methods and ideas expressing the dialectical unity of process. Similarly, old methods of art could not express the new man developing under socialism .

There seemed, and seems, then, to me a deep conflict between the socialist struggle for the new man and the methods which a socialist society is compelled to take over in order to develop its science and its art. This conflict seems to me to have been recognized so far only in its superficial aspects. But I had faith, and still have, that the conflict will grow powerfully in due time, and that from it will emerge the single line of thought-feeling which will unify science and art in undreamed-of ways and finally dispose of the heresy that being and thinking are the same, without succumbing to existentialist dilemmas or irrationalities.

I should like to follow out these problems further in their general bearing; but here I must restrict my remarks to the struggle rending me in 1936. I felt the existentialist stress on the unceasing urgencies of choice to be essential, but I wanted to discard the abstract mechanism that made the moment of choice a repetition-compulsion going round in a vicious circle where one chose nothing, one merely vindicated the right or liberty to keep on choosing. That abstract mechanism is what vitiates existentialism from Kierkegaard to Sartre (though the latter, as artist, continually breaks through it). Kierkegaard's system was the perfect consecration of the alienating process; for the person practising it went on as if nothing had happened and impacted on nothing outside himself; he had merely tied himself up in a knot of absolute anxiety. To choose abstractly is to choose nothing; it is to deify the *angst* of alienation as the only concrete aspect of experience. If, however, one straightens out the dogmatic kink in existentialism, one is left with a moral urgency and a sense of the immediate reality of living, which Marxism needs for the unfolding of its ethic and for a protection against all hardening of the arteries, all mechanist application of terms, methods, definitions, categories.

Through psycho-analysis, anthropology, and biology, I had broken down the divisions in my thinking between being-there, being-oneself, and being-in-itself; but I lacked terms adequate to grasp the inner conflict of the unitary process I was intuiting. I still could not satisfactorily explain the nature of real choice, which involved not only oneself but also others, not only the existential moment but also history. I needed Marxism to move from existence to history without losing the concrete texture of the moment. My struggle since then, often leading me into confusions and mistakes, has been to hold true to the existential moment, in which the unexpurgated colour and richness of experience is alone preserved, without blurring the significance of the long-distance choice, the complete self-dedication to the work of achieving human unity through association with others in the field of history.

Thus Marxism released me from the spell of my relations with Elza; nothing else could have done so. For, though I might attempt, in works like *Birth and Will* or in the novels, to analyse my own motivation and to understand what moved Elza, I was not strictly concerned to assess my relations to her. Those relations came under the existentialist heading of a Nietzschean *amor fati*. I had made an absolute act of choice and was bound to it. In the last resort I was not interested in understanding it so that I could overcome it; I wanted to grasp it in order to give it more power, make it more fully an aspect of myself. True, each step I had made forwards had undermined our relations; but despite my temporary revolts or plans of escape I could not have broken the spell of the relationship without snapping the existentialist *huis clos* of which it was the expression. I had to make the full philosophical exploration and find the flaw in the existentialist position, find the dialectic which emerged from the full comprehension of the flaw, before I could feel free.

Also, there was a powerful life-and-death pressure driving me on. To those who feel no need to unify their life and to make a consistent relation of theory and practice, the above arguments must seem nonsensical. Why be bound by such a desperate need to find a coincidence of theory and practice? why tie oneself to an intensely difficult mode of life merely because of a philosophical point? I can only answer that I have never been able to live, have never seen any reason to live, except in a unity of idea and action. And so I carried over into my post-1930 relations with Elza my Nietzschean concept of tragedy, my acceptance of *amor fati*. In *Bussy* and *Hereward* the hero (poet) when brought to the end-of-the-tether of his existentialist contradictions can only affirm himself by a triumphant and mocking death. When, in 1930, my bluff was called, I had to decide how far my Bussy-Hereward role held. Heseltine committed suicide. Such an end was not possible for me; but the time-space I had entered was a death. That was why I could not make an easy re-adaptation to the world, go to Phil, Edgell and the others, and find some way of jogging along as they did. I accepted Elza as a form of death, of total isolation. I felt that only by such an acceptance could I live out my death and find some way back to life that was not a cowardly retreat from all my premises. I had to live out that death of isolation and existentially find my rebirth. That is, I had to make each step forward as a fiercely-contested victory over the existentialist contradictions; I had to invoke those contradictions at their strongest and most effective, and only then find if I could overcome them. And I could believe that I had overcome them only to the extent that they were concretely resolved in immediate experience, in love, in work, and in my relation to nature. My love was the discovery of otherness as a dialectical part of myself; my work was the creation of images in which this dialectical conflict was resolved; my relation to nature was the joy in love and in work, which supplanted the tragic ecstasy and slowly evolved a new sensuous harmony in my momentary living. The problem was to achieve love, work and joy in a time space that was their ceaseless negation, the death-isolation incarnated in Elza. All the while, the existentialist conflict was deepening into the Marxist conflict, converting otherness into my own life and thus making a dynamic unity of being-there, being-myself, and being-in-itself.

At the crucial point, reached round the New Year of 1936, the new balance triumphantly asserted itself as a definitely organized system, and I found it was Marxism: not simply the particular system labelled Marxism at that moment, but Marxism the vital stream of thought-feeling which in that system had reached the highest world-level then possible. Marxism as a vital stream broadening into the future and implying an ever greater unity of consciousness, unity of man and nature, unity of man and man. Not that I did not welcome and accept the system as it had evolved up to that moment. To do otherwise would have been to sever potentiality from existence, otherness from self—the primary existentialist errors. I had found the open gate into a united movement, which, however many errors, corruptions, distortions it might incidentally produce, held the only fully valid clue to past, present, and future alike, and the one compact that could not in its essence be corrupted. I was free, with all the new problems that freedom raised— the relations to other people as well as the effects on myself that the moment of choice now brought about.

But in this digression I have omitted the events which went on as I wrote *Adam of a New World* and which had such a profound effect on the anti-fascist groupings: the conflict in Spain that led to the Civil War. In a newspaper of February 17 I read that shock-troops in Spain had disobeyed their officers and joined the mob. I wrote a rough poem, *Warning of the End*, which I sent to *The Eye*, a sort of trade-journal issued by Lawrence and Wishart. It has at least the interest of being a prophecy of the civil war to come in July and the first of the vast number of poems to be written on the Spanish theme; for me it meant the first direct expression of a new stirring loyalty.

About the same time, reading the review of a book by Allen Hutt in the *T.L.S.*, which remarked that what he said was all very well, but he didn't know the English, I wrote a longish declamatory poem. *Who are the English?* I sent it to *Left Review*, where it was published and received with such acclamation that it was reprinted in large numbers as a pamphlet. Also, a group at the recently-formed Unity Theatre, who wanted to develop a form of dance-mime together with spoken verse, took it up and produced a stage-version of it which was very successful and provided the basis of an English form of mass-declamation with mime and movement. When the Spanish Civil War broke out, Edgell wrote and asked me to do a similar sort of poem on the theme of the war, and I produced *On Guard for Spain*, which was also developed into a mass-declamation.

On Guard was even more successful than *Who are the English?* and in the following years was continually done all over England by Unity Theatre or groups connected with the Left Book Club. It was performed in Trafalgar Square and at countless rallies; the typical meeting in support of the Spanish Republic consisted of speeches by Victor Gollancz, Harry Pollitt, and the Duchess of Atholl, with a performance of *On Guard*. Harry once felt impelled to write to me after such a meeting that he had never in all his life seen an audience so powerfully affected as by the declamation.

The Civil War had itself affected me as no other event in my whole life. Coming just at the moment when I had discovered my new allegiance, it represented the new life with the immediate threat and attack it aroused from all the forces of evil, of power and property. Till the final defeat of the Republicans in 1939 my own aspirations were indistinguishable from what I felt of the Spanish people. There were, of course, over-simplifications in all this, but at the same time a profound element of truth. There was a peculiarly tragic quality in the struggle, with the Spanish people doomed from the outset through the help given by Mussolini and Hitler and the betrayal by the 'democracies', and with the anarchist spontaneities and confusions of the people themselves. I suffered extremely from a bad conscience at not being in the International Brigade, and yet at the same time felt an intensely urgent need to get on with my writings, to attempt to absorb into my own painfully evolved dialectics, and to express, the full meaning of proletarian unity. Perhaps I did not force the issue with Elza because my deepest need lay in my writing, and I felt underneath that if I joined the C.P. I would be hurried along by participation in the many activities of the day, thrown off my balance just as I was anxiously trying to find it in the new complexity of ideas and impulses that had gripped me. To join the C.P. was for me tantamount to going into the International Brigade—though in fact after the deaths of Fox, Cornford, Caudwell, every barrier was put in the way of intellectuals sacrificing themselves.

Also, for a while Elza listened to my political ideas and was moved by them; I had hopes that I had at last found a way of awakening her from her deathly withdrawals. It seemed that with a little patience I should be able to carry her with me, and that I must not frighten her too much by stressing the activities stemming from the ideas. However, she began to feel that contact with people would be the logical consequence, and at once closed herself against what I said.

Despite the sado-masochistic character of our relationship, I had escaped by facing the real nature of my isolation; she could not escape, could not work, because she had long given herself up to a retreat from reality in which she had staked her all on me as a 'magical helper'. She had lost all her spontaneity and waited for a miraculous moment that would restore it, restore her power to work (above all to write poetry) and her power to love; and that moment she had identified with the moment when I regained 'sanity'. But in this system of hers I could never regain sanity, for the test did not lie in anything I became, anything I said or did; it lay solely in the miraculous return of her spontaneity, her effective connection with the life-process. And as the miracle did not and could not happen without the effort it was beyond her to make, she could never consider that I had become 'sane'. So she was returned to her need to dominate me and the situation; but whereas I had freed myself from dependency through my work, she had grown ever more dependent on me, though this dependency took the form of her sense of domination. She needed me ever more as the one person with whom she could feel safe, the sole person she had as a symbol of the world and also as a victim. In fact I had now long lost my original sense of guilt towards her; I merely felt that by an involved set of circumstances I had become responsible for her; I pitied her and could not face the suicide or breakdown which I felt sure would result from my leaving her. It may be argued that this pity and this fear of what she would do if left alone were a delusion; and indeed a strong masochistic tincture pervaded the emotions. But after all there was the practical problem which no amount of chiding myself for self-pity and masochism could whisk away. I kept on hoping that one of my books would make a lot of money; I should then be able to take steps to see that she was well looked after when I went. But though after *Rome for Sale* I always had at least £5 a week, I could not advance beyond that level. Such extra sums as I made were swallowed up by our moves and similar expenses. The result was that I had to keep on working all the while if we were to subsist; and the unrelenting economic pressure had a great deal to do with my accepting the situation, because I feared any long break that would disorder my earning system. In the first years, when anxiety was strong, I had longed for illness, for a breakdown on my own part, which would solve the situation by putting me in hospital and forcing Elza to stand on her own feet. But, partly through my sparse vegetarian diet, my health could not have been better and I never came even remotely within reach of the coveted breakdown. Elza, on the other hand, was several times vaguely ill, though she always refused to see a doctor.

She, on her part, would have liked to stop me working. She recognized to a certain extent that I was escaping from our interlocked situation through my work. After Portobello Road, she never read a line I wrote. She knew that if she did she could not stop herself dictating and tearing up; and she had enough sense to know that if she did that, she would destroy my earning power and bring about a state of collapse in which she could not maintain her control. So, to maintain that control, she had to permit the process which made it impracticable. Her one resource was to dream of the miraculous day when she, too, would become 'creative', able to earn her living. But this dream was liable to fall away, leaving her with melancholic depressions or a sadic outburst in which she wanted to smash my typewriter. I realized that ever since she left Combe Martin, she had been seeking the magical helper who would restore her birthright and release her energies, her spontaneity and her expansiveness; and that her history had throughout been a series of disappointments and disillusions. Robert, who had introduced her into the refined world of his mother, the world of Ellen Terry and of Nicholson, had seemed for a while to offer her a key into a magical realm: but the inner release did not come. I had done more than anyone else to convince her that the release was possible, by my headstrong fantasies of our Fanfrolico purpose and our great aims, and by enabling her to begin writing poems. Therefore my letting her down had come with a decisive blow of derangement; and the fact that she discovered my 'betrayal' at the time when the Press was breaking down and I was going through a very painful and prolonged process of inner change, was crucial for bringing out her sado-masochistic components in the form of an effort to take complete charge of me. The economic decline and insolvency of the Press lay at the core of our spiritual fall; for she was thus led to a belief that I was a fraud, not at all the strong and fated character she had taken me to be, whose guidance had to some extent released her. The more I lost faith in what I had been and honestly sought to rid myself of my flaws and illusions, the more I convinced her that I was a weakling. Her respect for the demonic force of my Fanfrolico days (begotten in me by N.L.'s ideas and my feeling of a dedicated purpose in serving them) completely died away; and it was this ending of her respect for my 'power' which led her to feel the need of filling the vacuum with her own domination. To the extent that she had previously respected my demonic possession as the mark of her fated magical helper, she now feared and despised me. Her angers over Betty May had not been the key-thing at all; they had expressed her final conviction that I was a weakling and that she had discovered a means of dominating me. (I do not mean she thought consciously along those lines; I mean that that was how the situation worked on her.) In the same way, it was the economic collapse and the crisis of ideas which it precipitated that was the dynamic of my fall, not the guilty conscience over Betty in which I concentrated my dissatisfaction with my past self.

The plain proof of this analysis is to be found in the fact that the collision leading to the breakdown of our relations in 1930-1 occurred then, and not earlier, when I was still meeting Betty, or just after I had ended things with her. Elza was certainly feeling uneasy at that earlier period, as was shown by her sudden advent one morning to confront me and find out what was going on; yet she did not tackle me then, nor did I feel burdened by the sense of disaster and doom that made me 'confess'. Elza was still controlled by her respect for my strong sense of inner purpose. Long before she had heard the name Betty May she responded to the weakening purpose in myself to start petty tyrannies such as throwing out the Pentons. At the same time she made the vague effort to return to the persons she had known in her days of selling-herself—a further expression of the fact that she was beginning to feel she could not rely on me. But she found that she could not make a return to her old way of life, and that sharpened her sense of dependence on someone whom she no longer felt carried along by a magical aim.[1] She was impelled to begin direct attacks on me to find out just how weak I was, just how unlike her pristine image of me I had become. Her taking-up of the Betty-hints thrown out by Marie was the expression of this need to get inside me; and the cheat she felt was the discovery of the man-of-straw behind the Apollonian disguise. Therein lay my betrayal of her; the Betty-theme was the mere emblem of the deeper letting-down; her misery lay in feeling tied to someone

---

[1] In the first days at Forge Cottage, brooding over Donne's symbols of the Two Indies (gold and spice) and on Freud's idea of anal-eroticism, I said to Elza, 'Perhaps a man ought to give a woman money every time he lies with her.' The next moment I thought the idea a bad one (reducing all sex to the Baudelairean position of guilt); but Elza enthusiastically took it up and kept talking of it. Clearly it met her feeling of castration in the act that proved her woman.

who was now shown to be an imposter. She could not move forwards a poet or return to the one role, prostitution, where she could use her helplessness to get her own back on an outraging world. She felt the need to take whips and scorpions to my unreliable self; and thus it was, as I have said, that my vulnerable condition—ever more vulnerable the more I tried to change myself—provoked her distrust and hostility instead of making her feel that at last there was the basis of a stable and happy union between us.

Though I did not yet analyse things quite as bluntly as I have just done, I had steadily arrived at this position; and my discovery of Marxism, which was the natural completion of the process going on in me ever since 1928, brought me to the point of finally discarding the mechanism of guilt. But it did not, as I have said, solve the practical problem of what I was to do with Elza. I could not, now as before, accept a way-out which was an expression of my self-will and disregarded the consequences for her, however good a rationalization I could put up in its defence. My pity and my responsibility remained, however much their focus had changed.

25. CONCLUSIONS

In essence the conflict with Elza had been fought out and I had found the resolution of the contradictions which had been lurking in my thought and action since 1928, or more precisely since 1919. But to round off the story, I will rapidly describe what happened between 1936-7 and 1941, when I was called up. As usual, Elza's disconcerted mood found expression in a change of residence. We went to Dartmouth and stayed awhile in the upper storey of a long, thin house, packed with useless furniture. Then we found a small bungalow on the western side of the river, looking towards the sea, with a brewery deep below. Almost at once she wanted to move again. Fish had been driven into the estuary, shoals of them piling up in the shallows, and the fishermen were complaining that the dealers had dropped their prices so low it was best to sell the easy catches to the farmers for dunging the fields. The scream of excited gulls filled the river valley. Elza spent day on day away, looking for a house. I recall the posters saying that Madrid was on the eve of capture, and I grieved. For the first time since Forge Cottage I went into a pub and had a few half-pints. The local cinema-manager, acting the goat, was babbling about the gallons of pee that the kids left on his seats and floor on Saturday afternoons; I talked to a miserable-looking joiner and found that the P.A. officer had been telling him that he must sell his tools. I rowed up the river past the serried lines of chained ships rusting away.

Elza found a house at the end of the bay west of Paignton. We moved there. The beach was only about twenty yards distance and I bathed for a few moments all the year round. Still wrote to say that Nicholson had died, and he was arranging for me to go to Methuens. I wanted now to turn to English history, to use the novel to revive revolutionary traditions; and to finish off my Nicholson contract I wrote *Sue Verney* as a preparation for a large novel on the Cromwellian Revolution. *Sue*, based on the Verney Papers, dealt with the breakdown of the last stages of the manorial system; at the end Sue, married to a small landowner, finds that her hopes are based in the Cromwell whom she had once detested. Methuens asked me to do a biography of Bunyan: a proposition I was glad to accept, as it fitted in with my Cromwellian studies and enabled me to pay a tribute to a man whom I greatly admired as a character and as one of the founders of the novel. A reconsideration of *The Pilgrim's Progress* chimed in with my ponderings on the nature and form of a consciously revolutionary art which attempts a fresh start, a comprehensive vision of human activity and of the role of the individual breaking away in the struggle for a new life. Methuens also published, as *Anatomy of Spirit*, some essays I had written as part of a large book, *Homage to Bruno*, which I abandoned through the difficulty of reading and evaluing his Latin poems and his relation to Renascence mathematics. In *Anatomy* I tried to deal with the question of what elements of Freud remained useful for a Marxist.

I still had a considerable fan-mail; and two girls, without seeing me, fell in love. One I managed to divert into becoming a party-member; the other was not so easily interested in politics and kept on writing that she wanted to meet me. Luckily Elza had had one of her interfering bursts and had been abusive because she found I was in correspondence with Edgell, so I had all letters addressed to the bank in Paignton. The girl thus did not know where I lived; but she came down to stay in the neighbourhood and wrote urgently asking me to see her. I was in the habit of walking in to Paignton three mornings a week to buy food, and I arranged to have coffee with my pursuer, saying that I could only see her once and for an hour. We met and I did my best to make her feel the meaning of the Spanish struggle. She had banged into something the day before and injured her brow on one side: a handsome girl with a remarkably clear, frank look. Anyway, after our one brief meeting, she wrote less emotionally; I kept up my political arguments, and about three months later she stopped writing. In 1940 she sent me a short note with some wedding-cake.

Edgell asked me to review novels for *Left Review*; also to compile an anthology, *Handbook of Freedom*, which he himself cut and added to; it was later re-issued as *Spokesmen for Liberty*. The poetry section of the Left Book Club asked me to be chairman and I co-edited their monthly; I further suggested and edited verse broadsheets. I completed my novel *1649*, in which I sought to apply all I had learned through my Caesarian novels to the English Revolution, taking afresh the cycle of a year, attempting a multiple series of levels and angles and interspersing passages from contemporary writings. (One reason for this latter detail was to provide a touchstone which would show if the rest of the book had the tone and colour of the period. My method here as always was to avoid anachronisms, to be as factually correct as possible in all things large or small, but not to try for a pastiche of the period's style. Nothing must jar as out of period, but otherwise one should write in a modern style. The effect should be simultaneously: How like ourselves, how unlike.)

The reception of the Bruno novel and *1649* made me realize that nothing of what I was trying to do had got over to my fellow intellectuals, who saw only the political bearings. My Roman novels had been in general very well received, though without any insight into their intentions. Now, however, I came up against hostilities. I do not mean on the part of right-wing critics; for in these years almost the whole of the literary world had swung into support of the Spanish people and the anti-Hitler cause. But the element of whole-hearted acceptance which made the declamations so successful with audiences made me suspect with the intellectuals: and Spender attacked *On Guard for Spain* in *Fact*, taking some lines spoken by a dead man as a call on the part of the living for death. Calder-Marshall reviewed the Bruno book in *Left Review* without a flicker of penetration into what I had struggled to express. And so, oddly, from this moment when I had come through to an enduring sense of union with the revolutionary forces everywhere, I found myself odd-man-out, a continuing outsider, whose work was rejected by the conservative or liberal as crudely committed to the proletarian cause, and was not much welcomed on the Left, which complained steadily over the years about all sorts of unorthodox elements, overcomplex and subtle, overpsychological, mystical, overlyrical, lewd, overnaturalistic or psychopathological, overconcerned with sex, etcetera.[1] It was perhaps characteristic that at the moment Spender attacked me in *Fact*, John Allen, producer at Unity, wrote to me that he had been at the *Daily Worker* office to find why the report and photos of a performance of *On Guard* in Trafalgar Square had

---

[1] If I were asked to put in a phrase what my work since 1933 is about, I should answer: The Alienating Process (in Marx's sense) and the struggle against it. But even in the essay by my friend Alick West in his *Sunlight on the Mountain*, while he stresses the central significance of the relation to Nature in my work, he says nothing whatever of what this entails in method and how it involves the many-sided struggle against alienation, how the latter is artistically presented, what the total effect is, and so on. Instead, he queries some isolated passages without relating them to the central problem, in terms of which alone can the position and negative qualities be determined.

omitted my name, and had been told there was a rule I was not to be mentioned. But I went on doing my best to struggle ahead into the unknown by the light of my own experience, my deepest convictions, and Marx's critique of class-society. I have not been deaf to criticism; perhaps I have listened too much to it. I have often learned something from the letters or discussion of readers, and recently I have had letters from young people in the Soviet Union which reveal a clear understanding of my aims; this I find the most encouraging thing that has ever happened to me.

From *1649* on I worked direct on the typewriter, and till I was called up I made only a single draft of my historical novels. After long and thorough preparation I typed each work straight out and merely made local corrections before sending the MS off. I still, however, could not handle the contemporary scene. I roughed out a novel on the anti-conscription fight of 1917 in Australia; a semi-autobiographical novel of the Twenties set in Sydney, which I sank by putting too much into it; and part of a novel on Elza and Mrs Craig. Then I wrote *End of Cornwall*, which Cape published as by Richard Preston.

All the while I kept sketching out plays, some straightforward, some lyrical and fantastic, but my isolation from the theatre held me back from finding what I was after. I continued with many articles and stories, *e.g.* in *New Writing* and in anthologies edited by J. Rowland and E. Martin. Rowland worked for the *Literary Guide* and we corresponded a lot; Martin, enthusiastic for my philosophy, was working on a life of me and Phil. I also wrote articles for *New Masses* and a small book on Blake for the Critics Group, New York, which never came out on account of the war and is lost. Harry Moore and Isidore Schneider, whose writings I had liked in *Transition*, were my main correspondents; I think Moore at that time meant to follow up his work on Steinbeck by dealing with me. Further, taking up a request from John Sommerfield to protest against a narrow-minded Russian review of his *Mayday*, I was drawn into considerable article-writing and verse-translation for *International Literature*. I made the first English versions of the Ukrainean poet Shevchenko, and Partridge published some of the Provençal troubador-poems I translated. I was also continually composing declamations for small and large occasions. Strike-committees or trades-councils from all over England wrote in with requests; and I produced long poems for a Chinese event at the Phoenix Theatre and for the L.B.C. Theatre Guild in support of Soviet policy. The latter declamation, *Defend the Soviet Union*, was printed and performed fairly extensively. A boys' story about the Eureka Stockade was published by Lawrence and Wishart.[1]

Finally I accepted an invitation to speak at the L.B.C. summer-camp of 1938. When the time came, I simply told Elza what I was going to do, and said I'd be back in two days. She was so overwhelmed that she said nothing. In London I dropped in at 16 King Street—why, I cannot recall—and encountered Harry Pollitt in the street. Recognizing him from his photos, I introduced myself. At that moment a shower came up. I wore only a slight summer-suit, and he pulled off his raincoat and handed it to me, 'Here, lad, your need is greater than mine.' At the camp I gave a very bad lecture, but had the pleasure of meeting Norman Alford, whose friend Marley Denwood had written to me a couple of years back about my *Freethinker* articles. (The Denwoods were a remarkable Cumbrian family. The father, a village tailor, had been a follower of Ernest Jones in his last days and spent much time in Carlisle Gaol for poaching—a traditional defiance to which his poverty drove him. While in jail he wrote poems attacking the water-bailiffs and the landlords, which were printed as broadsheets and sold for the benefit of the family. Marley's brother, Jonathan, was the last important folk-poet in Britain, and Marley and John were keen collectors of Cumbrian lore.) Alford at this time was absorbed in poetry. He told me how he went round the pubs of Cumberland, reciting poems by Burns and myself: a compliment, which, however undeserved, I found pleasant. He was a tall eager fellow, so full of energy and ideas that he had to stride about as soon as he began talking. We paced up and down in the moon-shadows while he talked and talked. Once the subject of John Strachey came up, and, in reply to some derogatory remark, I protested about his Marxist staunchness: Alford replied, 'You just wait. As soon as things grow more entangled and set new problems, he'll turn to the Labour Party.'

But I was pleased to drive back next morning to London with Strachey. Gollancz had recently accepted my summary of a book I wanted to write, *A Short History of Culture*. I tried to discuss it, but Strachey didn't seem interested. On my arrival back home, Elza made

---

[1] My seclusion seems to have made me rather a mysterious figure at this time. Various efforts were made to visit me, which I baffled. In 1939 one of the many young poets with whom I corresponded, Maurice Carpenter, set out to walk down from London to find my lair, but was caught in Bristol by the war, married a working-class girl, and went into an aircraft-factory.

no complaints and I felt that after all nothing had been needed beyond decisive action on my part. However in a few days she was restless and wanted to move. We found a bungalow with large grounds on the eastern side of the Teign. The first night after we had moved she lay out in the dews and contracted severe rheumatism. For three or four months she was unable to leave bed. I did all the housework, cooking, washing. After a few weeks in the big room at one end of the long front corridor, she said that the wall-panelling was driving her mad with its smell; so I took it all down, leaving the roughly-finished brickwork underneath. Myself, I loved the place, with its broad gardens sweeping down towards the river, and would have liked to stay on for good. I rowed up the river and thought of Keats and talked with the old ferryman who had a tame seagull perched on his shoulder.

Here at Teignmouth I finished *A Short History*, which was sent back as about three times too long. I hacked it about, which was one of the reasons for the unsatisfactory form in which it appeared. But in any event I had bitten off more than I could chew, and oversimplified a number of anthropological and cultural issues. I next worked on the second novel of what I meant to be an English trilogy: *Lost Birthright*, set in the 1760's during the Wilkite agitations. I attempted a form that corresponded to the period's tensions and outlook, working at extreme pressure. In the middle I was diverted by an urgent request from Randall Swingler, who had taken over the editing of *Left Review* and was about to start a series of Key Books for mass-circulation at the price of 2d. He wanted to start off with a selection of Haldane's scientific articles and a long essay by myself on the revolutionary side of the English tradition, which I composed and called *England my England*. Randall wrote that he would be passing through Teignmouth on his way back from a farm-holiday in the West and would like to see me. I met him at the station and we walked back to the house across the toll-bridge; after a too-short chat he had to rush to catch another train. The tract sold some 80,000 and had a strong effect in the factories.

We were still in the house when the Munich crisis arrived. There was a small party-group in the town, led by a man with a fried-fish shop. I used to call in and discuss things with him, as also with the workers at the railway-station; and I should have joined up if Elza had not been bed-ridden. I was sure that though she had certainly been suffering at first from rheumatism, she was kept in bed by the simple fear of getting up again. But suddenly she decided that she could not bear the house. I

was faced with the problem of restoring the panelling in her large room
—a job that would have taken me weeks on my own. I found an un-
employed carpenter at the Labour Exchange, and the two of us re-
panelled the room in four days. Elza couldn't bear to stay in the house
another moment; she was sure it had developed all sorts of hostile
smells. So we moved to some rooms down nearer the river and the
bridge. I felt that we were in for a wandering period; and as I had been
put behind my schedule by Elza's illness, I drank coffee and worked for
about a week without more than a few hours of snatched sleep. I thus
completed *Lost Birthright* and sent it in to Methuens.

No sooner had I done so than Elza wanted to move into a house on the
other side of the river. We were there only a few days and she wanted to
move again. We had a look at houses along the coast, at Dawlish and
Exmouth, and ended by taking some temporary rooms at Exeter.
There we looked round and almost leased a lonely place inland to the
west, which was owned by a titled descendant of the Shelley family (who
had watercolours of appalling taste in her house). Elza, however, decided
to revisit her home-area of North Devon. We went to Barnstaple and
then Ilfracombe, where we found a small furnished bungalow and
visited various houses to let in the neighbourhood. I recall one place in
Ilfracombe of truly palatial dimensions—huge ballrooms and the like—
which we could have had for 30/- a week if we had undertaken repairs.
(The reader of the 1960's may wonder at the ease with which we
changed our residence; but at this time there was no difficulty in finding
houses or rooms almost anywhere, and thirty shillings a week provided
one with quite fine houses.) At Ilfracombe I was able only to write
stories and articles. One article, which I did for *Life and Letters* on
Savage, a book of whose poems I had picked up for sixpence in a small
bookshop, started me off on an enquiry into our 18th-century poetry
(and thence into that of the 17th and 19th century) which has now
extended into many million words, though I have published only a few
chapters of the various sections as essays.

Elza suddenly decided that she wanted to go back to Torquay. We
found a barnlike house a little inland; and while we were there, on
March 7th, the Spanish War ended. With a feeling as of world-end, I
read the report in an evening paper bought near the sea-front. The
Negrin Government had fallen. Stricken on a seat, I watched the
unconcerned passers and tried to find words that would express my
sense of horror and disaster. When, next day, I heard some girls laughing

in the lane by our rambling house, I felt an anguish that seemed deeper than any pang I had ever known on my own behalf.

> . . . *And yet the laughter was lovely and unstained*
> *as poplar-fountains flutterleafed with blue.*
> *It was their scream I heard upon the day*
> *when fear comes true.*
> *They do not know the barrier's down which kept*
> *the blackbird-whistle safe, the cherry-snow.*
> *They do not know what foulness roots the earth,*
> *but soon they'll know.*

In six months our war was to come. That afternoon I read, again on the sea-front, 'Communist troops refused to accept the coup against Negrin and were bombed in Madrid by forces that included Anarchists.'

> . . . *Out of the newsprint blows this wind of honour,*
> *pause reading amid the traffic-blast, seal down*
> *red as the heart the oath that we must swear*
> *if we are still to live on such an earth,*
> *and so it ends and ending so begins.*

We moved to a bungalow in a new estate being built on high ground to the west of Torquay. I did not like this locality and was pleased enough when Elza wanted to move again. (Here I corrected the proofs of *A Short History* hastily, missing many errors.) We went to Bournemouth and stayed awhile in the dim dank lower storey of a house in one of the central chines. Here I reduced to normal novel-size and method the strange vast MS of Dorothy Johnson about Giuliano Medici for Dakers. He and Ludovici were the persons in Methuens with whom I had been dealing; and during my visit to London in 1938 I had met Ludovici and discussed my work with him. About this time Dakers left Methuens and Ludovici went with him. Still wrote and told me to transfer to the new firm they were setting up, as they were particularly keen on my work and would give it special attention. I did so, but still owed Methuens two novels: the first of which I now wrote, *Bright Light*, on the life of Catullus, a companion-piece to *Despoiling Venus*. Elza found a house in the northern part of Bournemouth, unpleasantly surburban. One day, out walking, we stopped in a small café for lemonade and heard the depressed voice of Chamberlain announcing that Britain was at war with Germany.

Ever since the days of Munich, the inevitability of war had been obvious; and that was another reason why I felt I had to do my best to help Elza. We now moved out to a small bungalow on the sandbanks close to the ferry across the mouth of Poole Harbour. Soon the rigours of the 1939-40 winter closed in and the Harbour froze. In walking up to the shops I passed through some woodland and scattered for the birds, all the scraps of food I had. The grocer was an Italian, terrified that Mussolini would come into the war and that he himself would be interned, losing all the work he had put into the shop. I was working at a large book, *Mirror of Antiquity*, in which I tried to overcome the weaknesses of *A Short History* and in particular to grapple with the phases between the totemic tribe and class-society, which I felt to be a crucial and little-explored matter for anthropology. (Dakers, however, held this work on account of the war and it was never published.) I also completed my contract with Methuens by writing the third novel of my English trilogy, *Men of Forty-eight*. In those bitter days of the phoney-war, with the feeling that at any moment hell would be let loose, I strove to let myself go and to pack my deepest emotions about alienation and the class-world into the novel.

We had a look round Swanage, then moved over to Upwey, half-way between Weymouth and Dorchester. For thirty shillings a week we got a fine solidly-built Victorian house with a big garden. To save money, I used to walk into Dorchester for the public library, and sometimes visited Maiden Castle on the way. I wrote *Hannibal Takes a Hand* for Dakers, dealing with the situation at Carthage when the defeated Hannibal turns on his class, the nobles, and attempts to build a city-democracy on the remnants of the old clan-elements; the nobles call in the enemy Rome against their own disarmed city. Writing in the period of the *drôle de guerre*, I was symbolizing the betrayal of the anti-fascist cause by the French Government and prophesying the fall to Hitler; but at the same time I tried to develop from several angles the theme of ancient religion turned back in on itself, as the social situation grows more complex and the original bases break down. Then I did *Stormy Violence*, using for the first section a long-short I had written for an anthology edited by E. Martin, about one of the branded bondmen or slaves of Elizabethan times. To this story, in which human desperation was carried to its limits, I added a second half about the bondman after he had escaped to London and been pressed into service as a sailor; the ship is captured by Moors and practically single-handed he regains it—

driven solely by his love of one of his fellow-sailors and of the ship itself; he has regained his humanity through comradeship and work, regained his sense of a place in nature. Dakers wrote that the book was rather short; so, without even the MS of the two parts before me to check, in four days I wrote a middle part describing the man's experiences among the poor in London, when his hand is still against all others and it seems likely he will succumb to crime. This work, which sold well, I wrote in less than three weeks.

My contract with Dakers was now ended, and I wrote to Gollancz, who commissioned two novels: *Light in Italy*, centred on a painter in Italy about 1816, and *The Barriers are Down* dealing with a world in collapse and renewal (the Western part of the Roman Empire round A.D. 450). In these years I was reading a great deal of archaeology and anthropology, making full notes from scores of books. I found that by writing very fast, in a small script, I could get down in one day practically all the argument and the illustrative facts, with references, of a book of about 250 pages. I tried to persuade Lawrence and Wishart to publish a collection of my mass-declamations, including *Defend the Soviet Union*, as an expression of my unchanged political position; but perhaps they disliked the preface in which I declared that the war would become genuinely anti-fascist as it developed. This attitude I had expressed in many letters to the newspapers. Though I held the phoney-war with its efforts to mobilize political opinion against the Soviet Union rather than against Hitler, to express an imperialist stand, I never doubted that the dynamic contradictions of the situation would develop the war along anti-fascist lines; and I stated this in print. Which meant that as usual I was odd-man out. I also tried to concentrate in a simple form my ideas on *The Pattern of History*. This, too, was rejected as unorthodox. I made a fresh start on my theses about English Poetry, in *Decay and Renewal* attempting to show how the poets from Thomson on, while generally acclaiming the Newtonian universe, in fact were reacting against it; and that this reaction was a key-aspect of the Romantic Movement, which begins with Thomson—the moments of elemental change such as dawn, moon-rise, storm-flare, and dusk (especially the latter) being taken as symbols of a total transformation of life; the same struggle, I showed, was going on in the fields of science, psychology, history, art, as well as literature. I sent this to the Cambridge University Press, which rejected it—though eight years later, in Cracow, Waddington told me that he fought to get the Syndics to publish it. I continued amassing material for a large-scale extension of my theses; tried to tackle what seemed to me the fundamental problems of cultural anthropology (above all, the sequence of motives, the interrelation of ritual, society, and myth in an historical series—all that was ignored in the scholastic method of Frazer's compilation). I particularly sought to grapple with the origin, meaning and development of the Bear's Son motive, starting from an analysis of *Beowulf*—much stirred by the Chadwicks' *Growth of Literature*, which had brought out the enormous significance of the mantic or shamanist individual in the phases between the totemic tribe and the settled literate society. And so on.

I had the feeling that I must somehow conquer all the problems of culture before I was called up. Almost nightly the German planes came over, sometimes seeking to bomb Portland, sometimes using the landmark of Weymouth-Portland to give them their bearings as they struck inland. All round us were powerful anti-aircraft guns, which made the house tremble and shook down the strongly-built brick barn at the back. I had my curtains well drawn and my light shaded, but did not stop work even when the bombs and the shrapnel were falling around us. And when I went to bed, I slept at once, waking only with the light of day.

I was called up for my medical inspection at Dorchester the day after Hitler launched his attack on the Soviet Union. Elza was not much perturbed, as she assumed that I would be rejected. I said nothing. Some weeks later came my call-up papers, telling me to go to Trowbridge. At Dorchester, in reply to questions, I had said, 'Put me in the infantry.' But I found that I was directed to Signals, presumably because I had a university degree and Signals were counted the Brains of the Army. In my squad were a number of postmen, considered likely to prove good signallers because post offices had once used Morse a lot. But I do not want to tell the story of my life in the Army. What matters here is simply that a force against which arguments and screams had no effect had intervened to snatch me from Elza. I was pleased that the parting had come, even in such an ignominious way; yet I felt utterly miserable that Elza was being thrown back on her poor resources in such a difficult situation and that I had not been able to find some rational method of settling things. One of the chaps in my intake told me later that he had never seen anyone so stricken as I looked that first day in the barrack-room. But my misery was wholly about Elza and the way she would be feeling at that moment. At Trowbridge I soon joined the Party, though as soldier I could not hold a card or attend branch-meetings.

I was ashamed that I should so crudely express in my life that element in men which made them accept and even long for war, as the only release from the intolerable but unrealized tensions of their daily existence. My failure to find a way-out from my Elza-conflicts by my own exertions showed me as all-too-clearly representative of the very worst aspects of the *angst* of alienation, which made war possible; I had been in the divided state of realizing this weakness in myself while fighting against the drift to war. But now at least that division was over. I had failed to carry Elza with me; the struggle against war had failed; I was in the Army. But the war, for all its confusions and complex trends, was in its strongest aspect an anti-fascist war; and so, beyond all the remnants of unresolved conflicts, I could assent to my position and be happy in it.

It must have taken Elza some time to realize I had really become a soldier and was thriving on it. She would have assumed I must break down under a strain that would have broken her; I think the fact of my being at home in the Army baffled, perplexed, and wore her down. The impersonal nature of the force separating us did, however, make her accept the situation without violence or complaint. She became much more emotionally settled than she had been at any time since 1930, but also shrunken, deflated, as if she had at last awoke from a painful dream to find herself changed from a beautiful girl to an ageing chubby countrywoman who lacked charm, culture, or any reason for existence. She bought a wireless and tried to follow what was happening. She even attempted to write verse again, but could not manage it: only a few fragments, about the planes continually overhead like silver bees enigmatically burning. The doctor who lived next door to us at Upwey had promised to keep an eye on her; I had had a long talk with him before leaving. After a while, at his advice, she voluntarily went into a mental home close to Dorchester. I got special leave to see her there. She was not happy, but had no strong dislike of the place, no clear objections, no alternative to propose. Before long, however, she left and went to Brighton. There she wrote me long confused letters of detailed incoherent complaints about the people around her. (From the time I left her I wrote daily to her as encouragingly as I could.) She wilted away and died of cancer.

Thus sadly and undramatically our relation ended. What I felt and still feel was the intolerable waste of fine human material. It was so pathetically pointless that she should have fought her way up from the misery and degradation of her childhood and youth into the world of Ellen Terry, into the creation of the strange dream-charm that Edith Young has recorded in *Lisa*, into the limited but deeply original poetry of our days in Museum Street—only to decline into the desperate manic-depressions of the last decade. Endlessly I proved to myself that there was something warped and crippled in her from early days and that if she hadn't gone to pieces one way she'd have done it some other way; endlessly I found myself convinced that in 1926-8 she had made a deep-going effort to draw herself out of the slough, and while helping her out with one hand, I had pushed her back with the other. An equally good case could be made out for my exoneration and for my condemnation. But remorse was useless. Beyond both exoneration and condemnation was the image of the beautiful girl with her dream-charm, her childlike pathos.

The poem of hers in the *Aphrodite* defined the lyrical dream which had persisted through her early defeats:

> She walks with the drunken wind for lover, this girl——
> this mad girl who can't tell the thighs of shadows
> from those of Dick and Tom and drunken Harry
> as she goes walking with the wind along the meadows.
>
> This girl is a spirit who is not yet born,
> but wed to sun and air and to the drunken wind.
> She cares not how she treads, so young are her thoughts,
> and nobody knows how young is her unborn mind.
>
> She lays her languid body out under the trees;
> and lying with the drunken wind, round her lover's eyes
> she curls her slender body, round and round,
> like a young tree curling its branches round the skies.
>
> The wind runs up out of the grass and over her.
> She listens to the wind running up out of the grass,
> and sighs to hear the shepherd's pipe, and sighs,
> shutting her eyes, and waits for him to pass.

And there is a passage in *Lisa*, which subtly suggests the peculiarly magical strength of her presence in those years: the power she had to make of her body an immediately convincing thing of spiritual depth and integrity:

I noticed then the thin border of lawn—or was it lace ?—that topped Liza's bodice and lay next to her skin: it showed more of her nature to me than much of what she said and probably all she did; by it I knew her delicacy, and I also knew that the fineness of her complexion showed her sensitivity. What did it matter, I said to myself, how many men she has lived with, what experiments she has made in her search after some kind of fulfilment, some satisfying beauty between man and woman ? She herself is so sensitive that the most subtle of life's impacts are registered by her, are woven into this fabric of herself, and because of this she becomes subtle herself, her mind fine, made so by the acute registration of the most delicate shades of feeling.

The image of her fine dreaming self haunted and haunts me; and I have written this book, not to exorcise the ghost, but to give it a home. How could I pay her a fitting tribute except by attempting to tell the whole truth as far as I understood it in my long wrestling with her, my long brooding over her ? To obscure her failings and the darker sides of her life would be to belittle the desperate struggle that she ceaselessly waged, and to make a doll-thing out of her poor bruised humanity and her achievement, for a while, of a rare beauty. Even the years of her derangement had something of stark moral nobility, in her hopeless search for nothing less than complete freedom and harmony. She herself wanted the truth, and nothing but it. Let me end with one of her last poems written in 1930:

> How like to Satan is this hand of mine.
> How cunning these fingers, twisting these words
> to shapes I never guessed at, dragged from me,
> and jeers at my remaining fears, so pitiless.
> I see my hand stretched forth to take the pen
> to wring from me remorselessly all secrets
> that I had longed to keep from common ears.
> Yet I cannot stay my hand, nor would I.
> I have my pride and laugh at it—
> the devil may take me.

1. *Fauns and Ladies*, poems, 1923
2. Aristophanes' *Lysistrata*, translation, 1925; 1926 (later pirated in U.S.A.; and printed by Bantam Books)
3. Petronius' *Satyricon and Poems*, translation, 1927 (pirated in U.S.A.)
4. *Propertius in Love*, translations, 1927
5. *Marino Faliero*, verse play, 1927
6. *Helen Comes of Age*, three verse plays, 1927
7. *William Blake*, 1927
8. *Dionysos: Nietsche contra Nietzsche*, 1928
9. *Homage to Sappho*, translations and adaptations, 1928
10. *The ocritos*, translation, 1929
11. *Women in Parliament*, translation of Aristophanes' *Ecclesiazusai*, 1929
12. *William Blake*, reprint with an extra chapter, 1929
13. *Catullus*, translations, 1929
14. *Mimes of Herondas*, translations, 1930
15. *The Passionate Neatherd*, lyrics, 1930
16. *Hereward*, verse play, 1930
17. *Homer's Hymn to Aphrodite*, translation, 1930
18. *Patchwork Quilt*, translations from Ausonius, 1930
19. *Golden Ass*, Apuleius, translation, 1931; revised edition with essay, 1960
20. *Cressida's First Lover*, a fantasy-novel set in ancient Greece, 1931
21. *Rome for Sale*, novel on the period of Catalina, 1934
22. *Caesar is Dead*, historical novel, 1934
23. *I am a Roman*, translations, 1934
24. *Medieval Latin Poets*, translations, 1934
25. *Last Days with Cleopatra*, historical novel, 1935
26. *Despoiling Venus*, historical novel on Clodia and Caelius Rufus, 1935
27. *Storm at Sea*, long short story set in the early Roman Empire (Golden Cockerel Press), 1935
28. *Runaway*, novel for boys, period of Spartacus, 1935
29. *The Romans*, 1935

30. *Wanderings of Wenamen,* novel set near the end of the second millenium B.C., 1936
31. *Come Home at Last,* short stories of the Graeco-Roman world, 1936
32. *Adam of a New World,* novel on Giordano Bruno, 1936
33. *Who are the English?* verse-declamation, 1936
34. *Shadow and Flame,* contemporary novel published under the name of Richard Preston, 1936
35. *Mark Antony,* biography, 1936
36. *Rebels of the Goldfields,* boys' novel in the Eureka Stockade, 1936
37. *Sue Verney,* novel set in the Cromwellian period, 1937.
38. *End of Cornwall,* contemporary novel published under the name of Richard Preston, 1937.
39. *John Bunyan,* biography, 1937
40. *Anatomy of Spirit,* 1937
41. *1649,* the novel of a year, 1938
42. *To Arms,* boys' book set in ancient Gaul, 1938
43. *England my England,* long pamphlet on the English tradition, 1939
44. *Short History of Culture,* 1939
45. *Brief Light,* historical novel, on Catullus, 1939
46. *Lost Birthright,* novel set in the 1760's, 1940
47. *Guiliano the Magnificent* (version of a novel by D. Johnson), 1940
48. *Light in Italy,* novel set in 1816, 1941
49. *Hannibal Takes a Hand,* novel set in ancient Carthage, 1941
50. *The Stormy Violence,* novel set in early Elizabethan period, 1941
51. *The Dons Sight Devon,* boys' book (Elizabethan period), 1941
52. *Into Action,* long poem on Dieppe, 1942
53. *We Shall Return,* novel on the Dunkirk campaign, 1942
54. *Beyond Terror,* novel on the Cretan campaign, 1943
55. *Second Front,* army-poems, 1944
56. *Perspective of Poetry,* critical survey, 1944
57. *The Barriers are Down,* novel on the collapse of the Roman Empire in the West, *c.* 450 (written 1941), 1945
58. *Hello Stranger,* novel on women in war-industry, 1945
59. *British Achievement in Art and Music* (in series on developments during the war), 1945
60. *Time to Live,* contemporary novel, 1946
61. *The Subtle Knot,* contemporary novel, 1947
62. *Men of Forty-eight,* historical novel (written 1939), 1948
63. Longus' *Daphnis and Chloe,* translation, 1948

64. *Catullus*, completely new translation and essay, 1948
65. *Song of a Falling World*, account of Latin poetry 4th-8th centuries, with translations, 1948
66. *Clue of Darkness*, poem (Theseus theme), 1949
67. *Marxism and Contemporary Science*, 1949
68. *Fires in Smithfield*, novel set in reign of Mary, 1950
69. *A World Ahead* (account of travels in Russia and the Pushkin Celebrations), 1950
70. *Charles Dickens*, biography, 1950
71. *Peace is Our Aim*, poems, 1950
72. *The Passionate Pastoral*, 18th-century novel, 1951
73. *Three Letters to Nikolai Tikhonov*, poems, 1951
74. *Song of Peace* by V. Nezval, translation from Czech (with S. Jolly), 1951
75. *Byzantium into Europe*, history, 1952
76. *Betrayed Spring*, contemporary novel, 1953
77. *Rising Tide*, contemporary novel, 1953
78. *Rumanian Summer*, travels in Rumania (with chapters by M. Cornforth), 1953
79. *Civil War in England*, the Cromwellian Revolution, 1954
80. *Moment of Choice*, contemporary novel, 1955
81. *George Meredith*, biography, 1956
82. *Three Elegies*, poems, 1956
83. *After the Thirties*, critical survey, 1956
84. *The Romans were Here*, history of Roman period in Britain, 1956
85. *Russian Poetry 1917-55*, translations, 1956
86. *A Local Habitation*, contemporary novel, 1957
87. *Life Rarely Tells*, autobiography, 1957
88. *Poems of Adam Mickiewicz*, translations from Polish, 1957
89. *The Great Oak*, novel on the peasants' revolt of 1949, 1957
90. *Arthur and his Times*, history, Britain in the 5th century A.D., 1958
91. *Discovery of Britain*, field-archaeology, 1958
92. *1764*, a day-by-day account of the year, 1959
93. *Revolt of the Sons*, contemporary novel, 1960
94. *Petronius*, new translation, with essay, 1960
95. *The Writing on the Wall*, history, account of Pompeii, 1960
96. *The Roaring Twenties*, autobiography, 1960
97. *Asklepiades in Love*, translations, 1960

98. *Modern Russian Poetry*, translations, 1960
99. *All on the Never-never*, contemporary novel, 1961
100. *William Morris, Writer* (lecture, W. M. Society), 1961
101. *The Death of the Hero*, French painting from David to Delacroix, 1961
102. *Ribaldry of Rome*, translations of Roman writers, 1961
103. *Ribaldry of Greece*, translations of Greek writers, 1961
104. *The Way the Ball Bounces*, contemporary novel, 1962
105. *Celtic Heritage*, history, 1962
106. *A Short History of Culture*, a completely new work, 1962
107. *Cause, Principle and Unity*, by G. Bruno, translation with essay, 1962
108. *Fanfrolico and After*, autobiography, 1962

MAGAZINES EDITED
109. *Vision* (with K. Slessor and F. Johnstone), 1923
110. *The London Aphrodite* (with P. R. Stephensen), 1928-9
111. *Arena* (with J. Davenport and R. Swingler), 1949-51

WORKS EDITED
112. *Poetry in Australia* (with K. Slessor), 1923
113. *Metamorphosis of Aiax* by Sir John Harrington (with P. Warlock), 1927
114. *Loving Mad Tom*, Bedlamite poems of the 17th century, 1927
115. Eliot's *Parlement of Pratlers*, 1928
116. Herrick, *Delighted Earth* (as Peter Meadows), 1928
117. *Inspiration*, anthology of statements on the creative process, 1928
118. *Letters of Philip Stanhope*, second Earl of Chesterfield, 1930
119. *Handbook of Freedom*, anthology (with E. Rickword), 1939: re-issued as *Spokesmen for Liberty*
120. *New Lyrical Ballads* (with M. Carpenter and H. Arundel), 1945
121. *Anvil*, miscellany, 1947
122. *New Development Series* (the Bodley Head), 1947-8
123. *Herrick*, selection with essay (Crown Poets), 1948
124. *William Morris*, ditto
125. *Key Poets* (with R. Swingler), 1950
126. *Paintings and Drawings of Leslie Hurry*, 1950
127. Z. Stancu's *Barefoot* (Rumanian novel), 1950
128. Introductory Essay for Edith Sitwell's *Façade*, 1950

Among many essays and contributions to periodicals there are the long essays on the novels of Vance Palmer (*Meanjin* 1960) and K. S. Pritchard (*Meanjin* 1962); scripts for documentary films and for ABCA plays; plays, *Robin of England*, performed 1944; *The Whole Armour of God* 1944; *Face of Coal* (with B. Coombes) 1946; *Lysistrata* 1948, &c.